VIA OKLAHOMA

And Still the Music Flows

MABEL HOVDAHL ALEXANDER

SERIES EDITOR: GINI MOORE CAMPBELL

OKLAHOMA HERITAGE ASSOCIATION   OKLAHOMA CITY

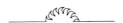

THE OKLAHOMA HERITAGE ASSOCIATION
IS THANKFUL
FOR THE SUPPORT OF

THE FAMILY OF MABEL HOVDAHL ALEXANDER
THE AD ASTRA FOUNDATION
MRS. WANDA BASS
MR. AND MRS. GENE RAINBOLT
MR. AND MRS. GEORGE SEMINOFF
MR. AND MRS. DICK SIAS
MR. AND MRS. PHIL PIPPIN

OKLAHOMA HERITAGE ASSOCIATION

201 NORTHWEST 14TH STREET

OKLAHOMA CITY, OKLAHOMA 73103

1.888.501.2059

Library of Congress Number 2003111373

ISBN 1-885596-32-4

Printed in China

EDITORIAL ASSISTANCE AND INTERIOR/JACKET DESIGN: CAROL HARALSON

IN MEMORY OF

Mabel Hovdahl Alexander

14 JANUARY 1920 ~ 5 AUGUST 2002

CONTENTS

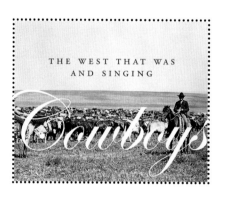

MUSIC IS PORTABLE. It can travel anywhere. It was carried to Oklahoma in the hearts, minds, and souls of men, women, and children of all colors and ethnic groups. *Via Oklahoma: And Still the Music Flows* takes the reader along on the journey with the thousands of people who came here for a new life and for those Native Americans whose roots were already here or who were moved from every direction on trails of tears to the land that was to become Oklahoma.

Music was a common thread, a way of communicating in the most eloquent way with each other and with those whose language and customs were a barrier. Music lifted the spirits of the pioneers to this land called Oklahoma and in this book, Mabel Hovdahl Alexander traces the history and the gift of music and talent from Oklahoma that has enriched the lives of people throughout the world.

The author likens the research for *Via Oklahoma* to the gathering of bits and pieces of information that fit together like a patchwork quilt. The story her "quilt" tells is an enjoyable documentation of the diverse and rich musical underpinnings of a strong and resilient society. It traces the contributions of the "self taught" and the "trained" musicians beginning with the Indian flute players, drums, and singers. It explores the romantic infusion of music ranging from spiritual to the classics followed by the color and diversity of jazz musicians, folk singers, singing cowboys, opera divas, and classical musicians, many of whom gained national and international fame. And it includes the role of stalwart individuals who cared deeply about providing fine music for this young state and the political intrigue that was interspersed in their efforts.

There will be surprises for many readers as the author gives her own gift of carefully researched information identifying world-renowned opera singers such as Lushanya Mobley that are many times "best kept secrets" in our state. There will be memories for readers who heard the superb performances of the Oklahoma City Symphony Orchestra as it was broadcast on radio throughout the world.

International recognition also came through voices such as Woody Guthrie, Leona Mitchell, Thomas Carey, Te Ata Thompson, Jimmy Rushing, Gene Autry, instrumentalists Chet Baker, Charlie Christian, Bob Wills, Woody Crumbo, Doc Tate Neva-quaya, and numerous fine orchestras and bands.

On their toes to music ranging from *The Firebird* to *Gaite Parisian,* five magnificent Indian women who became world famous ballerinas. The fame of Yvonne Chouteau, Rosella Hightower, Moscelyn Larkin, and Maria and Marjorie Tallchief will live on in the mural "Flight of Spirit" by Chickasaw artist Mike Larsen, a beautiful jewel in the high arch of the Great Rotunda of the Oklahoma State Capitol. Governor Frank Keating and the Oklahoma Arts Council later named the talented women "Oklahoma Treasures."

Via Oklahoma: And Still the Music Flows is, in its own way, a treasure of musical facts melded with the uniquely talented people who made them real.

BETTY PRICE

AFTER I COMPLETED a Master of Arts thesis in the history of music at the University of Central Oklahoma in Edmond, I realized that I had included little about contributions made to the state by American Indians, African Americans, and other early settlers.

My subsequent search to fill the vacuum became a fascinating learning experience. Like most non-Oklahomans, I had considered early Oklahoma to be a land of savage Indians, desperados, and wild cowboys. But with the help of archivists, librarians, and friends all over Oklahoma, I began to collect bits of information that eventually fit together, like pieces for a patchwork quilt, to tell a much more surprising story about the history, music, and character of Oklahomans. Perhaps it is only in Oklahoma, an area once judged too rough for human habitation, that the longings of the human spirit could culminate in such a story.

The diversity of the individuals who populated or traveled through the area is especially noted in the pages that follow. The music of the many Indian tribes, Africans, Europeans, Asians, and others from all points of the compass seemed, over time, to quite naturally blend together. Pioneer women, with determination, vision and the help of many volunteers who enjoyed music, also laid a foundation and sustained early dreams for the cultivation of opera and symphonic music in Oklahoma.

This manuscript has dealt primarily with music before statehood and during the early 1900s. The rich musical foundation inherited by modern Oklahoma has been emphasized and some later music has been included to show that Oklahoma-born musicians are still contributing to the world of music.

Perhaps this general consideration of music in the state will encourage interest, more research and an appreciation for the power of music in the history of Oklahoma. Meanwhile, the varied people who settled in the area have surprised the world and possibly themselves with their musical abilities. Oklahoma, like other hometown communities throughout the centuries, has been slow to recognize and appreciate its native prodigies. Consequently, there is a need to locate, record, and preserve old manuscripts and photographs before they are lost forever.

Special thanks to my family for their patience and understanding while I have been almost totally absorbed in this effort. My husband, Alex, a native Oklahoman, has been an unfailing reference source with his comprehensive knowledge of history. A special thank you also goes to Betty Price, executive director of the Oklahoma Arts Council, for writing the foreword and for locating some hard-to-find photographs.

I am also grateful to Royce Peterson, a history professor at the University of Central Oklahoma in Edmond, Oklahoma, who inspired me to appreciate history enough to switch my major from psychology. Maestro Joel Levine and my sons Michael, Patrick, and William were invaluable contributors.

Special acknowledgements go to volunteers who over the years clipped and preserved newspaper and magazine articles and other memorabilia about the Oklahoma Symphony Orchestra and early music in Oklahoma. My debt to those anonymous people who shared a common interest in classical music is beyond measure.

Dr. Patrick E. McGinnis, chairman of my graduate thesis preparation at the University of Central Oklahoma, gave generously of his time and expertise. He and a fellow mentor, Professor Gene J. Hellstern, encouraged me to publish my work.

Librarians Dr. Brad Robinson, Geneva Hoover, and Tame Wilson at the Oklahoma Christian University of Sciences and Arts in Oklahoma City allowed me to spend countless hours in their Archives of Contemporary History before the materials were catalogued. The staff at the Records Division of the National Archives in Washington, D.C., was also very helpful in my search for information about the Federal Music Project in Oklahoma.

I want to thank Scharlotte Myers for taking my typewritten manuscript and keying it for publication.

This publication would not have been possible without the support of the Oklahoma Heritage Association. Thanks to Gini Moore Campbell and Paul Lambert for their dedication to preserving Oklahoma's incredible history.

Mabel Hovdahl Alexander

Editor's note: Mabel Hovhahl Alexander passed away on August 5, 2002. Her family dedicates this book to her memory.

The flute represented the breath of life to Native Americans for centuries. In the 1930s, Kiowa Belo Cozad passed on the right to make and play the sacred flute to Woodrow M. Crumbo, a Potawatomi by birth, who had also learned the language, cultural, and ceremonial customs of the Creek, Sioux, and Kiowa Indians. Crumbo returned the Sacred Medicine Bundle to the Kiowa in the 1980s. Comanche Doc Tate Nevaquaya, Kiowa Tommy Ware, Seminole Woodrow Haney, and James Black of the Cheyenne Bowstring Society are also well-known twentieth-century flute players.[4]

A modern-day maker and player of flutes, Professor George Stevenson, talked about and demonstrated the capabilities of the flute to a spellbound audience at the Oklahoma Historical Society 1994 Annual Meeting. Stevenson noted that when Cabeza de Vaca wandered among the Indians along the Gulf of Mexico in the sixteenth century, he was often met by Indian flute players. The musicians accompanied welcoming processions, merry-making affairs, and also used their flutes to bewitch opposing athletic teams or to spur their own players on to victory. Their two-holed flutes did not accompany singing but substituted for the human voice. For example, an Indian lover would serenade the maiden of his dreams with the seductive sounds of his flute. Stevenson commented that, unfortunately, the telephone had replaced the flute in the courting ritual.[5]

An elder explained the high-pitched wailing characteristic of Comanche flutes. He related that a young Indian man who had lost his wife and children was told in a dream that music would help him to overcome his sorrow. Later, the young man discovered that a wailing musical sound coming from a nearby grove of cedar trees was actually caused by wind blowing through a hole in one of the tree limbs.

Woody Crumbo held the right to make and play the sacred flute of the Kiowa from the 1930s to the mid-1980s. Courtesy Lillian, Woody M., and Minisa Crumbo.

This painting of an Indian riding on a horse and playing a flute vibrantly portrays the power of music. The artist, Woodrow M. Crumbo (1912-1987), a Potawatomi Indian and an internationally famous artist and musician, created art masterpieces that portray the rich culture of the American Indians and preserve their ancient traditions. Photograph by John Southern. Courtesy Lillian, Woody M., and Minisa Crumbo.

Remembering his dream, he cut off the limb and fashioned a flute. The elder said that the young man had turned his sorrow into something beautiful as he played his flute. Although the Comanche had used the flute for personal enjoyment and inspiration to achieve inner serenity, flute playing eventually became a near-forgotten art. Fortunately, it experienced a revival.[6]

The Plains Indians made a wooden flute-like instrument called a flageolet. Its six main holes were sometimes covered with keys. Like earlier Indian lovers, the young men used the flageolet primarily during courtship. They also had rhythm instruments such as drums, rattles, and rasps to accompany singing, dancing, religious ceremonies, and social occasions. In 1832, the artist George Catlin sketched rattles, drums, tambourines, flutes, and bone whistles that were used by Indians living along the Missouri River.[7]

After the United States received the area of present-day Oklahoma as a part of the Louisiana Purchase in 1803, the federal government used it for a resettlement zone. Between 1820 and 1880, more than 60 different Indian tribes were relocated there to live among the few indigenous groups already present. Some of the Indians were agricultural and peaceful while others were migratory and warlike. Regardless of the cultural levels, there were diversities and similarities in their languages, music, and ceremonies.[8]

Missionary educators had influenced the culture and music of eastern American Indians before they affected the Plains Indians to a significant degree. Eastern tribal leaders and their tribal councils had begun to invite missionaries to establish schools and churches in the Cherokee Nation, East by the beginning of the nineteenth century. Consequently, the Five Civilized Tribes—Cherokee, Choctaw, Chickasaw, Creek, and Seminole—had experienced considerable cultural change before they were moved to Oklahoma. Substantial mixed-blood communities had developed in each tribe. The children had usually become culturally more like their white fathers than their Indian mothers.[9]

Several factors encouraged the rapid cultural progress of the Cherokees and the other Civilized Tribes living west of the Mississippi River, but none was of greater importance than the development of the Cherokee alphabet or syllabary by a Cherokee named Sequoyah, or George Guess. Sequoyah, a silversmith, had never attended school and could not speak English but he admired the missionaries, their books, and their schools. He called books "talking leaves." He determined to develop a system that would provide a written language for his people so that they could read and write in their own mother tongue.[10]

Many non-Indian male settlers married Indian women. The women and children usually adapted to the non-Indian culture. Fiddlers and their music were welcomed at their family gatherings. Kaw County, ca. 1892. Thomas N. Athey Collection. Courtesy Archives and Manuscript Division, the Oklahoma Historical Society.

Through approximately 12 years of study, Sequoyah isolated 86 consonant and vowel sounds in the Cherokee language. After refining and identifying each with a symbol, he had 86 characters for his alphabet or syllabary. When his wife burned his work because she regarded it as "bad medicine," he patiently restored the system.[11]

The Cherokee National Council was impressed with Sequoyah's work. Books were soon published in the Cherokee language. Samuel Worcester, a missionary, translated and published the Christian Bible and hymnals in Cherokee.[12]

In 1822, Sequoyah went to live with the Cherokee Nation, West in Arkansas and introduced the alphabet to them. After the Cherokee Treaty of 1828, he moved on to Oklahoma. The Cherokees soon became a literate people and the best-informed Indians in America. Sequoyah also shared his work with the other Indian tribes in the area.[13]

After the devastating experience of being forced to leave their eastern homes and relocate in Indian Territory, the Five Civilized Tribes poured much of the annuities they received from sale of their eastern lands into an extensive public education system for their children. During that period, it was possible in most of the Indian nations for every Indian child to attend school through the equivalent of modern-day high school and sometimes the first few years of college. Students were taught vocational skills in addition to traditional subjects that included astronomy, Latin, Greek, and philosophy. Boys were trained in animal husbandry, carpentry, agriculture, and mechanical arts. Girls received instruction in childcare, sewing, cooking, and other domestic arts. Schools for the mentally ill, orphans, the blind, and the deaf served the special education needs of the children. Saturday and Sabbath Schools, taught by native teachers, were also well received by the full-blood Indian population. Nearly all learned to read and write in their own language.[14]

The first public school at Tahlequah was located on the east side of Spring Branch (south of the present American Legion Hut), ca., 1874. The Ballenger Collection. Courtesy Western History Collections, University of Oklahoma Libraries.

Men and women of three different races were represented among the students at Oklahoma's Cherokee Teacher's Institute held at the Cherokee Female Seminary at Tahlequah, Cherokee Nation, ca. 1890. Left to right, Front Row: 1. Anna Richards (Mrs. Oscar Goddard), 2. Sallie Morris Pendelton, 3. Sallie Dick, 4. J.T. Parks, 5. Simon Walkingstick, 6. Isaac Hitchcock, 7. W.W. Hastings, 8. Sue Thompson Hamilton, 9. Herbert Neeland, 10. James D. Wilson, 11. Jim Ward. Back Row: 1. Unidentified, 2. Fannie Lowry, 3. and 4. unidentified, 5. Ellen Wilson McSpadden, 6. W.H. "Kenny" Davis, 7., 8. & 9. unidentified. Letitia Fields Wilson (Standing behind H. Neeland). The rest are not identified. The Ballenger Collection. Courtesy Western History Collections, University of Oklahoma Libraries.

The Cherokee Indians built this orphanage in Salina, Cherokee Nation. Many Indian children lost their parents during the tragic relocations from the eastern states to west of the Mississippi River, and later during the Civil War and during reconstruction. The building was destroyed by fire in 1903. The Ballenger Collection. Courtesy Western History Collections, University of Oklahoma Libraries.

Class of 1895. Cherokee Male Seminary. Left to right: Bottom Row: Samuel W. Mills, William Henry Clark, William Elliot, W.E. Davis (Principal). Top Row: Walter Adair Frye, J.W. Stokes, James W. Duncan, Jesse Stevens Lamar. Ballenger Collection. Courtesy Western History Collections, University of Oklahoma Libraries.

Missionary churches were often required by the Five Civilized Tribes to furnish qualified teachers for the Indian schools in exchange for the privilege of spreading their gospel in Indian country. The required number of teachers usually equaled the number of preachers the church wanted to send. Consequently, historians have found it difficult to distinguish between public and private schools in the region. However, the tribal education systems and the influence of various missionary groups accelerated acculturation and quite naturally affected music. Even some of the more conservative full-blood Indians began to read the Bible and became familiar with Christian religious music. When the more successful planters replaced their log houses with mansions, music rooms and libraries became common.[15]

During the early 1800s, Indian educators and missionaries of different faiths developed a basic aim to "educate the head, heart, and hands of each Indian." They also strove to develop business, political, and social leaders among the Indians and to train more Indian teachers for the private and public schools that were being built in Indian Territory. The devoted service of tribal government workers and special missionaries helped the Five Civilized Tribes to better adjust to their uprooted lives and lost economies. Emphasis on temperance and education served to lessen the hate, sorrow, and despair of the transplanted people.

In 1837, Park Hill Mission School was established by the Cherokees with the help of Samuel Austin Worcester, remembered as "the giant among Cherokee educators." The facility became known as the "Athens of the Southwest." Before Worcester died in 1857, his printing plant had done a massive volume of work, turning out more than 14 million pages for the Cherokees, more than 11 million pages for the Choctaws, and additional printing for the Creeks and Chickasaws. Worcester considered his greatest works to have been the translation and printing of the Bible and various hymnals.[16]

The Cherokee Female Seminary, which opened in 1846 at Park Hill, and the Cherokee Male seminary in nearby Tahlequah provided advanced study for Indian students. Most of the teachers in the two institutions were college graduates from the East.[17]

The Choctaws shared their educational facilities with the Chickasaws during their early days in Indian country. The Spencer Academy for advanced study for boys was built near Doaksville by 1844 and New Hope Academy for Girls near Fort Coffee opened that same year. The Choctaw Academy was organized eight years later. Altogether, the Choctaw Council built three academies for boys and six schools for girls between 1841 and 1843. Several of the graduates were selected by the council to further their education at Dartmouth, Union, Yale, Roanoke, and other eastern colleges.[18]

The Creek Nation's Kowetah Mission was established in 1842. Seven years later, the Creek Nation began to subsidize a new school named Tullahasse near present-day Muskogee. The school became the principal learning center for the Creeks. It also had a printing press. The Oak Ridge Mission School near Holdenville opened circa 1848 in the Seminole Nation, and Bloomfield Academy, a school for Chickasaw girls, was built near Tishomingo in 1852.[19]

By 1842, the Cherokees had opened 11 public schools, and by 1859 the number had increased to 30. During 1842, it had also become safe for the Chickasaws to move west onto their land, and they began to establish elementary schools in their area. They constructed McKendree Academy, later named Chickasaw Manual Labor Academy, and then Harley Institute near Emet. Additional academies were constructed by the Chickasaws during the 1850s.[20]

The Osage Indian School building with the Boy's Band in the foreground, at Pawhuska, Osage Nation, 1902. Courtesy Archives and Manuscripts Division of Oklahoma Historical Society.

The area along the Red River between Oklahoma and Texas where the Chickasaws lived was called a "culture spot" in the early 1800s. Bloomfield Academy was staffed with graduates from eastern colleges. Since the Red River was navigable in the 1800s, musical instruments such as pianos, organs, violins, banjos, and mandolins, as well as beautiful furnishings, were brought in and freighted inland to the spacious homes of well-to-do Chickasaws. Attorneys, physicians, merchants, and other educated people lived in the area. Stringed instruments were found in most homes. Isolated farmers sometimes made their own instruments from local materials.[21]

Square dancing to fiddle music was popular. Uncle Allen Latti, a Chickasaw Indian from Emet, fiddled for square dances in the 1800s. The girls thought it was "great fun" to go to the settlement of Bromide to dance with the cowboys, especially because they kept their spurs on. Fiddlers accompanied by guitar, banjo, or mandolin played for special Indian and non-Indian dances. Waltzes, two-step polkas, and popular music were played. Hoedown type fiddle tunes were enjoyed during intermissions.[22]

(MUSIC IN INDIAN COUNTRY)

Tribal music was not popular among the younger and the more acculturated members of the Cherokee Nation, West in the period between 1839 and 1907. At Park Hill, Samuel Worcester realized that the people responded well to his ability to sing and to teach others to vocalize. Worcester composed hymns in the Cherokee language and printed them in his *Cherokee Hymn Book.* By 1844, vocal and instrumental music had become important entertainment for the Cherokees. By 1845, Worcester had put out a seventh edition of the Cherokee hymnal. Not content with just teaching words, he finally managed to produce the *Cherokee Singing Book* with which the Cherokees could learn to read musical notes.[23]

An early Cherokee law required that music be taught at the Cherokee Female Seminary. A tenor viol and seraphine were sent to the Worcester children from Boston, Massachusetts. Vocal music became important because the seminary students sang at concerts to raise money for charitable needs and also for entertainment. When the girls went home to visit during their vacations, they were expected to give local concerts. Nearly every girl learned to play the piano at Park Hill. The original requirement for one part-time singing teacher soon called for a staff of three full-time instructors in music.[24]

Bloomfield Academy, 1900. This second structure that housed the school was built in 1896 and was destroyed by fire in 1914. The Hill Collection. Courtesy Western History Collections, University of Oklahoma Libraries.

A group of students at the Cherokee Female Seminary, after it was rebuilt. Left to right: 1. Florence McSpadden (Mrs. Phil Samuel), 2. Patsy Hayes Pointer, 3. Bluie Adair (Mrs. J.A. Lawrence), 4. unidentified, 5. Mattie Miller, 6. Lulu Starr (Mrs. W.W. Hastings), 7. Ella Prather, 8. unidentified, In Front Row: 9. Babe Thompson (Mrs. P. Phillips), 10. In Rear Row: Bunt Schimpsher, 11., Mae Duncan (Mrs. Harvey Shelton), 12. Ella Carter, 13. Fannie Nash, In Rear: 14. Ingram ?, 15. Llewellyn Morgan (Mrs. Cullis Mayes), 16. Lulu Duckworth Jones, 17. & 18. unidentified, 19. Josie Crittenden Satain, 20. Maggie Smith, 21. Laura Fields, 22. Minnie Wetzel, 23. Julia Phillips Edmondson. Ballenger Collection. Courtesy Western History Collections, University of Oklahoma Libraries.

Park Hill, 1851. The Cherokee Female Seminary was completed in 1849. It closed during the Civil War but re-opened in 1871, then was destroyed by fire in 1887. Columns still stand at Tsa-La-Gi near Tahlequah. The Balyeat Collection. Courtesy Western History Collections, University of Oklahoma Libraries.

Music Class at Bloomfield Academy, ca. 1900. The Hill Collection. Courtesy Western History Collections, University of Oklahoma Libraries.

The seminary flourished between 1875 and 1901, the years that Miss Florence A. Wilson was its principal. She "couldn't carry a tune, nor did she know one note from another," but she loved to listen to music. She insisted on dignified conduct and high scholarship, and she encouraged the arts. Miss Wilson enjoyed telling stories about music in the earlier days of Indian Territory, noting that Fort Gibson, first established in 1824, had been built on higher ground in the middle of the 1840s and had become not only the center of military activity but of social life for the area as well.[25]

One evening, when a gathering to listen to piano music was underway, an Indian man in native clothes came in and sat down at the back of the room. No one spoke to him, but when a spirited girl finished playing, she whirled around on the piano stool, jumped up, turned to the Indian, and said laughingly, "Maybe you'd like to play for us." The Indian stood, bowed, and said, "If you'd care to hear me." He removed his blanket, sat down at the piano, and played classical music for more than an hour. When he stopped, the audience was silent for a few moments and then applauded enthusiastically. The man is remembered only as belonging to the Ross family and as having graduated from an eastern school where he had studied music.

Some of the early music teachers at the seminary were Fannie Cummins, Nell Taylor, Florence Caleb, Carlotta Archer, Cora McNair, Bluie Adair, Cherrie Adair, and Mrs. Marlin R. Chauncey.[26]

The Cherokee girls were taught only music that was considered to be acceptable for Victorian young ladies. "Thrilling runs" and "powerful chords," the more the better, were popular. *Polka de concert, marches de concert, galops de concert, valses de concert* and *morceaux de concert* permitted the girls to show their fancy fingerwork. Duets, trios, and quartets were also popular at the Indian schools. Cherrie Edmondson, who married R. B. Garrett, taught music for five years at the Cherokee Orphan asylum. She appreciated those combinations because they allowed more children to participate. She said that the boys and girls at the asylum had "music in their souls" and they were always "picking out little tunes." The asylum building burned and was never rebuilt, but some of the printed music for the duets was saved as well as some music of an earlier period.[27]

Pianos, music boxes, guitars, mandolins, and other musical instruments were included in the household goods of families migrating to the area and also of the army families accompanying soldiers and officers to Indian Territory. In 1851, Mrs. William P. Ross, known to her friends as Mary Jane or Molly, used some of her son's headright money to buy a piano from Brigadier General William G. Belknap that she had wanted "more than anything else in the world." The general had brought the small spinet from Fort Leavenworth in Kansas to Fort Gibson by oxcart. It remained in Mrs. Ross's home in Fort Gibson until she died. Her son, Hubbard, inherited it and passed it on to his oldest daughter, Marjorie, who lent it to the George H. Murrell Home. An early piece entitled "Beethoven's Dream, Grand Waltz, Especially Composed for the Pianoforte" was placed on the music rack of Mary Jane's piano. Amanda M. Ross had studied that piece of music in 1844 while she was in school in the East.[28]

(MUSIC IN INDIAN COUNTRY)

Mary Jane had also played a Chickering piano for Ethan Allen Hitchcock when he visited the Lewis Ross family during 1842 in their Park Hill home. Later, the family moved to Grand Saline and may have taken the piano there. However, it is also speculated that the piano may have been burned during the Civil War.[29]

Another, much larger piano, was brought into Indian Territory by Narcissa Owen, the wife of Colonel Robert Latham Owen of Lynchburg, Virginia, and mother to Robert L. Owen, an early United States senator from Oklahoma. Mrs. Owen gave piano lessons on it after her husband died. When she came to the Female Seminary to teach, it was brought to Park Hill, where it escaped the fire that destroyed the seminary in 1887. Later, it was transferred as a gift from one family member to another until it was placed in the Cherokee Museum, John Vaughn Library, Northeastern State College, Tahlequah. The scrollwork carved on the music rack included the name Stieff.[30]

Practice time for the Friars, ca. 1898. The St. Gregory's Abbey Collection. Courtesy Western History Collections, University of Oklahoma Libraries.

Girl's Orchestra at Sacred Heart School in Pottawatomie County, ca. 1910. Courtesy Santa Fe Depot Museum, Shawnee, Oklahoma.

Many families at Beattie's Prairie, Cherokee Nation, owned organs. Large parlor organs with elaborate overboards, mirrors, and alcoves for vases, oil lamps, and family pictures were as plentiful as small, portable organs. Many Cherokees became adept at playing the instruments by ear. Fiddling also seemed to be a natural skill. The boys of the Male Seminary serenaded the Female Seminary girls by singing, fiddling, or both. The "delighted" girls would throw down bouquets of flowers to their admirers. Mandolins and guitars were also favorite instruments. E. Goldman of Tahlequah taught the mandolin to seminary boys for many years. Fiddling families such as John E. Red Cloud's family were popular entertainers.[31]

The public schools of the Cherokees and private schools of the missionaries, offered some musical study courses, encouraged participation in musical activities, and always welcomed and respected performers. Church music also meant a great deal to the families in the Cherokee Nation. Ministers were scarce, but there were many "singing meetings." If no instrument was available, the singing would be started with a tuning fork.[32]

Indian composers of hymns more than 150 years ago included original words in the Indian language. Some Indian singers became well known nationally. The Choctaw School for small boys in Norwalk was noted for its voice training and singing classes. A beautiful piano from France reached the Rose Hill home of the Choctaw planter Robert M. Jones in the 1840s. A melodian was a special item in the home of Allen Wright and his bride, Harriet Mitchell Wright. Choruses from the Wheelock Mission and the Goodland Mission in the Choctaw Nation were popular. Alfred Wright and Loring S. Williams revised the Choctaw hymn book in 1833, enlarging the collection to 123 hymns because the Choctaw children had responded favorably to singing.[33]

In 1889, one of the first musical compositions from Indian Territory, "New Hope Waltz" for piano or cabinet organ, was dedicated to the "young Ladies of New Hope," a seminary established in 1842 near Old Skullyville in the Choctaw Nation. Later, the site became a post office called Oak Lodge.[34]

Meanwhile, events were occurring that would end the "golden years" the Indian nations had first enjoyed after their removals to Indian Territory. With the onset of the Civil War, most fine homes in the Cherokee Nation were destroyed. The Choctaw and Chickasaw nations were not as damaged because only their northern perimeters were invaded, and they had not been debilitated by factional tribal politics.[35]

Following the war, Confederate Indian refugees were often afraid to move back to their homes north of the Arkansas and Canadian rivers because of possible problems with former Union tribesmen. Choctaws and Chickasaws used much of their own resources to ease the suffering of the Creek, Cherokee, and Seminole refugees. Meanwhile, the federal government began to use appropriated land as a "dumping

The people of the Creek Nation gathered together and held dances, ca., 1910. The De Venny Collection. Courtesy Western History Collections, University of Oklahoma Libraries.

ground" for other Indian tribes from all over the country in relocations that became known as "Second Trails of Tears." An influx of non-Indians created an economy that was a mixture of legal commercial activity, criminality, and tribal exploitation.[36]

In 1866, delegations from the Five Civilized Tribes reluctantly submitted to the Reconstruction treaties that were made in Washington, D.C. Only four agreements were negotiated because the Choctaws and the Chickasaws signed a joint treaty. Their Reconstruction treaty provided that the name of any unified Indian community established would be "The Territory of Oklahoma." Allen Wright, a Choctaw Presbyterian minister and a delegate to the proceedings, was credited with proposing the name. "I would like to call the new territory 'Oklahoma', " he said, because " 'Okla' in my language means people or tribe, and 'homma' means red. 'Oklahoma' then means 'Red People.' Would this not be an appropriate name for a territory formed from land taken from the red man?" When Wright returned to his home, he was met at the gate by his wife. He responded to her query of "Allen, did we get to keep our land?" by saying, "No, we lost our land—but we kept our name."[37]

Rapid economic development in the Choctaw and Chickasaw nations helped their recovery from the Civil War, but for the most part Indians found themselves in the midst of poverty and ruin. They began to experience what seemed to be inevitable forces of destruction as railroads created a revolution in the transport of both people and goods. Mining, farming, ranching, oil, and other enterprises drew outsiders to Indian Territory.[38]

The newcomers brought varied political, cultural, religious, and musical traditions. A mining boom in the Choctaw Nation in the 1870s attracted Italian, Welsh, Polish, Greek, Slav, and Russian miners from Europe. Scattered German Mennonite and Czech settlements with their Old World customs and colorful festivals added to a variety of music and entertainment in the area.

When the Potawatomi Indians invited French, Belgian, and English monks from the Order of St. Benedict to set up schools for Indian children, the monks added a "definite European flavor" to central Oklahoma. Their mission, a favorite stop for travelers on the California Road, could house 300 people. It became a center for education with its St. Benedict's School For Boys and St. Mary's School For Girls, operated by the Sisters of Mercy. Poor and homeless children and local non-Indians were educated there alongside the elite of the Indian tribes. Olympian Jim Thorpe and mystery writer Tony Hillerman attended the school. But by 1915, the monks had established St. Gregory's Abbey and College in Shawnee in order to be closer to a railroad, and in 1943 St. Mary's was relocated to Oklahoma City. Vandalism, earthquake, and fire have erased nearly all signs of the original mission site. Only a few indications of the Benedictines' fabled Versailles-style formal garden can be found.[39]

The lack of law and order in the Indian nations attracted renegades. Most of the big names in western crime finally did experience swift justice in the federal court at Fort Smith, Arkansas, after Judge Isaac Parker was appointed to serve there. He sentenced 164 men to the gallows. The sentences of all but 79 were commuted to long prison terms, usually for life. The tune "Judge Parker" alluded with typical buffoonery to gunfighters and desperados.[40]

The chanteys of sailors, cowboy ballads, French and Creole songs, the tunes of the workplace, lumberjacks, trappers, Englishmen, railroad workers, and settlers all began to blend in the Southwest. This "cross fertilization of folk songs" led to a new, varied, and democratic type of music. Class distinctions began to disappear as the

Te Ata attended Chickasaw tribal schools and Oklahoma College for Women in Chickasha. Her father was the tribal treasurer elected prior to statehood, and her uncle was a governor of the Chickasaw Nation. As a young girl, Te Ata worked summers in chautauquas while she studied drama and art at the Carnegie School of Art in Pennsylvania. With mime, dance, and song, she shared Native American music and stories with audiences. She also started a Broadway stage career. The talented Te Ata was very proud of her heritage and offered dramatic interpretations of American Indian folklore to her audiences. Later, she performed before European royalty and many other distinguished people. A frequent guest of Franklin Delano Roosevelt, Te Ata was asked to perform one of her Indian programs at Eleanor Roosevelt's first formal dinner in the White House. The Roosevelts named a New York lake in her honor.[52]

After watching her perform, an eastern music reviewer wrote, "Te Ata, an Indian from the Southwest, has eyes that vision, tones that ring deep. Her poses take instinctive line and meaning. She above all others was the artist of the evening." Other critics, in America and abroad, seemed equally impressed with her talents. She was seen as a special kind of interpreter who left the audience "with a better understanding of the beauty and spiritual qualities of those founders of America's first culture."[53] Another commentator in Stratford, England, described the "weird half chant of her singing, ever seeking a minor note in preference to the natural key" as "both inspiring and impressive." The reviewer reported that the English audience appreciated the dramas she beat from her old and sacred drum. The writer deplored the great loss experienced in the decline of a nation "responsible for so rare a dramatic idea, no matter what compensations may be offered us by progress."[54]

"Te Ata" Mary Thompson fascinated classmates and later audiences, in America and abroad, with traditional stories and lore about her Native-American ancestry. Courtesy *Oklahoma Today*.

In the character of the drummer, Te Ata beat out stories from the old sacred drum so that the ancient tales might live for the listener. Photograph courtesy of Sally Gray, Ardmore, Oklahoma.

The English audience especially liked her "Program of Indian Masks." As the listeners heard the words "caressed" by Te Ata's tongue, they seemed to understand that her expressively inexpressive face was the mask worn by a nation that lived so close to nature that "the slightest emotion dare not be shown thereon." Therefore, to hear the words expressed by Te Ata was "to hear the saga of a whole race, the glories of which we of the East can merely guess."[55]

In her ordinary conversations, Te Ata frequently shared stories told to her by Indian grandmothers. The women of her tribe seemed to have been, except in matters of war, the real leaders of their people. One once said to Te Ata, "All of my life I have been trying to learn as the Chickadee learns." Te Ata asked, "How does the Chickadee learn." "By keeping still, and listening," was the answer. As for hospitality and putting their guests at ease, it would be hard to match the Chickasaw women. When Indian travelers came to visit, it was customary for the women of the village to rub their own clothes with dirt or ashes so the visitors would not be embarrassed by their own travel-stained attire. On the subject of peace among themselves? Te Ata said, "Every year, they dug a deep hole in which they ceremoniously buried all their unkind thoughts.[56]

When she was a young girl, Te Ata swore she would never marry a non-Indian, but in 1933 she married Dr. Clyde Fisher, director of the Hayden Planetarium, a division of the American Museum of Natural History in New York City. The pair shared a mutual love of plants and botany. Dr. Fisher, often amazed by his wife's keen knowledge of plants, would ask, "You didn't study botany?" "Only from mama," she would say.[57] The Fishers traveled extensively, met famous people, and participated in many cultural activities. Te Ata continued to go on tours to perform and help her people. After her husband died, she returned to Oklahoma City to live near her sister and her niece, state Senator Helen Cole. She died October 28, 1995, just 36 days before what would have been her 100th birthday on December 3, 1995.[58]

Te Ata's cousin Mary Ataloa Stone McClendan, who was one year younger than Te Ata, was born March 27, 1896, near Duncan in the Chickasaw Nation. Ataloa, "Little Flower," became a nationally known classical vocalist, educator, humanitarian, philosopher, and artist. She was admired for the beautiful quality of her voice, her personality, and her grace. Her recitals of Indian songs and stories were considered to be more than entertainment as she lifted her audiences into the spiritual beauty of the old Indian life with her cultivated voice and pure diction.[59]

Mary spent most of her early life with her Chickasaw grandmother who taught her much about Indian history and lore. She was told that she was a descendant of the Randolphs of Virginia, who traced their ancestry back to Pocahontas. After graduating from Duncan High School, she attended the College for Women at Chickasha and married Ralph McClendan, who died during military service in World War I. After the war ended, Mary moved to California with her mother. In California she earned an undergraduate degree from the University of Redlands and later completed a master's degree from Columbia University in New York. She also attended Union Theological Seminary and the Damrosch Art Institute in New York City.[60]

Mary was well received as a concert contralto on both coasts of the United States during her student years. She was offered several scholarships to study classical music and to perform in Europe, but she chose to teach Indian children rather than pursue a career abroad. She did accept an honorary scholarship from the International Institute to do research work and travel with a group of educators from 30 other nations. She was the only American in the group.[61]

Later, Mary received a Research Fellowship in Indian Art from the Rockefeller Foundation and was a delegate and lecturer at international seminar conferences at Yale University and the University of Hawaii. Her life interest was the conservation and interpretation of the arts, lore, and traditions of her people. She believed education that prepared young Indians for leadership roles would help build better cultural relationships in the world.[62]

When she accepted a position in the Language Arts Department at Bacone College in Muskogee, Oklahoma, it was the only school of higher education for Indian students at the time. She organized a school newspaper and later became head of the Arts Department. Students who participated in the glee club wore native dress when they traveled throughout the country presenting concerts on radio and at conventions. Mary sang for the Sesqui-Centennial Convention held in Philadelphia for four weeks during 1926.[63]

Concert singer and educator "Ataloa" Mary Stone McClendan (1896-1967) of Bacone College in Oklahoma, "stood as a beacon of light – seeing all people as one people," said Maurine Moore. Courtesy Chickasaw Council House Museum, Indian Nation, and the Archives and Manuscript Division of the Oklahoma Historical Society.

In 1929, Gordon Berger, a concert artist, organized a choir called "The Singing Redmen" at the college. Mary performed with them under her middle name Ataloa. At first, she gave concerts for free but later accepted donations which she used to provide scholarships for Indian students.[64]

Ataloa performed for Eleanor Roosevelt in Albany, New York, and later at the White House. Such national recognition helped Bacone College to grow even during the days of the Great Depression. As field secretary, she interested philanthropists in Indian culture and was successful in fundraising.[65]

Before each of her songs, Ataloa would tell a story. She explained that everything meant a song to the Indian. The song "Miniahoten," which translated as "Crying Water," became well known to her audiences. Many non-Indians were surprised to learn that Indian songs were often performed in a complex counter rhythm. In her lectures, she tried to dispel myths about her people. She noted that Indians did not acquire all their notions of social progress from non-Indians. She pointed out that the Chickasaw and some other tribes had constitutions and compulsory education long before non-Indians did in America.[66]

Ataloa realized her dream to make Bacone College a center for Indian music and art when Ataloa Lodge was built in 1932 on the grounds of the college. She had planned every detail of the stone and log building, including its furnishings, and had collected the stones for its fireplace when she traveled. More than 500 additional stones were sent to her from all over the country. A stone from the grave of Sitting Bull, a Hunkpapa Lakota chief, one from the birthplace of Sequoyah, and one from the Little Big Horn battlefield were embedded in the massive structure. Eleanor Roosevelt sent a stone from Oyster Bay, Long Island, to represent her husband's interest in and friendship with Native Americans. Rocks were also sent from New England to commemorate the Old Mohawk and Deerfield Trails. Stones from old mission fireplaces, pioneer forts, and frontier stockades were also included.[67]

In 1935, Acee Blue Eagle, a former student at Bacone College, became director of arts at the school. Bacone was the first American college to offer art instruction to Indian students. Ataloa also rediscovered the finger weaving of horsehair and other lost Indian arts and crafts. Students representing 40 tribes were present on campus by 1936.[68]

Ataloa's hobby was collecting Native American music. The year she received her fellowship from the Rockefeller Foundation, she drove some 50,000 miles across the United States and Canada to visit every Indian nation and learn firsthand about its culture. She sang and played her flute at gatherings that formed along the way. Around 1941, she discovered an extensive, ancient, very mildewed collection of Native American music in the Library of Congress. She was hired to clean and classify the collection. During that time, she also made recordings for Helen Keller to be used for the Talking Book Series for the blind.[69]

She was an officer of the National Congress of American Indians. Although the general poverty and poor health of the country's 400,000 Indians concerned her deeply in 1932, she maintained great faith in the sense of justice of the American people. Although well-meaning teachers had taught the Indian children to forget their culture and language, she hoped the image of the American Indian would change from enemy, nuisance, and problem to contributor to American culture.[70]

Ataloa was grateful for her early education from her Chickasaw grandmother and the later formal education she received. She was quoted as saying that the tribes could never get the Indian land back, but it was never too late to give the Indian a good education. She stressed the worth of a Christian education that trained young people for positions of leadership.[71]

After she retired from Bacone College she moved to Santa Fe, New Mexico, where she and her cousin, Te Ata, purchased a house. Ataloa started the International Hospitality Group and was hostess to many foreign visitors. She also counseled students at the Institute of American Arts and taught extension courses in American Indian culture at the University of California in Los Angeles. Together with Mac and Bee Krone, she started the Idyllwild School of Music and Fine Arts in California. She taught there every summer from 1950 to 1963. Her graceful influence and genuine love for people seemed to permeate every corner of the campus, and her campfire programs with Indian songs and music touched the hearts of all her listeners. The Sunday night sunset services she held at Inspiration Point in California were known to be exceptional. A friend, Maurine Moore, said that Ataloa stood as a beacon of light and that light remained a steady inspiration and challenge to them all.[72]

Another gifted Oklahoma Indian musician, Tsianina Blackstone, was born of Cherokee-Creek heritage in the Creek Nation, near Oktaha, in 1892. She became a world-famous concert singer and received many honors in her lifetime. In 1970, she

Tsianina Blackstone, a world-famous Creek and Cherokee concert singer, who was born in Oktaha, Creek Nation, in 1892, received many honors in her lifetime. Charles Wakefield Cadman also composed the opera *Shanewis* (The Robin Woman) about Tsianina's life. (Metropolitan Opera, 1918). George Rainey Collection. Courtesy Western History Collections. University of Oklahoma Libraries.

Lushanya Mobley in Giuseppe
Verdi's *Aida* presented by the
Chicago Opera Company.
Courtesy Archives of Greater
Southwest Historical Museum,
Ardmore, Oklahoma.

Clockwise: Lushanya Mobley in *Madame Butterfly*, *Lushanya*, and *Il Trovatore*. Courtesy Greater Southwest Historical Museum, Ardmore, Oklahoma.

was recognized as the only living American woman whose life had been made the subject of an opera.[73]

Tsianina grew up in the Oktaha area and rode the M-K-T train to the Indian school in Eufaula. She learned to play piano at the school. After graduating at the age of 16, she left Oklahoma to study voice and piano in Denver, Colorado.[74]

While in Colorado, she took time out from her studies to tour the United States with the composer Charles Wakefield Cadman to interpret his Indian songs. Later, she became known as an outstanding singer of classical songs. She appeared as a soloist with New York, Minneapolis, and Russian symphony orchestras. Cadman composed the opera *Shanewis, The Robin Woman* about Tsianina's life. He believed that the only true American voice was that of the Native American. Although the opera was well received at its first hearing at New York's Metropolitan Opera in 1918, Indian works did not sustain long popularity at that time in history.[75]

When the United States entered World War I, Tsianina volunteered to help in the war effort. She toured Europe with the American Expeditionary Forces and received special permission to wear her Indian clothes instead of the usual khaki uniform. She was the first American girl to cross the Rhine River with the Army of Occupation and she was adopted as a Daughter of the Regiment of the Second Division, commanded by Major General John A. Lejune. Later, she had the distinction of being the first woman permitted to join the American Legion.[76]

Tsianina wrote a book called *Where the Trails Have Led Me* in which she told stories of her childhood, Indian life, and the special relationships her family had with non-Indians. The book contained many photographs and included one of Alice Robertson, Oklahoma's first congresswoman, who was also a good friend and mentor to Tsianina.[77]

After Tsianina retired, she lived in Burbank, California. Despite her advanced years, she continued to be active in Daughters of the American Revolution work. Profits from her book were used to send Indian boys to Bacone College. Tsianina's aim in life was to represent her people with dignity. She tried to fulfill a true image of the American Indian.[78]

In 1964, reporter Roy P. Stewart remembered the time that he and a friend had dared to provoke a pretty Chickasaw Indian girl named Tessie Mobley, who sat in front of him when he was a sixth grader in the First Ward Grade School at Ardmore, Oklahoma, in the early 1900s. Stewart shared a desk, which in those days had ink wells, with another boy. One of the two boys succumbed to temptation and dipped one of Tessie's beautiful black braids into the convenient receptacle. The pretty little girl promptly whirled around and with one quick swoop knocked both boys out onto the aisle floor. The teacher came back to investigate and only said, "Humpf!—serves you right!" Stewart reminisced about the epidsode years later in "Pigtails to Opera, Now Hall of Fame," one of his regular newspaper columns.[79]

Tessie was born in Ardmore in December of 1906. The name Lushanya was given to her by a neighboring Indian tribe, the Cherokee, in whose language it meant "Sweet Singing Bird." She began her musical studies at the age of six. The 1923 Ardmore High School yearbook listed many of her achievements, with the comment "She made opera singers jealous."[80]

After further studies at Christian College in Columbus, Missouri, the University of Oklahoma, and Georgia University in Athens, she continued her education in California where she was soloist with the Hollywood Symphony Orchestra and the Griffith Park Greek Theatre. She played in motion pictures and was a technical advisor for one film. For four years, she sang the leading role in *First American,* produced in Albuquerque, New Mexico. She toured the South, Midwest, and western states giving concerts and appearing on radio. Early in 1932, she toured Europe on a concert tour and remained to study at the State Academy of Music in Berlin, Germany, for two years. She sang on radio programs in Berlin and in Rome, Italy. She won a competitive scholarship offered by Premier Benito Mussolini for study at the Royal Academy, St. Cecilia in Rome. She was the only foreigner in attendance at the academy that year. When she made her operatic debut at La Scala in Milan, Italy, she was the first American Indian to sing there. The crowd went wild and kissed her hands and feet to show their enthusiasm over her performance. Six European critics predicted a brilliant future for her when she sang the title role of Giuseppe Verdi's *Aida* at the Rosetti Theatre in Trieste. Canadian and American reviews of Lushanya's performances were equally favorable, especially for her role as Aida. The *Los Angeles Daily News* declared that "Miss Lushanya makes a beautiful Aida. . . But most gratifying of all is that she has succeeded in investing Aida with glamour. Her Aida would surely have been the pin-up girl of the Pharaohs."[81]

World leaders recognized Lushanya's talents. The mezzo-soprano was chosen to sing before crowned heads of state and other dignitaries in Europe. In London, she sang the role of Minnehaha in a production of *Hiawatha* at Albert Hall in London. During World War II, she was asked by President Roosevelt to help the United Service Organization entertain soldiers and defense workers on behalf of the war effort.[82]

The Ardmore singer was painted by several European and American artists. One painting became part of a collection in the Royal Academy of Art in London. The Italian sculptor Galileo Parisini did several figures of Lushanya. One of the statues was placed in the Quirinal Palace in Rome, Italy. Oklahoma artist Brunetta Griffith did a portrait entitled *Lushanya, Sweet Singing Bird.*[83]

Tessie retired after marrying Ramon Vinay, a leading tenor for the Metropolitan Opera. She traveled with him on his overseas and American tours and served as his manager, promoting him in his career. Vinay continued to perform for charities and benefits after he became Chile's counsel to Spain. The couple lived in a house that overlooked the Mediterranean Sea near Calibas, Spain.[84]

A collection of Lushanya's costumes has been put on display at the Chickasaw Council House Museum in Tishomingo, Oklahoma. Tessie is recognized as a link between American Indian and European cultures. Her remarkable beauty and talents enabled her to "walk with kings" and powerful leaders on both continents. Reporter Ruth Lewis wrote that whenever and wherever Lushanya was interviewed, she never hesitated to say with pride that she "was born in Ardmore, Oklahoma." Tessie "Lushanya" Mobley Vinay was inducted into the Oklahoma Hall of Fame in 1964.[85]

Five Indian girls, all born in Oklahoma, received much recognition, nationally and internationally, for their superb talent and artistry in the field of classical ballet. The famous ballerinas were Yvonne Chouteau, Cherokee-Shawnee; Moscelyn Larkin, Shawnee-Peoria; Rosella Hightower, Choctaw; and Maria and Marjorie Tallchief, Osage. In November 1991 all five gathered in the rotunda of the Oklahoma State Capitol to help dedicate a 20-foot ceiling mural by Mike Larsen, a Chickasaw artist from Oklahoma City. The work, called *Flight of Spirit,* portrays the five dancers symbolically in white ballet costumes. The background depicts the historical Trail of Tears with young dancers, tribal ancestors, and five flying geese. The geese represent the "grace and spirit" of the ballerinas.[86]

Six years later, the Oklahoma Arts Council invited the five ballerinas to the 1997 Governors Arts Awards where Governor Frank Keating announced the designation that placed them among the extraordinary group of gifted Oklahomas called Oklahoma Treasures.[87]

Yvonne Chouteau became the youngest dancer ever accepted into the company of the Ballet Russe de Monte Carlo in Paris, France, when she began her career at the age of 14. For eight years she was the troupe's celebrated ballerina. Later, she became an artist-in-residence at the University of Oklahoma. She was inducted into the Oklahoma Hall of Fame in 1947.[88]

Moscelyn Larkin, choreographer, teacher of ballet, and the daughter of a Russian dancer, joined the original Ballet Russe before her 16th birthday. She toured Europe, South America, and the United States as a soloist and later as a ballerina. She also performed with the Ballet Russe de Monte Carlo. She possessed a wide knowledge of classical repertoire and an exceptional memory. Frequently featured with

"Flight of Spirit," a 20-foot mural in the Oklahoma State Capitol, was dedicated on November 18, 1991. Artist Mike Larsen had symbolically portrayed the "grace and spirit" of Oklahoma's five internationally famous ballerinas against a background that depicted the historical "Trail of Tears," young dancers, and tribal ancestors. From left to right in the foreground: Yvonne Choteau, artist Mike Larsen, Rosella Hightower, Maria Tallchief, Marjorie Tallchief, and Moscelyn Larkin. Courtesy Oklahoma Publishing Company.

Radio City Ballet, in New York City and on television, she also served as artistic director of the Tulsa Civic Ballet and taught ballet in a number of Tulsa schools. She conceived the idea for the Oklahoma Indian Ballerina Festival of 1957. She appeared in the premier of Louis Ballard's *The Four Moons* in Tulsa to commemorate Oklahoma's 60 years of statehood in 1967. She was installed in the Oklahoma Hall of Fame in 1979.[89]

Rosella Hightower had an outstanding career with the Ballet Russe de Monte Carlo, as a soloist with the American Ballet Theatre, touring in North and South America with the original Ballet Russe, and as grand ballerina with the Marquis de Cuevas Company in Monte Carlo. At the request of the United States government, she also toured two years with the Ballet Theatre of Lucie Chase. Later, she formed her own Center of Classical Music in Cannes, France. In 1967, she came back to Oklahoma to perform in the world premier of Ballard's *The Four Moons* in Tulsa.[90]

Marjorie Tallchief, said to be the most "versatile" of the great ballerinas, danced leading roles in both traditional classical and contemporary repertoires. She was a member of the American Ballet and, at 18, she became a ballerina with the Marquis de Cuevas in Monte Carlo. She was the first American dancer to perform at the Bolshoi Theatre in Russia and the first American dancer to become a "Danseuse Etoile" with the Theatre National de la Opera de Paris. She was inducted into the Oklahoma Hall of Fame in 1991.[91]

Marjorie's sister, Maria Tallchief, joined the Ballet Russe de Monte Carlo after high school. At the end of the first season, she danced the premier role in a Frederick Chopin concerto. She made her New York debut in the same role, and soon advanced to ranking soloist. When she became a member of the Balanchine Ballet Society, now known as the New York City Ballet, she was recognized as the equal of top dancers in the United States and abroad. She was the first American dancer to receive the title of prima ballerina and she became accepted as one of the world's greatest dancers. Although tormented by shyness, Maria changed herself, by self-discipline, into a woman of "authority and radiance." She was inducted into the Oklahoma Hall of Fame in 1968 and received many other honors in her lifetime.[92]

Young Indian men were also contributing to the musical scene in Oklahoma. Outstanding figures in American music included Albert Stewart, Chickasaw; Lynn Riggs, Cherokee; Louis Ballard, Quapaw-Cherokee; Woodrow William Haney, Sr., Creek-Seminole; Tom Mauchahty-Ware, Kiowa-Comanche; Woodrow Wilson Crumbo, Potawatomi; and Doc Tate Nevaquaya, Comanche.[93]

Albert Stewart, born in Wynnewood, Oklahoma, in 1909, earned his way through college with his rich bass-baritone voice of remarkable range and power. He became a popular platform and concert artist who was known to thousands of people all over the country. He was also featured on television programs for children and in *Rhythm,* a film produced by *Encyclopedia Britannica* for school distribution.[94]

Stewart was related to Robert Harris, governor of the Chickasaw Nation, and was a descendant of Frances Folsom, the wife of President Grover Cleveland. He was a winner in the Chicago Music Festival of 1939. He served as director of the Chicago Program Service, two terms as president of the Indian Council Fire, and on the International Platform of Lecturers and Concert Artists.[95]

A tune that made musical history appeared on the scene in the mid-1930s. Lynn Riggs, a young Cherokee playwright, had written a play based on his book *Green Grow the Lilacs.* It had a short run on Broadway but attracted the attention of the Theater Guild, which suggested to composer Richard Rodgers that it might have material for a new musical show.[96]

Rodgers was interested. He collaborated with Oscar Hammerstein II to produce *Oklahoma!* with a ballet directed by Agnes de Mille, lyrics by Hammerstein, and music by Rodgers. From opening night in March of 1943 until it closed on May 29, 1948, the show was an unprecedented triumph in the history of American theater, presenting more than 2,200 performances. No other musical entertainment in the history of the theater had run as long. The play, with its rollicking, jubilant expression of pioneer life, became a part of American tradition.[97]

Rodgers placed his well penciled and autographed original manuscript in the Library of Congress. In 1953, Oklahoma state representative George Nigh, who later became governor, authored a bill that made "Oklahoma!" the official state song. Representatives Glen Ham of Pauls Valley and Ira D. Humphreys of Chickasha co-

Lynn Riggs at Yaddo. Poet and playwright Lynn Riggs (1889-1954) wrote the play *Green Grow the Lilacs* on which the musical *Oklahoma!* was based. The Campbell Collection. Courtesy Western History Collections, University of Oklahoma Libraries.

He was self-taught in both specialties. He used the two-dimensional style of painting to emphasize mood with a sophisticated use of color. He reflected a deep attachment to the past and to his family upbringing.[132]

The more Nevaquaya played the flute, the more his style of painting subtly changed. His works became less busy and more rhythmic as mood and atmosphere became more important to him. He became proficient at painting over black where no under-sketching or erasing was possible. Complete technical control was necessary to make every stroke final and meaningful.[133]

Numerous awards, honors, and financial rewards did not cause Nevaquaya to change his lifestyle. He continued to paint in his home at a table in his bedroom. Whenever he needed inspiration or help, he would pick up his flute and play it for a while. His paintings and the music of his Indian flute seemed to naturally blend together. Julie Pearson, an Indian art critic, noted, "… the faster the world spins, the more his style of art remains a source of beauty and reflectivness . . . a place to come home to."[134]

The appreciation and the study of Indian music and art has been difficult for European-Americans because the structure and purpose of Native-American compositions have been alien to them. Unlike much European singing and dancing, Native American music and art is not primarily intended to entertain. Rather, songs and dances traditionally called upon the spiritual world for help. As the original Indian religions were challenged by a changing world, the old ceremonies were practiced less. Medicine men managed to preserve some old songs, but as the younger people cared less about them, the original significance of the singing and dancing was almost lost.[135]

Writer Clyde Ellis lectured that to the Indian, the world of sound was immense, compelling, and filled with power. Song was fundamental to Indian culture, and was called the cornerstone of its identity. He observed that to hear music in the Indian way was "to see with our ears." Carol K. Rachlin wrote that if a person would keep listening to the old Indian music, the melodies of the other era would emerge.[136]

Natalie Curtis, who lived from 1875 to 1921, was one of the few pioneers who helped to pave the way for the scholarly study of Indian culture and music. A family friend, President Theodore Roosevelt, helped Curtis in her work, although it was contrary to the prevailing beliefs and attitudes of American society and also to government policy. When Natalie, who had studied and composed music in America and Europe, heard the music of the Southwest Indians, she declared it to be distinctly American music that was "the spontaneous and sincere expression of the soul of a people." She found Southwest native cultures to possess a sophistication, with definite art forms, highly stylistic song-poems, and elaborate detailed ceremonies that had taken centuries to evolve. She collected songs, art, poetry, lore, and history that became more meaningful as the years passed.[137]

Curtis believed that the histories and unique cultures of American Indians were of great value, not only to America but to the human race. She recognized how Indian music differed from European. She declared that no European music had as complex, elaborate, and changing rhythm as that of the American Indian. She found the music and singing of the different tribes to be as varied as their individual lifestyles and customs. Their early music was compatible with the sounds of nature and the cries of animals, and their lives were so linked with nature that for them it became an unconscious harmonic background in their music that non-Indians could not hear and so considered lacking. She pointed out that to hear Indian songs and

Watonga, Oklahoma's James Black, a member of the Cheyenne Bowstring Society, teaches Native American traditional values, beliefs, and cultures through his music on his red cedar flutes, in the latter 1900s. He explained, "We believe all things have a spirit of their own . . . Each flute has a different sound the way we, as human beings, all have a different voice. The spirit of the flute is alive and vibrating in my hands when I play. Courtesy *Persimmon Hill Magazine.*

music in their own natural environment, under the big sky, on the open prairie, with the feel of the wind and the grasses, and the sounds of animal life, was to hear a symphony of nature complete with a rhythm, melody, and harmony.[138]

Some Oklahoma Indians have been able to maintain tribal traditions as they have adapted to changing times. Plains Indians have kept the old practice of gathering together in powwows for spiritual renewal. The festivals tend to make the participants feel good, mentally and physically, as they sing, dance, and feast while visiting, making new friends, and sometimes competing for prizes. Athletic events are often sponsored. Artists and craftspeople also have an opportunity to display their work. During the 1990s, Red Earth Festivals in Oklahoma City vividly demonstrated a dramatic legacy from the past. Costumed Indians from more than 100 American tribes have gathered together to celebrate life in colorful, happy celebrations with dance competitions.[139]

The set, formal ceremonies of the past have become more a combination of family reunions and celebrations of family events with singing and dance competitions. Months of preparations usually precede a powwow to practice drumming, singing, dancing, to make dance regalia, prepare give-away items, and to set up the campsite or arena. The festivals are held wherever the space is available, from a cow pasture to a large modern convention center.[140]

The ceremonies constantly change and vary as cultural traditions and religious experiences are shared from generation to generation. The powwows serve as popular social and cultural activities in Oklahoma. Non-Indians who attend often find them to be interesting experiences.[141]

The drum and the singers always hold center stage and are vital to a good powwow. Good drums are in demand and attract good dancers which can make for a more successful gathering. Every song is unique, though most follow the same structure with a lead, a second, a chorus, and honor beats.[142]

The original North American Indians are remembered as religious people who were instinctive environmentalists with a song for everything and every occasion.

Historians are noting that their contributions to the music of America and to the world are considerable. The poetry and the death songs of the old chiefs have, quite naturally, gone into mythology.

William Brandon wrote, "The wars of the plains are America's *Illiad*....all poetry, for poetry is really made of blood and not of daffodils. It will outlive sober history and never quite die...." He added that Red Cloud, Roman Nose, and other great Indian leaders will "very likely, still touch a light to the spirit as long as America is remembered." Author Marian Wallace Ney also pointed out that the Indian as a myth-god protector could not have been shown greater respect than during World War II when paratroopers jumped from their planes into combat with what was perhaps their last word on their lips—"Geronimo."[143]

AFRICAN AMERICAN

Music

IN OKLAHOMA

2

Black people were among the earliest non-Indian settlers in

Oklahoma. They came with their Indian slave owners when the

eastern Indian tribes were relocated to Indian Territory during the

early 1800s. Their African music, which had already been exposed to

Latin American and European harmonies, helped to change all

musical styles and to create new patterns of modern music.

Researchers have noted that Oklahoma, a geographical "crossroads"

for travelers, became a sort of "musical passage" for the creative new

styles that blended music of the different cultures.[1]

Most of the Black slaves who came to Indian Territory had their roots in Africa. When they were brought to America, they were able to make crude musical instruments from trees, reeds, and bones. By clapping and patting, they were able to beat an improvised drum to bring the words and the beat together at one time. The intricacy of the rhythm and the words they spoke were difficult for Europeans to understand. An African would be talking and then burst into song to express himself better. African music and conversation often swung back and forth between speaking and singing with hand-foot stomping and an involvement of the entire body. Above all, the music was rhythmic. The rhythm was usually like tapping one's foot twice while beating the hands three times, keeping the rhythm of the feet steady, and dividing each of the hand beats into two or three beats, which is called syncopating the notes. All of this was easy for Africans but usually difficult for musicians of the western world.[2]

Music in African society served almost the same role as speech because the actual pitch of the syllables in African words influenced their meaning. For example, if both syllables in the Yoruba word "oko" were pitched the same, the word meant "husband." However, it meant "hoe" if the first syllable was lower than the second, "canoe" if the second syllable was lower than the first, and "spear" if both were low. African drums "talked," not because of some Morse Code but because the drummer sounded the pitch of the actual words. African drumming used to be a form of sign language that developed so that people of different tribes and dialects could understand each other.[3]

The same plantation, slave, or work songs were used for rowing, revival shouts, burials, hymns of consolation, signals, and for the purpose of escaping to freedom in the northern states or Canada. For example, when singing "O Canaan, Sweet Canaan, I Am Bound For the Land of Canaan," Africans were sometimes expressing their determination to reach the North or Canada, their "Canaan." Moses of the Christian Bible at times had religious significance as a deliverer that the slaves begged to come to America. Moses could stretch out his rod to create a path of dry land on which the slaves might walk back to Africa. Many of the American slave songs were set to tunes that closely resembled old African melodies. Set to the religious songs of the western world, the spirituals were not just songs of sorrow but covered a wide range of subjects. The harmony was not regular—each singing might be a new creation. Because every singer tried to express his or her own feelings, harmony and disharmony, shifting keys, and broken time made up the songs.[4]

Drums and horns were generally banned by southern slave owners because of fear that they might be used for signaling. Musicologist Dena Epstein believed that the banjo came into use when drums and horns were forbidden. Africans played any piece of wood or metal across which a few strings could be strung to mimic the rough plunking of the banjo or guitar. One theory about the origin of ragtime suggests that the distinctive ragtime piano rhythm initially imitated the African banjo. With the addition of a brass band, jazz was born.[5]

Many Black traditions survived in America because Blacks were permitted to sing and dance to their old African music in the North and, despite the ban in the South, Black festivals were allowed every Sunday at Congo Square in New Orleans, Louisiana. African-American folk music began to develop when Blacks were exposed to European music in the 1600s and the 1700s. European Americans did not sing as they worked, but they allowed the slaves to sing because they thought that meant they were happy, and a happy slave would not try to escape. Research has also shown that before 1865 American Black spirituals were not always simple affirmations of faith; they were sometimes used with great skill, strength, and intelligence by plantation Blacks to communicate with each other. It was also noted that African-Americans adopted white customs and music, but wherever possible they integrated them with their own traditions.[6]

The years between 1845 and 1865 were the "heyday" for spirituals in America. More than a priceless heritage from the past, the spirituals were promising material for later Black music and perhaps for great liturgical music.[7]

Most of the music on the large plantations in the Red River area of Indian Territory was group singing. One Indian owner had as many as 500 Black slaves. Early Black music in Oklahoma was researched by the WPA Writers Project in the 1930s. Much of the project's work was preserved and has become a valuable reference resource.[8]

Jesse Irvin, a writer for the project, discovered that the song "Swing Low Sweet Chariot" was sung long before the Civil War by Wallace Willis, better known as "Uncle Wallace," and his wife "Aunt Minerva." The two slaves were brought to an area near Doaksville in the southern part of the Choctaw Nation by Brit Willis, a prominent Choctaw who had owned a plantation along the banks of the Mississippi River. One sultry afternoon during the 1840s, Wallace looked ahead to where the Red River lay shimmering in the distance. As he gazed past the cotton field to the waters beyond, he was reminded of old friends and of days gone by. Engulfed by homesickness, he broke into a song that expressed the longings of his soul:

> Swing low, sweet chariot,
> Comin' fo' to carry me home....

His wife leaned on her hoe and joined in his crooning as she too looked far away. Together they sang:

> I look over Jordan, an' what do I see,
> Comin' fo' to carry me home....
> Swing low, sweet chariot....[9]

During the winter months of 1851-1859, the two were rented out as servants to the Old Spencer Academy, a boarding school for Choctaw boys in the Choctaw Nation. Although the school superintendent Reverend Alexander Reid abhorred slavery, he needed to hire Black slaves from their Indian owners because the Choctaw did few menial tasks. The slave servants were treated as more than just field hands and became an intricate part of life at the academy. Uncle Wallace and Aunt Minerva were well known in the area and delighted others with their singing. They have been credited with the oral composition of "Steal Away to Jesus," "The Angels are Coming," "I'm a Rolling," and "Roll Jordan Roll," songs that evoked the feelings of oppressed souls. The missionaries were especially pleased to note the inspirations that the slaves derived from Christian hymns, Bible readings, and missionary preaching.[10]

Reverend Reid left Indian Territory at the beginning of the Civil War. While living in the North, he attended a program given by a group of Black singers from Fisk University in Tennessee. Although the chorus was singing mostly European-style music such as "Home Sweet Home," "There's Moonlight on the Lake" "Patrick McCuishla," "Annie Laurie," and temperance songs like "Wine Is a Mocker," Reverend Reid was impressed with the musical ability of the students. He became inspired, with the help of his wife and sons, to remember the words and music of Uncle Wallace's songs. Under the direction of the missionary and Professor George L. White of Fisk University, the chorus practiced and learned about five or six of Uncle Wallace's songs. The group made history when they began singing the slave songs at a religious conference in Oberlin, Ohio, in 1871. Strains of "Steal Away to Jesus" transfixed the delegates. They called for more and more singing from the chorus. From then on, the group continued to sing in public the plantation songs which soon became known as spirituals—American folk songs in the truest sense, as they arose from a culture known only in America.[11]

The songs usually originated spontaneously in the heat of religious fervor or under oppression. After hearing the old plantation songs, people began to understand and appreciate the spiritual quality that Blacks contributed to the culture of America. The old slave songs show such a remarkable knowledge of the Bible that it has been said it could be reconstructed from them. In 1872, spirituals were first made available to the public in written form with Thomas F. Steward's book *Jubilee Songs as Sung by the Jubilee Singers of Fisk University.*[12]

Three of Uncle Wallace and Aunt Minerva's orally composed songs, "Steal Away to Jesus," "Swing Low Sweet Chariot," and "I'm a Rollin'," became popular not only in America but worldwide. In 1873, Queen Victoria of England asked for an encore of "Steal Away to Jesus" when it was one of two spirituals sung before her by the Jubilee Singers. Weeping, she said nothing had comforted her more since the death of her husband, Prince Albert. The Jubilee Singers continued to be famous throughout the western world. Before Reverend Reid died in 1890, Professor White, director of the Jubilee Singers, told him that by giving the slave songs to the group at the time he did, he had made the most valuable contribution to Fisk University ever made by any one person.[13]

Archival records note that in 1883 Reverend Reid "secured" photographs of Uncle Wallace and Aunt Minerva for the walls of Fisk University, but there is no further mention of the portraits. A few months later, Uncle Wallace died and was buried in a Black cemetery west of Boggy Depot in Oklahoma. In 1959, the Oklahoma Historical Society placed a stone monument on the original site of the Old Spencer Academy. The red granite boulder, located on the original site of the school eight miles north and one-half mile east of Sawyer in Choctaw County, one-half mile west of Spencerville, near the center of Section 6, T55-R19E, bore the following inscription:

> This noted school for Choctaw boys, established by the Choctaw
> Council, was named for John C. Spencer, U.S. Secretary of War.
> Subjects through high school were taught. The first graduates
> went to eastern colleges in 1848. Large buildings were erected.
> In a quadrangle here including Jones Hall, Pitchlynn Hall,
> Armstrong Hall, a school building and dining hall, with houses
> for employees, storehouses and barns adjacent.
> It was here at Old Spencer Academy that "Steal Away to Jesus,"
> "Roll, Jordan Roll," "Swing Low, Sweet Chariot," spirituals now
> sung throughout America, were composed by the old Negro, Uncle
> Wallace who first sang them with his wife, Aunt Minerva to the
> delight of all who heard them. The two old slaves were hired
> out by their owner to work for the Reverend Alexander Reid,
> Superintendent of Spencer Academy 1851-61.
>
> ---
>
> *Oklahoma Historical Society, 1959*[14]

Another WPA slave narrative from the 1930s recorded that during or shortly after the Civil War, some 100 Black slaves were enlisted with the promise of freedom to help drive horses and cattle north to Kansas from Grand River in Indian Territory. Inspired by the hopes of the Black drovers, one of Benjamin Franklin Landrum's educated slaves "composed the celebrated violin piece, 'I tell you, Marse Ben, your nigger's gwine to leave you' " shortly before they departed. By the time the group reached Kansas, it had been joined by some 400 more Blacks, all seeking the promised freedom. However, many disappointed and disillusioned Blacks came back later to Indian Territory to work again for their former masters.[15]

After the Civil War, Black immigrants from the South began to arrive in Indian Territory. Some took part in the land runs beginning in 1889. After the Dawes Commission carried out the change of land titles to individual ownerships in the Indian nations during the 1890s, songs of Black experience began to blend with Indian music as societal relationships changed. The Black population in Oklahoma reached 137,000 between 1890 and 1910. The boomtown era of the petroleum industry also brought increased Black immigration.[16]

Musical tastes were considered to have been quite low in America before 1875. Over the next 20 years, music became even more gaudy and gross. One writer

After the Civil War, groups of Northern skilled, educated, and professional Black people came to Oklahoma Territory to build their own towns and communities. The education of their children was a priority. This photograph shows a music class preparing for a musical pageant, ca. 1890. Courtesy Western History Collections, University of Oklahoma Libraries.

referred to the period as "the circus age of music" when music was hitched to the circus chariot. Caricatured versions of Blacks and their music became popular. Popular music was cut off from its classical roots, and a bitter feud developed between popular and classical music. Composer Stephen Foster came into favor as the minstrel vogue was ending. His music, a diluted version of Black melodies and dialect ditties, started the country humming, whistling, playing, and singing Black tunes. However, true Black music might have been lost forever but for the work of the Fisk University Jubilee Singers who toured the United States and Europe during the late 1800s and early 1900s. Their programs showed the artistry, beauty, and rhythm of the old spirituals to the world.[17]

Most of Oklahoma's considerable musical contributions, especially to American jazz, went relatively unrecognized for years. The majority of the territorial traveling dance bands were made up of African-Americans. As they traveled around the various Indian nations and non-Indian areas, musicians of different cultural backgrounds experimented, improvised, and freely borrowed from each other to develop new techniques

(AFRICAN-AMERICAN MUSIC IN OKLAHOMA)

and styles. Folklorist Alan Lomax wrote that "the map sings" was a description of music in Oklahoma during those early days.[18]

In the 1890s, the town of El Reno in Oklahoma Territory became a center for ragtime music and a place where musicians, songwriters, and performers congregated. S. Brunson Campbell, a professional piano player, remembered El Reno as a wide-open town and "a beehive of gamblers." In 1900, 16-year-old Campbell played Scott Joplin's "Maple Leaf Rag" for the famous Gordon W. "Pawnee Bill" Lillie at El Reno's Kerfoot Hotel. Twenty years later, when they met again in Tulsa, Pawnee Bill asked the popular "Ragtime Kid" to play it again for him.[19]

Older musicians and jazz enthusiasts remember jazz appearing almost spontaneously in Oklahoma at more or less the same time as it did in other parts of the country. The marching brass bands in Oklahoma and other areas of the Southwest and Midwest are considered to have played important roles in its development.[20]

Teachers in Guthrie, Oklahoma Territory, 1890. Courtesy Western History Collections, University of Oklahoma Libraries.

One factor was the popularity of "cakewalks" around the 1890s. At these social events, dressed-up couples promenaded to the music of brass bands for prizes of cake. The lively music naturally led to dancing, which in turn caused dance halls to spring up. The distinctive musical style of the cakewalk went from ragtime to jazz and from "spontaneous" music to a formalized written music for ballroom dancing. A musician who was born in 1883 remembered that brisk ragtime music was often played at funerals in his native Baltimore, Maryland, especially in the streets on the way back from the cemetery.[21]

The advent of musical recordings of jazz and a federal order helped to usher in the new musical era. The first recorded jazz discs were made by the Original Dixieland Jazz Band in 1917. The same year, a federal order closed the bordellos in the Storyville area of New Orleans, throwing musicians out of work. Jobless musicians formed traveling bands that moved all over the country to wherever they could find work playing for dances and concerts.[22]

In the early stages of the phenomenon, eastern jazz sounded quite different from Dixieland, or New Orleans, jazz, but as musicians traveled back and forth through Oklahoma on their way to musical engagements on the West or East coasts, they shared the music with local musicians as well as other traveling musicians and their dance bands. Consequently, Black folk music, Acadian, or Cajun, folk music, and European folk music were brought together, and jazz ceased to sound as regional as it had before. Meanwhile, younger people turned to newer dances like the fox-trot and turkey-trot that were influenced by the African-American style of dancing.[23]

The first blues recordings were not made until the 1920s. Because nineteenth-century writings about Black music do not seem to include anything about such music, the early blues songs appear to have evolved from work songs, prison songs, and spirituals around the turn of the century. Spirituals reflected the social conditions under which Blacks were forced to live as slaves and later under freedom. When Black people appeared light-hearted, they were often broken-hearted.[24]

Black individuals have tried to explain blues songs. One wrote that blues songs expressed the pain of being Black and the melodies brought a relief even though the relief was "a joy born from pain." Another offered that the singing of Black people was often a desperate attempt to keep from crying. One Black female writer reasoned that it took much spiritual strength to express bad experiences and at the same time recall and recreate that same sorrow or bad memory time and time again in song. She considered the ability to be a powerful tool that exhibited a toughness and a talent for articulation that helped to maintain personal status and self-respect. She wrote that the singing of the blues not only demonstrated a toughness that exhilarated and renewed the singer but also evoked and enhanced the feelings of the listener. The blues artist seemed to reach out to people who had suffered and to assure them that they were not alone, that someone else understood their troubles and heartaches.[25]

A blues pianist said that the intent of the blues was not to escape from reality but to express deep feelings artistically. Some researchers have observed that listening to the four-four beat of jazz recordings seemed to make it easier, then and later, to endure some of the harsh realities of life—drought and dust, crop failures, the Ku Klux Klan, and the incredible carnage and loss, both human and financial, suffered by the African-Americans in the 1921 Tulsa race riot.[26]

Writer Ralph Ellison, who was born in Oklahoma City in 1914 and grew up there, wrote vividly about his childhood, recounting how he and his fellow Black children were caught between different musical styles and cultures. He observed that

Claude Williams, born in Muskogee, Oklahoma in 1908, played with Oklahoma City's Twelve Clouds of Joy Orchestra in 1933. He soon became known as Claude "Fiddler" Williams. Williams played his fiddle all over the world and the United States for special occasions. He entertained for President Bill Clinton and the First Lady in the White House in 1994 and again in 1998.

everything was mixed culturally for the children "and anything and everything was to be found in the chaos of Oklahoma." He described his neighborhood as "chaotic" and still characterized by frontier attitudes, a mixture of naivity and sophistication, good and bad, that was puzzling and often confusing.[27]

Ellison remembers that Black veterans of the Spanish-American War taught complicated drill patterns to the neighborhood boys on summer evenings on the Bryant School grounds. Before long, a jazz feeling would come into the marching and they would be "swinging." He wrote that the veterans raised military discipline to a low art form, almost a dance, and the spirit was jazz.[28]

Slave, or work, songs conflicted with the European classical music that was taught in the public schools. The folk song tradition of Black music demanded the playing of what was heard and felt while the teachers of classical music insisted that musicians play strictly by the music book and express only what they were "supposed" to feel. Often strong clashes resulted.[29]

The Langston University Band, 1906, with director Zelia N. Page (middle) and her sister, Mary Page, at the far right of the photo.

Ellison reminisced about a third grade music appreciation class in which a classmate insisted that he saw a large green snake swimming down a quiet brook instead of the large white bird that the teacher saw when they were listening to Saint Saens' *Carnival of the Animals.* The rest of the class, including Ralph, "lied like black, brown, and yellow Trojans about that swan," but his classmate held firm to his vision. When the episode ended, the classmate had been spanked, and the teacher was crying. Ellison was satisfied that reality and environment had been redeemed and were intact because all of the children were more familiar with snakes than they were with beautiful white swans. Ellison often marveled that in spite of such teaching methods, some of the children, including himself, had grown up with a sincere appreciation of classical music.[31]

Ellison also wrote about the Oklahoma jazz dances, jam sessions at Halley Richardson's place on Deep Deuce, or Second Street, in Oklahoma City, phonographs blaring the blues in the back alleys he knew as a boy delivering groceries, and the watermelon vendors and other peddlers who shouted out their wares to the rhythm of their horses' hooves. Washerwomen sang work songs as they bent over tubs in sunny yards. The public school programs tuned ears to classical music with music

Ca. 1907, the Langston University Band traveled in a wagon that was drawn by six large white horses. Courtesy Archives and Manuscripts Division of the Oklahoma Historical Society.

appreciation classes, free musical instruments for the children to use, and basic musical instructions for any child who cared to learn classical music. Uniforms were furnished for all who qualified for the band. Ellison observed that Oklahoma City Black children were heirs to all ages and styles of music, and he was confident that those who knew their native culture would not be lost when they encountered the unfamiliar.[31]

Although ragtime, blues, and jazz could be heard in respectable places, the lively music became associated with saloons, gambling, and houses of ill repute. Consequently, social and other pressures were attempted to curb such musical expressions. Most school programs from elementary through university level taught only classical music.[32]

In the mid-1800s, traditional spirituals were sung without musical accompaniment except for hand-clapping or foot-tapping. After the Civil War, three- and four-part harmony became popular, along with the unaccompanied singing of sacred songs in close harmony, as the Fisk University Jubilee Singers were doing.[33]

In the latter 1800s, groups of African-Americans, sometimes numbering as many as 100 and including various skilled workers and professionals, had come to the Indian and Oklahoma territories and settled together. Concerned parents in the resulting all-Black towns such as Langston, Clearview, and Boley realized their chil-

The Langston University Choir, 1916. Courtesy Currie Ballard, Langston University.

dren had many social, political, and economic problems to face. Therefore, they tried to ensure that children and young adults heard only music that was "decent." When jazz music was in vogue and "swinging," Langston University students were not allowed to form off-campus bands or to participate in any such musical organizations without faculty approval. Blues, jazz, and even spirituals were frowned upon. However, the music seemed to be everywhere. Although spirituals had become popular nationally in the late 1800s, the general population of Blacks in Oklahoma were still singing the same songs they had sung as slaves. Ellison remembered that Oklahoma schoolteachers at the time would "have destroyed blues, jazz, and even spirituals" and "scattered the pieces" if it had been possible for them to do so.[34]

The first singing conventions with itinerant teachers were started in Indian Territory in the 1870s by an organization called the Union Singing Convention. Not much is known about the original group but their tradition has survived. Two other singing conventions, the New Harmony and the New State, were organized later.[35]

Black Indian freedmen and freedwomen were taught to read shaped notes, four- and seven-note. Shape-note singing is considered indigenous to the United States but the classical European round-note characters gradually replaced the shape-notes for hymnals. However, the more fundamental and conservative churches continued the shape-note tradition with their singing conventions.[36]

The New Harmony Singing Convention was organized in 1911 in Wewoka, Oklahoma. The singers continued to sing the same four-note shape-note hymns that their ancestors had brought to Oklahoma from Mississippi. Their goal was to perpetuate the singing classes. Their membership spread over a large area in east central Oklahoma but new groups began to decrease as the more popular gospel music attracted more people. The shape-note tradition is not limited to Black singing conventions but the style has generally been used less as religious denominations have changed.[37]

Much credit for the survival of the New Harmony group is given to Henry Samilton, the original singing master of the singers in Oklahoma. Samilton, who had learned his craft in a shape-note school in Mississippi in the early 1900s, had a disciplined credo. He taught his students restraint, intonation, diction, and an appreciation for the enjoyment and satisfaction derived from that style of singing.[38]

Consequently, the New Harmony singers are reported to have practiced enthusiastically on Friday evenings in different churches in the Wewoka and Weleetka, Oklahoma, area. Samilton's daughter, Ruth, and the other dedicated New Harmony singers have provided hope that the threatened art form will survive in the modern technological world.[39]

After World War II, music groups began to use pianos, organs, drums, and electric lead and bass guitars as musical and rhythm aids to their voices. Microphones increased the power and volume of the singers. No longer were the singers dependent on their voices alone to lay down the base line and carry the beat. The new style of music caught on, was called gospel, and became popular.[40]

Many Oklahoma churches nurtured outstanding *a capella* quartets, large singing groups, and soloists. Oklahoma City's Jessie Mae Renfro Sapp and Reverend Matthew McClarty of Ada, Oklahoma, became well-known soloists and performers of Black sacred music. The church

Rockers in Tulsa have kept the *a capella* quartet singing alive. The Truthettes from Oklahoma City became nationally known female gospel singers. Dennis Williams of North Carolina brought out-of-state gospel traditions when he moved to Oklahoma. Checotah, Oklahoma's Tony Matthews played both gospel and the blues. His vital blend of Oklahoma's Black music traditions and contemporary styles was heard in his album *Tony Matthews: Condition Blue.*[41]

The Reverend Matthew McClarty had learned to play music on his brother's guitar under rather difficult circumstances. Forbidden to even touch his older brother's guitar, little Matthew would climb up and play the instrument where it was hanging high on a wall when his brother was away. His early picking style and chording reflected the unusual method he had used to make music, but he learned to ably play and sing the blues. Later he influenced gospel singing with his style of blues and rhythm. In 1982, he represented Oklahoma at the Smithsonian Folklife Festival in Washington, D.C., and was one of the most popular entertainers at the event.[42]

About 40 percent of Oklahoma's Black population lived in the mid-east section of the state during the first decades of the 1900s, and that area became historically important as a source of the development of blues music. Pianists and band vocalists often came from the urban areas of Muskogee, Guthrie, Oklahoma City, and Tulsa where small clubs, social functions, and large musical events were more plentiful, but music was heard in homes and at outdoor dances in the rural areas where musicians would meet to just "jam" and socialize.[43]

Trees were plentiful in that area and people would often cut them down to make platforms for outdoor dances. Enterprising vendors would sell food, refreshments, and, during Prohibition, sometimes "bootleg booze." Guitars, fiddles, and accordions were used to play waltzes, and the traditional Black and white country dance music. The faster tunes were sometime called "stomp music." Men often danced by themselves to the stomp music which became know as "clogging" or "buck dancing." Toasts, boasts, rhyming, and storytelling to music were common. A rag stuffed into a kerosene-filled bottle usually provided the lighting. Chicken and fish were available for food. Popular country blues songs were "Corinne, Corrina" and "Settin' on the Top of the World."[44]

Oklahomans Verbie Gene Terry, born near Inola, native Tulsan Lowell Thomas, and Jimmie Nolan, who grew up near Weleetka, all were popular blues artists. They represent just a few of the rural Oklahoma blues-style musicians. Others include D.C. Miner of Rentiesville, Jay McShann of Tulsa, and Jimmy Ellis, who recorded "Work With What You've Got" and "Ain't Gonna Cry No More."[45]

Many blues and jazz musicians not born in Oklahoma came to the state and formed strong musical connections with the local entertainers. Oklahoma musicians and their traveling friends created a freer, more complex, style of music out of their own traditions, imaginations, and emotions in spite of discouragements and restrictive social and political factors. Sometimes they experienced an "outrageous and irreverent sense of freedom." Bassist Walter Page, who was an organizer and leader of the Blue Devils Orchestra, trumpeter Icky Lawrence, and several other musicians had training in classical music as well as jazz. They did not feel the need to draw a line between the two kinds of music. Their ideal was to master both.[46]

After statehood, Oklahoma City, Tulsa, and Muskogee served as training areas for jazz artists who later migrated to Los Angeles, New York City, Chicago, Kansas City, Detroit, or Milwaukee, where the new styles of music were more appreciated, acceptable, and popular during the Jazz Age of the 1920s. Family and school signif-

icantly influenced these musicians. Often one or both parents or a sibling played a
musical instrument or had vocal talent. The majority of Oklahoma jazz musicians
were Black males with high school educations. Several had attended Douglass High
School in Oklahoma City or Booker T. Washington High School in Tulsa.[47]

Between 1923 and 1933, the Oklahoma City Blue Devils Orchestra was known
for its unforgettable music. Ernie Field's Orchestra in Tulsa between 1930 and 1950
also gained national distinction. Oklahoma musicians were found everywhere on the
national and international jazz scenes. Their music often affected other well-known
performers. In 1928, Jimmy Rushing, an Oklahoma City vocalist, recruited William
"Count" Basie, a bandleader, pianist, organizer, and composer born in New Jersey in
1904, for the Blue Devils Orchestra. After the group disbanded, Count Basie organized a band with some of the Oklahoma musicians. His orchestra ultimately revolu-
tionized American jazz. In 1982, Oklahoma's Governor George Nigh signed a proclamation that made Count Basie an honorary native son of the state. Basie reminisced
that the Blue Devils was "the happiest band" he ever played in.[48]

Industrial development in Oklahoma, combined with more and better automo-
biles, vans, buses, and roads, led to more than 100 "traveling" or "road" bands in the
state by the early 1920s. The phrase "one-night stand" indicated that the musicians
worked one night in a town and then traveled, sometimes more than a hundred
miles, to their next job on the following night.[49]

In the 1920s, the increasing use of written arrangements led to a larger proportion of jazz men who had studied music. However, until about the 1930s not much mention of jazz appeared in American magazines. If a jazz fan or musician wanted to read about jazz, there was a growing backlog of foreign books and periodicals about the new American music. In 1937 and 1938 the Commodore, H.R.S. (Hot Record Society), and Blue Note labels were founded. Finally, in 1939, a documentary book of jazz was published in America. Although jazz had been generally ignored in the United States up to the early 1940s, Europeans were said to know more about the individual recording careers of American jazz men than the musicians knew themselves. The jazz players and their orchestras had become very popular in Europe. Dozens of American jazz performers had been welcomed overseas as unofficial

Tulsa, Oklahoma's Ernie Field's Orchestra, 1930-1950, gained national distinctions in the jazz music world. Courtesy Guy Logsdon.

ambassadors of goodwill from the United States. No other American export had been received with more enthusiasm than jazz music and its performers.[50]

Although Blacks and whites in Oklahoma did not feel free to mingle in public during the early 1900s, they did so privately as musicians. Music was colorblind. People might have used the terms "Black music" and "white music" but researchers have pointed out that it should not be inferred that Oklahoma's musical history was culturally segregated. When musicians played non-segregated music to segregated audiences, they were primarily concerned with the sounds that came from their instruments, not the visual pigmentation of the players.[51]

Bob Wills, a Texan by birth, and Woody Guthrie of Okemah, Oklahoma, crossed racial lines and never forgot their roots. They had both learned much about music from Black musicians when they were growing up. A Black teenager had taught Guthrie to play the harmonica in Okemah. When Hart Wand, a young European-American in Oklahoma City, wrote the first published blues song, he was accompanied by an African-American whistler from Dallas, Texas. The song became universally identified as belonging to Black music. That racially shared creativity was typical of music in Oklahoma.[52]

However, when entertainer Bob Wills, who had freely borrowed from blues music as well as jazz, came to Oklahoma he quickly learned that Oklahomans were not ready to see a Black man playing in a white orchestra. He became popular in the state by entertaining white audiences in the 1930s with "St. Louis Blues," "Empty Bed Blues," "Basin Street Blues," and other blues and jazz songs. Meanwhile, Claude Williams, a Black fiddler with Andy Kirk's Twelve Clouds of Joy Orchestra, beguiled Black audiences with traditional country music. Woody Guthrie enthralled all sorts of audiences by playing both the blues and cowboy songs. Jack Teagarden, known as the "Blackest white jazzman" who ever lived, also imitated the sounds of the Indian powwow when he performed with Paul Whiteman and his orchestra at the Oklahoma fairgrounds.[53]

By the 1960s, jazz had earned an unprecedented national and international recognition and acknowledgment as America's one true native contribution to the world of music. Historians have noted that Oklahoma's contributions to the history of jazz have been greater than to any other aspect of American culture. Unfortunately, many pioneers in the Oklahoma jazz scene have been forgotten. However, the experiences of many of Oklahoma's jazz musicians have been eloquently expressed in Chet Baker's 1977 album *You Can't Go Home Again.*[54]

The following Oklahoma Jazz musicians are included in various published encyclopedias, books, and articles with their date of birth and hometown if known:

ARDMORE
Alva Lee "Bo" McCain, Sr., tenor saxophone
Howard Smith (1910), piano/composer

BEGGS
George James (1906), saxophone/clarinet

BESSIE
Elmer Reuben "Moe" Schneider (1919), trombone

BOLEY
Claude Jones (1901), trombone

BRISTOW
Joe Lee Wilson (1935), vocals/composer

CALUMET
Dempsey Wright (1929) guitar

DOUGHERTY
Kay Starr (1922, Kathryn Starks), vocals

EAGLE CITY
Edward "Big Ed" Lewis (1909), trumpet

EL RENO
Sam Rivers (1930), saxophone

ENID
Pat Moran (1934, Helen Mudgett), piano

FORT GIBSON
Lee Wiley (1915), vocalist/composer

GUTHRIE
Harold Breeden (1921), clarinet/saxophone
Joe Liggins (1915), piano/composer/leader

IDABEL
Hadley Coleman (1932), saxophone/clarinet/flute

HASKELL
John Jacob Simmons (1918), trumpet/bass

KINGFISHER
Elmer Crumley (1908), trombone/vocalist

MCALESTER
Berta Leah "Lea" Mathews (1925), vocalist
David Matthews (1911), composer/tenor/alto saxophones

MUSKOGEE
Samuel Aaron Bell (1922), bass/piano/trumpet
Carlos Wesley "Don" Byas (1912), tenor saxophone
Barney Kessel (1923), guitar
Clarence Love (1908), alto saxophone/bandleader
Jay "Hootie" McShann (1909), bandleader/piano
Joseph "Joe" Thomas, Jr. (1908), composer/tenor saxophone
Walter Purl "Foots" Thomas (1907), tenor/saxophone/flute/composer
Claude Williams (1908), violin/guitar

OKLAHOMA CITY
Buddy Anderson (1919), trumpet/piano
Abe Bolar (1909), bass
Henry Bridges (c. 1908), tenor saxophone
Donald E. "Don" Cherry (1936), trumpet
Theodore "Ted" Donnelly (1912), trombone
Wardell Gray (1921-1955), tenor saxophone
Lem C. Johnson (1909), saxophone/clarinet/vocals
Donald Douglas Lamond (1920), drums
Marilyn Moore (1931), vocals
James Andrew "Little Jimmy" Rushing (1903), piano/vocals
Stanley Wrightsman (1910), piano

OKMULGEE
Oscar Pettiford (1922), bass/cello/bandleader

SAPULPA
Marshal Royal (1912), clarinet/alto saxophone

TULSA
Earl Bostic (1913), alto saxophone/compser
Jim Keltner (1942), drums
Cecil McBee (1935), bass
Howard McGhee (1918), trumpet/composer
Harold "Hal" Singer (1919), clarinet

UNKNOWN TOWN OF BIRTH
Charles Brackeen (1940), saxophone
Laura Rucker (1903), piano/vocals

VALIANT
Sunny Murray (1937), drums

WYNNEWOOD
Roy Milton (1907), vocals/drums/bandleader

YALE
Chesney "Chet" Baker (1959), trumpet/singer.[55]

The following list contains a sampling of Oklahoma musicians and the nationally recognized ensembles they have played with:

Baker, Chesney (Gerry Mulligan)

Bell, Samuel (Lucky Millinder, Teddy Wilson, Lester Young)

Bolar, Abe (Count Basie, Lucky Millinder, Oran Thaddeus "Hot" Lips Page)

Bostic, Earl (Lionel Hampton)

Byas, "Don" (Count Basie, Duke Ellington, Lionel Hampton, Dizzy Gillespie, Coleman Hawkins)

Cherry, Donald (Ornette Coleman)

Crumbley, Elmer (Cab Calloway, Earl Hines, Jimmy Lunceford)

Donnelly, "Ted" (Count Basie)

Gray, Wardell (Count Basie, Benny Goodman, Charlie Parker, Earl Hines, Tad Dameron)

James, George (Lucky Millinder, Louis Armstrong, Teddy Wilson)

Johnson, Lem C. (Lucky Millinder, Louis Armstrong, Thomas "Fats" Waller)

Jones, Claude (Duke Ellington, Cab Calloway, Fletcher Henderson)

Kessel, Barney (Charlie Parker, Billie Holiday)

Lamond, Donald (Benny Goodman, Woody Herman, Charlie Parker, Quincy Jones, Stan Getz)

Lewis, "Big Ed" (Count Basie)

Matthews, David (Woody Herman)

McBee, Cecil (Miles Davis)

McGhee, Howard (Charlie Parker, Coleman Hawkins)

Moore, Marilyn (Woody Herman)

Murray, Sunny (John Coltrane)

Pettiford, Oscar (Duke Ellington, Woody Herman, Dizzy Gillespie)

Rivers, Sam (Miles Davis)

Royal, Marshal (Count Basie, Duke Ellington, Lionel Hampton)

Rushing, James (Count Basie, Benny Goodman)

Simmons, John (Duke Ellington, Benny Goodman, Louis Armstrong, Nat King Cole, Thelonias Monk)

Singer, "Hal" (Duke Ellington, Lucky Millinder)

Smith, Howard (Glenn Miller, Benny Goodman, Tommy Dorsey)

Thomas, Joe (Jelly Roll Morten)

Thomas, Walter "Foots" (Ferdinand "Jelly Roll" Morten, Benny Goodman, Count Basie, Cab Calloway)

Williams, Claude (Count Basie)

Wilson, Joe (Miles Davis).[56]

Jay McShann, a band leader and piano player from Muskogee, Oklahoma and Buddy Anderson, a trumpet and piano player from Oklahoma City, played at the world famous Savoy Ballroom in 1941. Front Row, L-R: Jay McShann, Lucky Enois, Gene Ramey (Bass), Water Brown (Singer), Bob Malone, Gus Johnson (drums), Charley Parker, John Jackson, Freddy Culiver, Frog Anderson, Joe Baird. Back Row, Left to right: Buddy Anderson, Harold Bower, and Orvill Minor.

Greenwood Jazz was called the foundation of the Kansas City School of Jazz. Tulsa, Oklahoma's jazz scene on Greenwood Avenue was vibrant and many musicians who began playing in clubs in that area became world famous. This photograph taken in the "3 Bears Club" of a local group in 1956, shows L-R: Tollie Moore, Jr., Harry Vann, Cecil McBee, Eddie Randell, Al Harrison, and Nickie Cato.

James Andrew "Little Jimmy" Rushing, who was born in Oklahoma City in 1903, fit the model of a vocal and jazz legend in Oklahoma. Jimmy, his trumpet-playing father, and his mother and brother, who were both pianists and vocalists, made music a family affair in their home and in the father's Deep Deuce Café on Northeast Second Street. Rushing, a graduate of Douglass High School, studied music theory with Zelia Breaux, the first music director at the school. Between 1920 and 1950, he was considered by many experts to be the eminent blues singer. While a member of the Count Basie Band from 1935 to 1950, he was especially known for singing "Good Morning Blues" and "Going To Chicago." Rushing was called "Mr. Five-by-Five" for his modest stature, but there was nothing vocally modest about the singing style he pioneered, known as "blues shouting," He received numerous awards for his vocal performances.[57]

In 1994, the town of Langston, Oklahoma, became the first city founded by African-Americans to host a stamp dedication ceremony when Langston University and the United States Postal Service honored Rushing with a First Day of Sale Recognition of the stamp that portrayed him. Reporter Charles Rush remarked that the knowledge of Rushing's contributions to music faded after his death in New York in 1972. Currie Ballard, historian-in-residence at Langston University noted, "I think Oklahomans forgot about Jimmy after his death because he had no family members in the state." Ralph Ellison observed that Rushing's ability to vocalize a sense of hard reality along with the feeling that it could be overcome was something that only Black living could produce. "Little Jimmy" seemed to remind his audiences of their human limitations while encouraging them to see how far they could go.[58]

Rushing was a member of Walter Page's band from 1925 to 1929, Benny Moten's band from 1929 to 1935, and count Basie's band from 1935 to 1950. He died June 8, 1972.[59]

Zelia Page Breaux, the daughter of Inman E. Page, the first president of the Colored Agricultural and Normal University in Langston, Oklahoma, taught formal music classes at the university from 1898 to 1918. Under her leadership, music became an integral part of campus life for African-American students. All students were enrolled in "vocal music," and courses in instrumental music were available. Daily chapel exercises and regular dormitory services included singing. Later, the institution of higher learning became known as Langston University.[60]

Zelia organized a seven-member university orchestra that began to give public performances in 1902. The piano, violin, and brass instruments were played by three female students. The clarinet, French horn, and a coronet were played by male students. By 1904, the orchestra had grown to 23 members. By that time, they were using drums, violas, flutes, a slide horn, a clarinet, saxophones, and brass instruments.[61]

Mrs. Zelia Page Breaux (1880-1950). Photograph by Harry Wattony. Courtesy Archives and Manuscript Division of the Oklahoma Historical Society.

Zelia also formed a choral society, and her efforts led to a Department of Music for instruction in voice and piano. Advanced students were required to play Johann Sebastian Bach, Franz Liszt, Wolfgang Amadeus Mozart, and Frederic Chopin. She added a band and a glee club to the Department of Music in 1907. Luther H. Henderson became her assistant. The band, composed mostly of males, traveled in an elegant wagon drawn by six large white horses.[62]

In her early years as an educator, Zelia taught both instrumental and vocal music with a strong emphasis on classical music. During her last years as a teacher, she headed up the music department at Douglass High School and directed the Douglass High School Stage Band. She later served as music director of the Oklahoma Separate School System. She featured big name jazz artists in her Aldridge Theater on Southeast Second Street in Oklahoma City. Zelia was inducted into the Oklahoma Women's Hall of Fame in 1983. She was also honored at the First Day of Sale Ceremonies for the Jazz and Blues Singers Stamps held at Langston University, September 17, 1994.[63]

Another important figure on Oklahoma's jazz scene was Charles "Charlie" Christian, born in Dallas, Texas, on July 29, 1916. He came to Oklahoma City with his family when he was five years old. Ralph Ellison, who knew him as a child, recalled that Christian was surrounded by many different musical influences and a respectable family. Before he could hold and play a guitar, Christian served as a guide for his father, a blind singer and guitarist. Later, he entertained with his father and two of his brothers, Clarence and Edward. They would go strolling in white middle-class neighborhoods and play serenades of light classical music or blues on request.[64]

After first playing the trumpet, Christian began concentrating on the guitar when he was twelve years old. He did not join the school band but he spent considerable time in the manual training department of his school where he made guitars from cigar boxes. He and his brother Clarence would often impress their classmates when they played for them with their hand-made instruments.[65]

When Christian was fifteen years old, he played at local clubs and with his brother Eddie's band, the Jolly Jugglers. He also worked as a tap dancer, baseball pitcher, prize fighter, singer, and pianist. After the family group disbanded, Charlie worked with other bands around Oklahoma City. He played, at times, with saxophonist Lester Young, Oran Page, and other musicians who were members of the Oklahoma City Blue Devils Orchestra. He also played bass with Alphonso Trent's sextet in 1934 and guitar with the Jeter-Pillars Orchestra in St. Louis. He returned to Oklahoma City in 1937.[66]

When Eddie Durham came to Oklahoma City to play with Count Basie's band in 1937, he took an interest in Christian, who was then working as a pianist. Durham showed Christian his new custom-built electric guitar and some new playing techniques. Jim Daddy Walker, a Kansas City guitarist, also helped Christian. Walker and Durham were impressed with how quickly Christian learned.[67]

Christian bought an electric guitar when the instrument first appeared on the local market in 1938. He joined Trent's band again. A year later, John Hammond, a jazz critic and columnist for *Downbeat* Magazine, discovered Christian playing with Trent's group in Oklahoma City. Hammond recommended Christian to Benny Goodman, who was one of the few white jazzmen to hire Black musicians to play in an integrated band. Christian began to perform for Goodman in September of 1939. The young musician introduced audiences to single-string solos on the amplified guitar. Although he was not the first musician to introduce the electric guitar, Christian changed the concept of guitar playing. Instead of using the guitar in the traditional manner to provide a steady rhythm pulse, he used it as a front-line instrument, as if it were a horn, creating long, flowing lines that he could sustain with amplification. In spite of being on the New York musical scene for a very brief time, Christian is considered to have been the unifying force that brought together the different individual jazz musical styles and propelled the music into a new phase of development. He is credited with having been the most important influence in the reshaping of the melodic line and the manner in which the rhythm section performed together with modern front-line soloists. He based ad-lib playing on the harmonic structure rather than the melodic source. As Christian sang "bebop, bebop, bebop," to the fall of notes from his instrument, he also gave a new name to the music of the 1940s.[68]

A question often asked was, "How could a young musician who brought southwestern blues to modern jazz manage to come musically mature into the New York jazz scene, and what kind of a musical environment could produce a musician like Charlie Christian?" To explain, researchers usually first recognize Christian's enormous natural talent and the overlapping diverse musical influences of the southwestern blues guitar, classical, and country music of the Texas, Oklahoma, and Kansas City regions. The Texas blues tradition is thought to predate the New Orleans music that is considered an original source of jazz. Christian's style of guitar playing represented a guitar tradition that had been used by southwestern musicians as they roamed throughout the area. Writer Ralph Ellison also pointed out that hundreds of musicians in the Southwest had been blending the classic, or "correct," music with the eclectic, or "unconscious," music in a fusion that led to the discovery of a new style of music called "jazz."[69]

John Hammond, Benny Goodman's talent scout, also played an important role with his ability to locate talent and bring it to Goodman's attention. In 1939, Hammond sneaked Christian onto Goodman's bandstand at the Victor Hugo Restaurant in Beverly Hills, California. When Goodman saw the poorly dressed intruder, he planned to quickly get rid of him by counting off "Rose Room," a tune he assumed that the young gutarist would not know. However, Christian took off into a 45-minute chorus-after-chorus extemporization that brought overwhelming applause from the audience, and Goodman hired him on the spot.[70]

Charlie had only a brief career. While on a Midwest tour with the Goodman Band, he became ill and was hospitalized in New York in June of 1941. He was diagnosed as having tuberculosis and died March 2, 1942. Unfortunately, he left only a few recordings. He recorded two tunes, "Honeysuckle Rose" and "Solo Flight," with Goodman's band. However, he had profoundly impressed his contemporaries and continued to influence later guitarists. He also won over music critics, who generally agreed that "the kid from Oklahoma was the best there ever was."[71]

Joachim E. Berendt in his *The Jazz Book: From Ragtime to Fusion and Beyond* wrote that great jazz musicians have felt the connection between their playing styles and the period of time in which they lived. They have also realized that the nature of jazz stands on its "being alive" and also on its being able to "change." They know that "whatever lives changes."[72]

Lester Young, a jazz musician from Mississippi, played with the Oklahoma City Blue Devils Orchestra and later the early Count Basie Band. Some years later, he declined an invitation to participate in a recording to demonstrate the Basie style of the 1930s. "I can't do it," Lester said. "I don't play that way anymore. I play different. I live different. This is later. That was then. We change, move on."[73]

Leona Mitchell, also a member of a musical family, was born to a mother who was a talented pianist and a father who was a musically-gifted Pentacostal minister. She grew up in a family that learned and played music by ear. As a young child living in Enid, Oklahoma, Leona, the tenth of fifteen children, was not aware that many people learned music by reading notes.[97]

Leona had been a winner of a Young Artist Competition sponsored by the Women's Committee of the Oklahoma Symphony Orchestra. In 1971, she won first place in a study program sponsored by the San Francisco Opera, and, a year later, she made her operatic debut as Micalea at the San Francisco Spring Opera Theater. Three years later, she appeared with the Metropolitan Opera in New York. Her European debuts were at the Geneva Opera in 1976, the Convent Garden in London and the Paris Opera in 1980. In April of 1982, she made a guest appearance with the Oklahoma Symphony Orchestra in Oklahoma City.[98]

A local reviewer quoted a New York critic as observing that Mitchell, "in just six years, has risen from an operatic type to probably the most impressive lyric soprano singing today." *The New Yorker* also noted the "silvered purity of her voice and the dynamic effect of the personality."[99]

Facing: Tulsa, Oklahoma's Clarence Love and his dance orchestra performed extensively in the Midwest during the 1930s. Courtesy Clarence Love.

Clarence Love was installed in the Greenwood Jazz Hall of Fame in Tulsa, Oklahoma, in 1990. Left to right: Unknown, Clarence Love, and Mabel Rice.

Stoney Edwards of Seminole, Oklahoma became one of the few Black performers in country music. His "Mississippi, You're On My Mind," and his "If I Had To Do It All Over Again" were especially popular. Courtesy Guy Logson.

Conductor Kenneth Kilgore, front right, with the Ambassadors Choir. They performed in Mexico City, D.F., during the summer of 1987. Courtesy the Oklahoma Publishing Company.

Thomas Carey, a professor of voice at the University of Oklahoma who had performed leading roles in Europe with the London Royal Opera Company and the Stuttgart Opera Company in Germany, organized the Cimarron Circuit Opera Company with the help of his wife, Carol Brice, an internationally famous contralto. In 1975, Carey had recognized a need to provide opportunities for Oklahoma's many talented young singers to develop their talents and also for older people and children in rural areas to learn to enjoy opera.[100]

At that time, the Careys' lives were already hectic with their own rehearsals and travel to opera openings in Munich, Germany, and Lisbon, Portugal. Organizing and keeping the new opera company alive was time-consuming and exhausting, but an experience following a performance in the small rural town of Copan, Oklahoma, made it all worthwhile.[101]

Carey had been tired after a long day. He had taught his classes at the university, driven the long distance to Copan, performed, and directed the evening performance. He was about ready to start his return drive to Norman when an old farmer came up to him and said, "My wife had to drag me to this performance tonight."[102]

Carey nodded. Suddenly feeling dejected and extremely tired, he turned to move on, but the older man stopped him and confided, "Next time, she won't have to."[103] The two men exchanged satisfied smiles and went their separate ways.

Leona Mitchell, a graduate of Oklahoma City University, became an internationally known opera singer. Courtesy Oklahoma Publishing Company.

Thomas Carey, a professor of music at the University of Oklahoma, and
his wife, Carol Brice, an internationally famous contralto, seemed to
interlock music and culture to stimulate new interests in their students
and audiences. Courtesy Oklahoma Publishing Company.

The possibility of stampedes on the drives was very real. Sometimes it took very little to "spook" an entire herd. A startled jackrabbit, the rattle of cooking pans, a bolt of lightning, or a horse's whinny could bring on chaos and the furious flight of thousands of panicked cattle. Consequently, singing and crooning often seemed to help calm a herd at night and also served to break the monotony of the open range for the cowboy. Old-timers have said that a cowboy who "couldn't carry a tune in a bucket when he began the long trip would often become a full-fledged troubador during his long months on the cattle drive."[4]

However, written accounts of "life on the trail" vary considerably. Not all old-timers remembered singing on the cattle trails they had worked. Some recalled that by the end of the day, the men were only interested in some food, rest, and sleep. It was pointed out that "hollering at cattle" and sleeping in the open did not nurture "good singing voices" and furthermore many cowboy songs were just obscene ditties. In retrospect, varied recollections were only to be expected as men of different backgrounds, ages, and former occupations traveled the old trails over a 20-year period.[5]

Cowboy songs were usually sung by just one person, and different lyrics were often substituted for ones the singer had heard while growing up. Cowboys delighted in making up songs to ridicule their inexperienced companions. "The Top Hand" made fun of a young cowboy who was "too big for his boots." "Banjo In the Cow Camps" contained references to cowboy songs and cowboy singing. "Dodgin' Joe" was about the "fastest cutting horse in Texas." The cowboy balladry that developed often contained references to musical instruments:

Come alive you fellers, hear the foreman shout,
    Drop your books and banjos, fetch your saddles out,
Shake that squeaky fiddle, Red, go and get your hoss,
    Dutch ain't you got duties, as the chuck-wagon boss?
Range is getting grassy, winter draws its claws,
    Calves are fat and sassy, teasin' of their maws
Loafin' days are over, dreamin' time is gone,
    No more life in clover, fer the round up's on.[6]

Most of the songs were made up of numerous, sometimes almost endless, verses that varied according to the locale or the experiences encountered. Some ballads were set to simple tunes popular at the time. Longings, laments, tribulations, and the constant danger of cattle on the run were usual themes. "John Gardner's Trial Herd," "The Old Chisholm Trail," and "When the Work is All Done in the Fall" were typical songs. One of the best-known of the many sentimental ballads was "Lasca," by Frank Desprez, about a cowhand's love for a girl who lost her life while trying to shield her wounded lover from an oncoming stampede of cattle. The song closed with the tender verses:

I gouged out a grave a few feet deep, and there in Earth's arms
    I laid her to sleep;
And there she is lying, and no one knows;
    And the summer shines, and the winter snows.

For many a day the flowers have spread a pall of flowers over her head;
  And the little grey hawk hangs aloft in the air
And the coyote trots here and there.

And the black snake glides and glitters and slides
  into the rift of the cottonwood tree;
And the buzzard sails on, and comes, and is gone,
  stately and still, like a ship at sea.

And I wonder why I do not care for the things that are
  like the things that were,
Does half my heart lie buried there in Texas,
  down by the Rio Grande?

About 35,000 longhorns were brought up from Texas to Abilene, Kansas, in 1867. More than 75,000 cattle came the following year, 300,000 in 1870, and 600,000 in 1871. During the first ten years of the drives, a total of more than three million cattle came through Oklahoma on the way to railroad shipping centers in Kansas.[8]

The same railroads that hauled Texas cattle to eastern markets also brought settlers to the West. As open range was fenced by small farmers around the cowtowns, cattle markets were forced to move farther west. Consequently, more and more open range began to disappear. The vast grasslands were a part of the federal public domain and soon attracted a steady stream of ranchers and homesteaders. About 1892, land companies that controlled thousands of acres of grazing land in the Texas Panhandle and other western areas began to sell their acreage. They had decided they could make more money by selling their land to small farmers than by leasing it to cattlemen.[9]

Cowboys were still needed to work the ranches and to handle the smaller herds shuffled between the grazing ranges in Texas and Montana, but the cattle being transferred were usually moved slowly to allow them to graze along the way and be in good

Cowboys moving a cattle herd in the Oklahoma and Texas panhandles, ca. 1885. The A.A. Forbes Collection. Courtesy Western History Collections, University of Oklahoma Libraries.

shape for the expected severe winter they would face in Montana. Panicky cattle and stampedes seemed to have become problems of the past.[10]

By 1892, cowboy work had changed. The drovers who worked with the cattle were beginning to be called "cowpunchers" or "cowpokes" because one of their primary tasks was to prod fallen cattle onto their feet in the railroad cars that carried the animals from loading pens to the market.[11]

The era of the open range and the movement of millions of Texas longhorns over the cattle trails of Oklahoma ended. Never again would 100 cowboys, ten chuckwagons, and 25,000 wild Texas longhorns travel one of the old cattle trails across seemingly endless lonely stretches of prairie except in imagination and the movies. However, the cowboys who herded the cattle have lived on in our myths, our songs, our music, and in our history.[12]

The singing cowboys of movies and television can be traced to the Spanish vaqueros. They were southern California mission Indians who had been enslaved by the Spanish to be horsemen. They were called vaqueros because the Spanish word "vaca" meant "cow." Later, the word vaquero sounded like buckaroo to Anglo-American ears. Many vaqueros were of mixed Spanish and Indian ancestry.[13]

Indian cowboys, possibly Caddo or Kickapoo, in Indian Territory. The Woodward County Collection. Courtesy Western History Collections, University of Oklahoma Libraries.

Despite later stereotypes, some of the cowboys were former Black slaves, Mexicans, or full-blood Indians. It was estimated that one out of seven cowboys on the trails across Indian Territory was Mexican, and about the same percentage was African-American. Although Indians have seldom been portrayed as active participants in the development of the American cattle industry, a considerable number of Seminole, Creek, and other Indians were experienced cowboys and cattlemen before they were forced to leave their plantations, ranches, and farms in Florida and other areas to move to Indian Territory.[14]

The early Spaniards had introduced large-scale ranching to Florida about 1650. They had trained Indians and Black slaves who had escaped from American colonies in the north to be cowhands. The Indians continued to maintain large herds of cattle after the Spanish vacated Florida in the mid-1700s. Some Indians were able to bring small herds to Indian Territory when they were forced to move in the early 1800s and continued to ranch and work cattle in the new area. A fully developed ranching culture had already been established by the Spanish to the south of Indian Territory in the later Texas region. The cowboys, or vaqueros, who worked the early ranches, or rancheros, were usually Indians and mestizos of Mexican, Indian, and Spanish ancestry.[15]

Meanwhile, the Plains Indians had become attracted to ranching, but as the vast grasslands disappeared into small fenced farms and the government leased thousands of acres of grazing land to large non-Indian cattle companies and foreign investors, the Indians could no longer compete as cattlemen. Some were able to find work in movies and Wild West shows, but others were finding it difficult to make a decent living. However, several Indians were among the top rodeo performers in the nation.

Many myths and ballads have celebrated the vaqueros and cowboys, and cowboy fans have pictured cowboys as especially noble, brave, and beholden to no one. But in truth there was little romance about the reason men rode over the cattle trails on the open range. Many of the cowboys were discharged Confederate soldiers—Indian, Black, or white—who had returned home to devastation and chaos in Indian Territory and in the South. Riding a dangerous, lonesome, dusty cattle trail was often the only work available to them.[16]

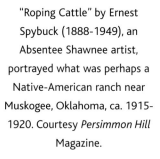

"Roping Cattle" by Ernest Spybuck (1888-1949), an Absentee Shawnee artist, portrayed what was perhaps a Native-American ranch near Muskogee, Oklahoma, ca. 1915-1920. Courtesy *Persimmon Hill* Magazine.

Over time, cowboys became the knights of western songs and ballads. The song "Cowboy Jack" heralded the cowboy, and "The Bucking Bronco" carried out the theme of many western romance tales in which the cowboy tamed a bronco and the "fair maiden" tamed the cowboy. However, women were a rarity in the early West, and, though cowboys might fall in love, they generally rode away when events took a serious domestic turn.[17]

Although movies and television have shown the guitar to have been the cowboy's musical instrument, the banjo and fiddle are likely to have been used more than the guitar in the Old West. They were more portable, and they were more common in the South, the birthplace of many cowboys. One old trail driver reminisced, "It was a poor cow outfit that did not have in its equipment at least one fiddle or banjo, and a man who could play the same."[18]

"I Ride Old Paint" was a favorite song of Charlie Willis, an ex-slave who began work as a cowboy about 1871. Willis taught the song to Jesse Morris, a cowhand on the XIT Ranch. Morris later started a popular cowboy band and recorded the song under the title of "Goodbye Old Paint" for John Lomax, a collector of cowboy songs. The well-liked ballad was often sung at the end of cowboy dances.[19]

A historical marker for the American folk-song classic "Home On the Range" denotes the final resting place of its composer, Dr. Brewster Higley, in Shawnee, Oklahoma. Courtesy Santa Fe Depot Museum.

"Git Along Little Dogies," perhaps one of the best-loved cowboy songs, told about the history of cattle-raising, the enterprise that had created the need for cowboys. Texas Longhorns, the tough half-ton cattle often called monsters, were regarded with wary affection by the cowboys. The song described how the cowboy always rode casually without cantering, trotting, or galloping. He always wore a hat and had one extravagance—fancy spurs with jinglebobs. Some cowboys claimed that the music created by the jinglebobs kept the cattle company.[20]

Both cowboys and Indians watched the arrival of the railroads with caution. Cowboys realized that railroads would end the need for cattle drives. Indians saw the locomotives as iron horses with human-sounding whistles. The engineers cultivated such distinctively individual sounds with their locomotive whistles that some listeners could name engineers they had never met personally. Although the railroad companies were seen to be criminal and greedy as they snatched up government grants and public lands, the trains themselves were considered to be benevolent and helpful. A popular song was "The Wabash Cannonball."[21]

After months on the trail, the cattle were herded into corrals adjacent to railroad tracks, and the cowboys were "turned loose on the town." The "Railroad Corral" was a rollicking, spirited song about the end of a long cattle drive near the Kansas towns of Abilene, Dodge City, or Ellsworth.[22]

"The Strawberry Roan" told about breaking wild horses to the saddle. The "Night Herding Song" and "Cowboy Lullaby" were about calming restless cattle. "Blood On the Saddle" related what could happen to an unlucky cowboy who was thrown from his saddle while "bustin' bronchos." "Bury Me Not On the Lone Prairie" was a haunting favorite of the cowboy. "Old Texas" lamented the end of the era of the great cattle drives. The American folk classic "Home On the Range" was originally a poem called "My Western Home" written by a 50-year-old, Indiana-born

A horse drawn calliope led the parade when a Miller Brothers Wild West Show came to an Oklahoma town in the late 1800s and early 1900s. Boys could work for admission tickets to the Wild West Shows. Both courtesy Western History Collections, University of Oklahoma Libraries.

physician, Brewster Higley IV, while he was homesteading near Athol, Kansas, in 1872. The words were set to music by Higley's nearest neighbor Daniel E. Kelley, a renowned banjo player. The song was published in the local newspaper in 1873 but it was many years later, after Higley had moved his family to Shawnee, Oklahoma, in 1886, where he died in 1911, that his up-beat song became one of the most popular in America during the Great Depression.[23]

Typical cowboy gear continued to include a fancy saddle, leather chaps, a bedroll or blanket, a coiled lariat, a poncho, and a large kerchief to wear about the neck, and nearly all cowboys were armed with pistols or rifles. The harmonica that had been well suited for the trail was still a popular musical instrument. Banjos and guitars were also common to ranch life and to public and family gatherings. Cowboys also played for local dances.[24]

Meanwhile, the cattle drives had not only given birth to a new group of Americans called cowboys but had also created new entertainments and competitions. When thousands of Texas Longhorns and hundreds of cowboys poured into towns at the end of their long journeys, competitive contests developed that included steer riding, "bronco busting," calf roping, and bulldogging. The contests were usually for prestige, not money. These events soon came to be called rodeos.[25]

In the 1890s, William "Buffalo Bill" Cody introduced the rodeo competitions to the public with his Wild West shows. By the 1900s, dramatizations of western life and musical entertainments were routinely included with the rodeo competitions. The

WORKING BOY TICKET

MILLER BROTHERS

101 RANCH

REAL WILD WEST
AND
GREAT FAR EAST
SHOWS

GENERAL OFFICES AND WINTER QUARTERS
MARLAND, OKLA.

ADMIT ONE WORKING BOY
GOOD ONLY FOR BOY WHO WORKED
VOID IF SOLD

26

1926   **OFFICIAL ROUTE**   **1926**

MILLER BROS

101 RANCH

REAL WILD WEST
AND
GREAT FAR EAST
HEADQUARTERS
MARLAND OKLA

No. 23

Date	City	Railroad	Miles
	TWENTY-SIXTH WEEK		
Oct. 18th	Oklahoma City, Okla.	Frisco	41
" 19	Sapulpa, Okla.	Frisco Ry.	104
" 20	Henryetta, Okla.	Frisco Ry.	45
" 21	Muskogee, Okla.	Frisco Ry.	52
" 22	Fort Smith, Ark.	Frisco Ry.	167
" 23	Hugo, Okla.	Frisco Ry.	143
	TWENTY-SEVENTH WEEK		
Oct. 25th	Paris, Texas,	Frisco Ry.	25
" 26th	Greenville, Tex.	T. M. Ry.	52
" 27th	Texakana, Ark.	Cotton Belt Ry.	132
" 28th	Hope, Ark.	M. P. Ry.	32
" 29th	El Dorado, Ark.	M. P. Ry.	88
" 30th	Monroe, La.	M. P. Ry.	89
" 31st	Vidalia, La. (Mat. only)	M. P. Ry.	113

"TEX" COOPER, Mail Agent

An advertising poster for the Miller Brothers' Wild West Show and an official route schedule of the 101 Ranch Show. Both courtesy Western History Collections, University of Oklahoma Libraries.

shows were glamorized to portray the harshness of pioneer life, the heroism of pioneer men and women, and to satisfy curiosity about Indians. The 101 Ranch Wild West Show traveled the nation in 150 railroad cars and carried, at one time, 126 cowboys, Indians, wild steers, horses, tents, parade wagons, a calliope, banners, and show equipment. In the 1920s, the 101 Ranch show purchased the Walter L. Main Circus

(THE WEST THAT WAS AND SINGING COWBOYS)

and included its animals and properties to present the 101 Ranch Real Wild West and Great Far East Show, which included 1,400 cowboys and Indians. The show did not survive the Great Depression. However, Buffalo Bill, Pawnee Bill, and the Miller brothers of the 101 Ranch near Ponca City all capitalized on the popularity of that kind of entertainment for about 20 years. At first, the showmen tried to present authentic portrayals of ranch and frontier days as they had been lived on the southwestern prairies. Joseph C. Miller of the 101 Ranch, particularly, wanted to present and record the hardships and bravery of pioneer men and women as a "reminder of a past that would never live again." However, imitators with shoddy sideshows and poor circus acts changed the Wild West shows to hybrids that were neither rodeo nor circus. Also, in the early 1900s, Oklahomans began to sponsor annual frontier events, including rodeos, that replaced the Wild West shows. They were community affairs that encouraged local talent.[26]

Meanwhile, technological developments were occurring that would diminish the need for traveling shows and at the same time contribute to the continued popularity of cowboys, Indians, and pioneer life. While the chaos of the first land run into the Unassigned Lands was being played out in Indian Territory, the famous inventor Thomas Alva Edison was demonstrating his latest invention, the Kinetoscope Viewer, in New Jersey. His friends were taking turns looking through a peephole in a cabinet to watch some 50 feet of picture film revolve on a series of spools while they listened to Edison's recently invented Kinetophonograph. The figures on the picture film appeared to move. The strange contraption later became recognized as the forerunner of the modern motion picture. Once the novelty of his "peepshow" abated, Edison thought of it as a passing fad. However, one of his engineers, Edwin S. Porter, kept working with it, and, in 1903, demonstrated an 11-minute classic called *The Great Train Robbery* produced using Edison's technology. The one-reeler cost $150 to produce and was played during intermissions in crowded music halls and vaudeville houses across the nation. The action-packed thriller was popular.[27]

When President Theodore Roosevelt participated in a wolf hunt in southwestern Oklahoma in 1905, he was impressed with the Oklahoma cowboy Jack Abernathy, who was known as "Catch 'em Alive Jack" because he claimed to be able to capture wolves with his bare hands. Back home in the East, Roosevelt was unable to convince his friends of the authenticity of Abernathy's exploits. To prove his point, he sent a telegram to Abernathy asking him to film one of his encounters with a wolf. The reluctant Abernathy, who had just been named a United States marshal to Oklahoma by Roosevelt, asked two of his deputies, Bill Tilghman and Chris

Gordon W. "Pawnee Bill" Lilly's Wild West and Great Far East Museum tents, with performers and the band posed in front. The G.W. Lillie Collection. Courtesy Western History Collections, University of Oklahoma Libraries.

Madsen, to help him. In 1908, they sent the film, *Wolf Hunt,* to President Roosevelt, who showed it in the East Room of the White House in 1909. Later, the amateur film crew produced *The Bank Robbery* at Cache, Oklahoma, about an early bank robbery in the town. Among the extras added to the cast was Quanah Parker, chief of the Comanche Indians. Other crude one-reel motion pictures were made. The producers were not especially concerned with historical accuracy but they captured death-defying exploits of cowboys, Indians, and villains on a silent screen that was accompanied with the music from a phonograph and special sound effects.[28]

Jack Hoxie, 1888–1965, and Art Acord, 1890–1931, rodeo actors in Oklahoma's Wild West shows, became popular stars of the silent screen. In February of 1926, the Wigwam Theater in Altus, Oklahoma, featured Hoxie in the "shoot 'em-up" movie *Bustin' Through.* A couple of months later, Blair, Oklahoma, proudly advertised Acord in *Sky High Corral.*[29]

Earlier, Acord had been a stuntman with the Bison Film Company in New Jersey, where he performed in some of the earliest one-reeler movies. In 1914, he played the starring role in Charles Van Loan's *Buck Parvin* series when the stories were adapted to motion pictures as two-reelers. Criterion Studios cast him in a series that included *When the Fiddler Came to the Big Horn* and *The Cowboy's Sweetheart.* After his heroic experiences in World War I, a three-year contract with Universal Studios, the top "horse opera" production company, proved him to be a "bonafide star." He became Universal's leading star in the 1920s.[30]

Hoxie's billing in Universal's *Man From Nowhere,* a two-reeler directed by William S. Hart, and *Johnny Get Your Gun* caused his star to rise. A 1917 cliffhanger, *Lightning Bryce,* a serial in which Hoxie co-starred with Ann Little, was a hit with the public. In 1922, he was hired by Universal Studios, where he worked with Acord and Edmund R. "Hoot" Gibson, all three trying to outdo each other with their hazardous stunts.[31] An estimated 2,000 films were made by Hoxie and Acord. Unfortunately, most have been lost.

By the 1930s, real cowboys were no longer needed. The rough and tumble, risk-taking, hard-riding cowboys were passed over for soft-spoken, singing cowboys who frequently had to be taught to ride a horse after they were hired. Stunt men were called in for the hard-action scenes. However, the mystique and drawing power of Jack Hoxie's white hat, all-white attire, white horse named Scout, and dog Bunkie, along with Acord's all-black clothing, black hat, famous dog, and horse named Black Jack were imitated by the "singing" cowboy actors who replaced them.[32]

In the early 1900s, some Oklahoma ranchers and cowboys began to organize small bands to play for local dances. In 1926, businessman Otto Gray of Stillwater, Oklahoma, began to manage William "Billy" McGinty's Cowboy Band, a string dance band made up of musicians who were real-life cowboys and lived in the Ripley, Oklahoma, area. At the time, no one foresaw that Gray's approach to management of the band would lead to the commercialization and acceptance of rural western music and to major changes in the music industry. Gray applied the techniques of big-time musical productions to rural dance music. He demonstrated the appeal and potential of southwestern string bands and in doing so introduced America to cowboy music. To date, the popular attraction of western music has lasted more than 70 years.[33]

Although neither Otto Gray nor Billy McGinty was a real musician, Gray did admit later in life to a secret desire to play with his band. Consequently, he practiced, continued to buy better fiddles, and all the while hoped that one day he would be able to play with them. However, when he happened to overhear some of the musicians talking about what they could do to "keep Otto from playing," he decided to concentrate on his trick roping and his work as the band's manager and emcee. Raised on a farm near Ripley, Gray was a real cowboy who had worked on a ranch in Wyoming, and he and his wife, Florence, were skilled trick ropers. Florence was usually called "Mommie." She and the Grays' son, Owen, both sang. Owen also composed songs.[34]

Billy McGinty was considered to have been a real cowboy by the age of 14. He later spent some years with Buffalo Bill's Wild West Show and as a Rough Rider in Cuba during the Spanish-American War. He had taken part in the famous charge up San Juan Hill with Theodore Roosevelt. Later, when he was a rancher, he became the sponsor of a string band, The Old Time Fiddlers, organized by a group of Ripley businessmen. The group had met in Ulys Moore's barber shop since about 1920. In 1925, when they needed someone to vouch for them before the group would be

Billy McGinty (1870-1960), one of America's early bronco-riding rodeo champions, organized a string dance band in Oklahoma in the 1920s. The original Billy McGinty Cowboy Band, 1925, is shown above with Billy seated third from the right. Courtesy Washington Irving Trail Museum, Stillwater, Oklahoma.

McGinty's Oklahoma Cowboy Band with Florence "Mommie" Gray, at the far left. Courtesy Washington Irving Trail Museum, Stillwater, Oklahoma.

permitted to sing over Radio Station KFRU Radio in Bristow, Oklahoma, George Youngblood, a radio salesman, asked his partner, O.W. "Jack" McGinty if his famous dad might be willing to help them. Jack's reply was, "We'll just tell him he's going to be the sponsor so everybody in Ripley can hear the band play over the air." The events that followed became significant in musical history.[35]

The hugely successful program, aired on May 7, 1925, is generally thought to have been America's first radio broadcast of a western string band. The band received congratulatory telegrams, telephone messages, and letters from throughout Oklahoma, Texas, Missouri, Arkansas, Kansas, and other states. At that time, the band included Billy McGinty as leader, Colonel Frank Sherrell on first fiddle, W. E. Moore on bass, Paul Harrison on guitar, Guy Messecar on the mandolin, H.C. Hackney on the banjo, Marie Mitchell playing the piano, and Ernst Bevins with his harmonica. The musicians played tunes like "Ride 'em Cowboy," "Hell Among the Yearlings," "Turkey in the Straw," "Who Stuck the Gum In Grandpa's Whiskers," "Arkansas Travelers," and others.[36]

4

By the 1870s, most of the good land in the trans-Mississippi West, with the exception of Indian land, had already been legally claimed. Consequently, land-hungry people, railroad companies, manufacturers of farm machinery, and officials of banking and mercantile interests in Kansas City, St. Louis, Wichita, and Topeka were casting covetous glances at Indian Territory. Because railroad companies, big business, and banks were generally unpopular, the homeseeker, "the image of American democracy," became a "likely stalking horse for the corporate interests." [1]

Professional promoters called Boomers were hired to attract homeseekers, to mobilize them, and to inspire them to "take matters into their own hands and go down there and occupy and cultivate those lands." The powerful interests argued that once the area was opened to settlement, all, including the homeseeker, would benefit. [2]

Although the cattlemen and most of the leaders of Indian nations were strongly opposed to the opening of Indian Territory to homesteaders, "tiny Boomer Camps" began to appear on the borders of Indian Territory in the spring of 1879. David Payne, an effective propagandist, organized thousands of homeseekers into well-disciplined groups with strong religious overtones that wore down congressional opposition. Federal courtrooms were used to popularize the movement. Eventually the organizers gained powerful friends in the United States Congress. Consequently, the stage was set for about 50,000 homeseekers to take part in the Land Run of 1889. [3]

The settlers who came added new folk songs, poems, dances, and music to the history of Oklahoma. David Payne had kept up the spirits of his followers for years with favorite Biblical quotes like "and the Lord commanded unto Moses, 'Go forth and possess the Promised Land.' " Promoters referred to the region as the "Garden of Eden" and "the Land of the Fair God." The enthusiastic campers often marched to a favorite song, "On to Beulah Land." Songs about the Boomers and later the Sooners, homeseekers, and speculators who entered the settlement zone before the run legally started, became popular.[4]

The first organized music group in Oklahoma City was a hymn-singing congregation seated on beer kegs and nail boxes in the open air on the first Sunday after the area was opened to settlement by the Land Run of 1889. The First Christian Church of Oklahoma City organized a choir a few days after the run. The First Methodist Church Choir was also organized in 1889, and the pastor's daughter, Pearl Murray, accompanied on the piano. Oklahomans were showing a remarkable interest in music by 1892.[5]

The day after the lots were staked out and claimed in Oklahoma City, fiddlers, harpists, and harmonica players showed up. Square dancing started on the open prairie. Church choirs were organized by "singing teachers" before churches were built in the rural areas. Quickly the choirs became singing societies. Members seldom had musical instruments, but they learned to read music by using the same shaped notes that their ancestors had used in the mountains of Kentucky, Tennessee, and Virginia. The singing schools led to singing conventions at which members met for all-day "sings."[6]

Songs of the settlers often portrayed the activities and attitudes associated with frontier living:

> Rise up my dearest dear
> And present to me your hand,
> And we'll go in pursuit
> Of some far and better land
> Where the buzzard will chase the crow
> And we'll ramble around the cane brake
> And chase the buffalo.[7]

One of the more popular party songs, "Skip to My Lou," had more than a hundred verses and sounded nonsensical but the verses were considered to be significant for their inventiveness. Typical verses were:

> Red Birds singin', two by two,
> Gone again, skipped to m'Lou,
> Skipped to m'Lou, m'darlin'.

> Corn in the corn crib, who is who,
> Gone again, skipped to m'Lou,
> Skipped to m'Lou, m'darlin'.[8]

One writer compared Oklahomans to mockingbirds and concluded that the people were more interested in getting the sounds out of their systems than in a finished performance. He contended that Oklahomans sang for fun, one tune after the other, not caring how it sounded. He further noted that the quality varied from the lively melodies of a rural genius who would rig up a contraption to hold a harmonica to his lips while leaving his hands free for playing a reed organ to the practiced oratorios sung by cultured groups that gathered together from the shacks and tents of Oklahoma City.[9]

About the time of the Land Run of 1889, "Ta-ra-ra-ra-Boom-de-ay," a London music hall song, was popular. A few years later, "Comrades," by J.L. Molly, and "Daisy," also from London, were especially well liked. The following words were often heard:

> It won't be a stylish marriage,
> I can't afford a carriage;
>   But you'll look sweet
>   Set up on the seat
> Of a bicycle built for two.[10]

In the rural areas, hymns and popular folk ballads were the most common forms of musical expression. No distinctive type evolved because the people tended to maintain their back-home influences.[11]

Generally, after statehood, the music was about the same as in other states. Oklahomans usually looked to Kansas City for their music supplies and for whatever was popular there. "Alexander's Ragtime Band" gave way to "Tipperary" and "Over There." "There'll Be a Hot Time in the Old Town Tonight" was replaced by "Chinatown." Many parodies about local interests were heard:

> And here all the ramshackle coaches,
> Of every make and design,
> And every worn-out locomotive
> May be found on the panhandle line.[12]

The same tune might be sung in other areas of the state or in other states to pillory any railroad line with a conveniently rhythmical name. Except for titles, there was often little to distinguish one parody from another.[13]

A steady stream of homeseekers came to Oklahoma Territory. The settlers in the new territory were more than 96 percent European-American in 1900. Indians and African-Americans were the only significant non-white groups. Most of the settlers had come from neighboring states.[14]

The last camp of David L. Payne, the leader of the Boomers. The man standing in the center of the photo to the left, holding an axe, is Payne. At that time, ca. 1883, the group was being detained by Black U.S. Cavalry soldiers. The Phillips Collection. Courtesy Western History Collections. University of Oklahoma Libraries.

(LIGHT AND LIVELY)

Bad climatic conditions in the 1890s that carried over into the early 1900s in some areas worked against the settlers and were almost disastrous for the farmers. Many left the area discouraged and penniless. The poverty-stricken people who remained were drawn together by hard times and isolation. The second decade of life in the territory was easier, but better times never completely erased the scars of human suffering and the loss of loved ones. Many settlers relied heavily on their religion and were sustained by confidence that a better life awaited their loved ones in the hereafter.[15]

Some early homesteaders turned to poetry and singing as an outlet for personal grief after a new grave marked a spot in the seemingly endless prairie grass. Local editors were usually happy to print poems and songs in their newspapers. Personal letters also often contained writings about losses and tragic happenings or the sense of satisfaction experienced in building a new state and better future. Correspondence also sometimes revealed the discomforts of living conditions—the spiders, snakes, mosquitoes, and bugs endured in sod houses—and the unrelenting loneliness of life on the prairie.[16]

Despite the early fierce contest for land, the uncertainty of life in rural areas brought about a spirit of concern for fellow sufferers. To survive the loneliness, desolation, and early poverty, settlers needed each other. When a homesteader felt "blue," even meager social contacts were cherished and had therapeutic value. The homesteaders did not wait until they had so-called "respectable" housing and a stable economy before they turned to a social life of music, get-togethers, protracted meetings, celebrations, singing, recitations, debates, religious worship, and dancing. Square dancing to tunes such as "Turkey In the Straw," "Buffalo Girls," and "Cotton-Eyed Joe" was popular. Play parties that substituted a group of singers for the conventional fiddler and caller satisfied those who opposed dancing for religious reasons.[17]

It was estimated that about one thousand different folk tunes and ballads were sung between 1880 and 1905 by the diverse people in the region. "Oklahoma Run," also known as "Old Purcell," "Red Bird," "Oklahoma Waltz," and "Slaton's Waltz" all originated within the boundaries of the newly settled land. Folk musicians often played improvisations from light opera and popular sheet music that they had learned by ear. Many tunes and melodies were only known locally and were named for their composers. "Slaton's Waltz" was a melody of Tom Slaton's own composition that became a popular dance number. It was said he came up with the tune when he was trying to outdo some women fiddlers because he thought it was not fitting for women to fiddle in public, especially for dances.[18]

When musicologist Marion H. Buchanan, a concert violinist known as Maria Costa, did a survey of fiddling music in the hill country for the Federal Music Project in 1936, she compiled perhaps the only authentic collection of old fiddle ditties and dance music indigenous to the pioneers of Oklahoma. The Shawnee, Oklahoma, native traveled over rugged roads and lived in the homes of her sources. When the foot tapping of the fiddlers jarred the needle off her recording machine, she solved the problem by placing pillows under the shoeless feet of the musicians. She transposed dozens of tunes into notes, clefs, and keys while the mountaineers fiddled away. Nine of the 420 musicians she interviewed were women. Only six of the more than 200 pieces she gathered had originated in Oklahoma. Strains and entire melodies from England, Scotland, Ireland, Norway, and Africa had been woven into the folk music of Oklahoma.[19]

Just before the 1892 Cheyenne-Arapaho Land Opening, C.G. King (far left), and other home seekers from Kansas, illustrated essential frontier activities near Kingfisher, Oklahoma. One man made music while another poured coffee. A third man roasted meat. The Forbes Collection. Courtesy Western History Collections, University of Oklahoma Libraries.

Buchanan came to realize that, in spite of difficulties, almost constant danger, and the worries experienced by the early pioneers, their music was light and lively. She observed that the lullabies sung to their babies were boisterous and lilting instead of soothing and sweet. She concluded that early Oklahomans just had to laugh and sing to endure the harsh realities of their daily lives and that reaction to stress had become a shared characteristic of Oklahomans.[20]

The energetic early music of the Southwest and of Oklahoma flourished as rural singers developed styles and techniques that they shared with friends and neighbors. The music tended toward novelty, with catchy and infectious rhythms.[21]

Old tunes survived as the lyrics changed. The words of rural music were more important than the instrumentation and were usually rendered in a rigidly pitched voice that was high rubato and nasal. Because women taught the boys as well as the girls to sing in the home, rural men usually sang in a higher tone than they did after radios became available and they heard other male singers.[22]

In territorial days, Oklahoma musicians seemed to be able to play any kind of musical instrument they could find or improvise, and the lively music and marches they played often started an impromptu dance. Homemade fiddles, guitars, and banjos were played if available. Brown jugs, bottles, hair combs, and all manner of other sound-producing objects joined them.[23]

When pianos became more available, ragtime developed. Ragtime was a type of rhythmic music that probably arose from military marches and the music of minstrel shows. Pianists played for social affairs and for family gatherings. Brass bands often played ragtime tunes as well. Marching and parade bands were popular additions to advertising wagons, circuses, carnivals, political, and fraternal occasions. Hometown bands were also enjoyed both by their members and their audiences.[24]

Sometimes an itinerant or local vocalist would offer singing lessons to men for a dollar each and to women and children for free. When classes were in session, one-room schoolhouse rafters would shake above enthusiastic renditions of "Nellie Gray," "Tumble-down Shanty," "On-the-Claim," "Red-Wing," or other favorites. Adults were too intent on having fun to do much disciplined study. The children, often referred to as "young-uns," would fall asleep on back benches.[25]

(LIGHT AND LIVELY)

When adults began to yawn, the "master" would turn down the damper on the pot-bellied stove and nod to the organist, pianist, or other musician to play a farewell song for all to join in before gathering their families for the trip home by foot, on horseback, or in their wagons.[26]

Oklahomans generally worked long hours so relaxation became an important part of their life. Interest in theater productions was traced back to the earliest

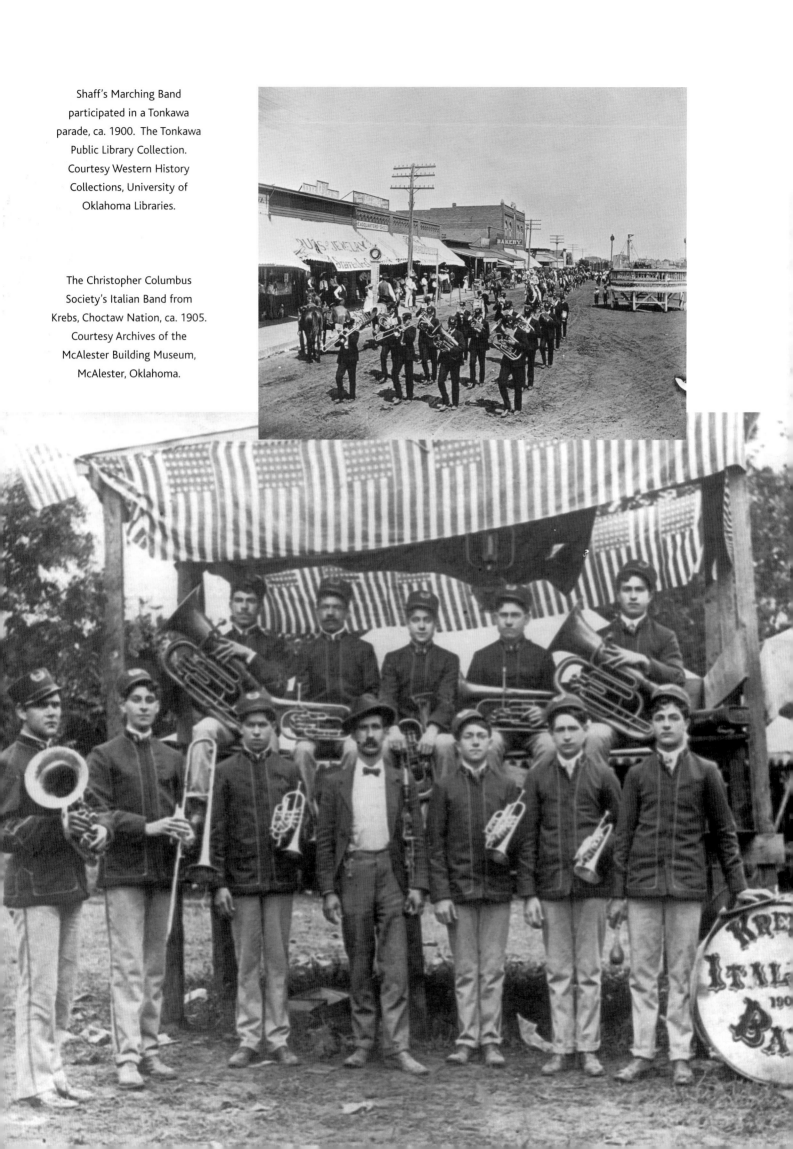

Shaff's Marching Band participated in a Tonkawa parade, ca. 1900. The Tonkawa Public Library Collection. Courtesy Western History Collections, University of Oklahoma Libraries.

The Christopher Columbus Society's Italian Band from Krebs, Choctaw Nation, ca. 1905. Courtesy Archives of the McAlester Building Museum, McAlester, Oklahoma.

Tishomingo's Woodmen of the World Band, September, 1916. Left to right: Back Row: Charles Hawkins, clarinet; Jess Enbe, trombone; Lem Richardson, baritone trombone; Jess Easley, trumpet; Professor Geck, trumpet. 2nd Row: Alton King, trombone; Van Thornton, clarinet; Alvie Moore, baritone trombone; George Moore, baritone trombone; Ross Lipe, baritone trombone; Frank Costiloe, French horn. 1st Row: Ernest Lucas, French horn; Jake Hacker, bass drum; Lem Burris, traps; Alfred DeCordova, trombone. Front Row: Huston Conklin, French horn. Chickasaw Council House Museum Collection. Courtesy Archives and Manuscripts Division of the Oklahoma Historical Society.

frontier days in Guthrie, Kingfisher, Oklahoma City, and other early towns and communities. In 1879, an opera house with a stage and rough board seats was set up in a Muskogee, Oklahoma, barn owned by Joshua Ross. The building was located near the railroad track by a downtown street since renamed Martin Luther King Street. Even the rough miners in the Choctaw Nation attended "crudely fashioned Shakespearean plays." Girls and women played both male and female Shakespearean roles.[27]

Many of the men were Italian, Slav, Greek, Welsh, Polish, and Russian miners recruited to work in the coal mines. Many of these brought their wives and families with them. Scattered German Mennonite and Czech settlements added to the richness of Oklahoma's ethnic community. The lack of cultural uniformity in early Oklahoma churches also led to the use of various hymnals in church services.[28]

All kinds of music seemed to flourish in Oklahoma. Singing schools continued to be popular. Rural areas looked forward to traveling medicine shows that would come to a community, set up tents, and sometimes stay as long as a week. The irresistible appeal of city life affected rural music. Street singers were popular and influential before town ordinances banned them from performing. City songs often were synthesized into rural songs. In pioneer life, oral songs usually became folk songs regardless of their own origin or quality.[29]

Although fiddle music was very popular among the early settlers, singing was substituted for fiddling if the group frowned upon musical instruments as tools of the devil. Because singing was a source of reassurance and comfort, people would travel several miles to sing with a group.[30]

Nearly every town had its own opera house in which no operas were expected to be produced but which hosted performances by local talent, traveling vaudevillians, entertainers, and lecturers. Blind Boone, an African-American pianist, was a popular Oklahoma performer who traveled around the area. The opera house was usually open only a few nights each week until the advent of silent movies. Entertainment was provided more often then, and a local musician, usually a pianist or violinist, was hired to furnish musical accompaniment for the adventures that were seen on the recently invented movie screens.[31]

In the late 1800s and early 1900s, Chautauqua and lyceum companies booked tours to appear in many rural towns. Chautauquas had originated in 1874 in Chautauqua, New York, and they made appearances all over the states and territories. They were defined as assemblies for the education of adults with lectures, concerts, and other entertainments. Often the events were held for several days in one place before moving on to another area. Lyceums were also traveling associations for instruction and entertainment through lectures, debates, and concerts.[32]

The Wanette, Oklahoma, National Band, ca. 1910-1920. Courtesy Santa Fe Depot Museum in Shawnee, Oklahoma.

Improved methods of transportation and the invention of the radio, phonograph, and silent movie all helped to alleviate the isolation of living in rural Oklahoma. People continued to come together to talk, sing, socialize, share food, and to make light of their troubles and inconveniences with lively music, energetic dancing, and local entertainments.

When the United States Congress awarded acreage to a group of Indians to do with as they chose, Thomas P. Richardville, the chief of the Miami Indians in northeast Indian Territory, sold the townsite of Miami, in 1891, to Colonel W. C. Lykins, a Kansas stockman. Lykins then formed the Miami Town Company and began to make plans to actualize his dream of building a new town on the frontier. A stagecoach stop on the Southwest Trail, later known as the Ozark Trail, on the route between Kansas City to Dallas helped the settlement to become a major trading area.[33]

In 1896, the St. Louis and San Francisco, or Frisco, Railroad came to Miami and, in 1901, it joined there with the Kansas, Oklahoma, and Gulf Railroad. The community became more accessible for traveling acting companies, and people were encouraged about their possibilities for the future.[34]

The Boys' Band in Shawnee, Oklahoma, ca.1934. Courtesy Santa Fe Depot Museum, Shawnee, Oklahoma.

Actress in costume for Shakespeare's *Twelfth Night,* above. Girls and women dressed in Shakespearean costumes and played both male and female roles in Oklahoma Territory, ca. 1900. The Coleman Collection. Courtesy Western History Collections, University of Oklahoma Libraries. At right, Touring actors and actresses in Oklahoma City, 1893. The Oklahoma Collection. Courtesy Western History Collections, University of Oklahoma Libraries.

The cast of *The Three Old Maids,* a play performed in Oklahoma City in 1892. The General Personalities Collections. Courtesy of Western History Collections, University of Oklahoma Libraries.

Facing, top. In 1889, the Guthrie Club Theater had a six-piece orchestra and "available actors of all ages." This photo was taken when the group was still housed in a tent. The A.P. Swearingen Collection. Courtesy Western History Collections., University of Oklahoma Libraries.

Three new theaters that were built after statehood in 1907, the Odeon, the Grand, and the Pastime, provided cheaper entertainment with vaudeville teams, single comedians, and brief showings of the new moving pictures. When the townspeople wanted more, a summer theater, Pleasure Park Playhouse, was built in 1908 by S.O. "Doc" Robinson. Before the following summer season, Robinson moved his first theater to Oak Street to become a skating rink and built a new roofless theater with a sloped floor and a well-equipped stage.[45]

On May 17, 1909, a large audience sat in the new summer theater under the stars and viewed the play *Down Where the Cotton Blossoms Grow.* Later, the top was roofed in and the name was changed to the Auditorium. The popular theater was especially patronized by younger people and soon gave McWilliams much competition.[46]

Lyceum circuits varied from the educational to pure entertainment. Minstrel shows, especially Al G. Field's Minstrels and his Uncle Tom shows, were big crowd pleasers. Other companies bringing minstrel shows to Miami included the Ray E. Fox Minstrels, the Orpheus Road Show, Richards and Pringles, and also some female minstrels known as LeGrange and Gordon's Lady Minstrels. The Ball Field Minstrel Show consisted of local amateur and professional talent. It was presented each year from the 1920s to the 1950s for the benefit of the local baseball team and was always one of the biggest events of the year. Lectures by visiting artists, entertainment professionals, and local theater supporters were well attended. Several churches also presented musical programs, plays, or an elocutionist to raise money.[47]

Animal acts, Salome dancers, barnyard and forest mimicry, chalk pictures drawn to music, and other theater acts were presented by professional and amateur performers in Miami during the late 1800s and early 1900s. People were also interested in reading about the theater. The *New York Clipper* ran ads in the local weekly newspaper and provided free copies when they were requested. A yearly subscription to the paper cost four dollars and a single copy cost ten cents.[48]

At the same time, concerned townspeople demanded strict morality from the visiting theater companies. The citizens believed that amusement was important, but they also expected entertainment to provide educational and moral values that were guaranteed not to offend anyone, regardless of religious denomination.[49]

The five-cent motion pictures particularly were viewed with suspicion at the time and sometimes were denounced from the pulpit. Thomas A. Edison was quoted in *Live Wire* as having prophesied that "the moving picture has not only come to stay and to become more deadly, but is also soon to speak. What now produces fantoms will soon be an inducement of permanent insanity."[50]

Because Chautauquas seemed to satisfy the moral concerns of the community, Dr. Ralph H. Cully organized 54 other concerned townspeople to encourage the Chautauqua circuit to include Miami in its schedules and to guarantee the company a profitable engagement in Miami. The educational assembly accepted the invitation and came to Miami for several summers, set up their tents on the high school grounds for six to ten days, and provided all-day events for children and evening performances for adults.[51]

The concerns for morality and high educational standards exhibited by the early settlers of Miami created a setting for family entertainments and also for family operated theaters. One such was the Marsh family—George D. and Lou Marsh, their daughter Sue Ann, and married daughter Jan Elizabeth with her husband John Giffin. Known as the "Auditorium Family," the Marshes became special to the people

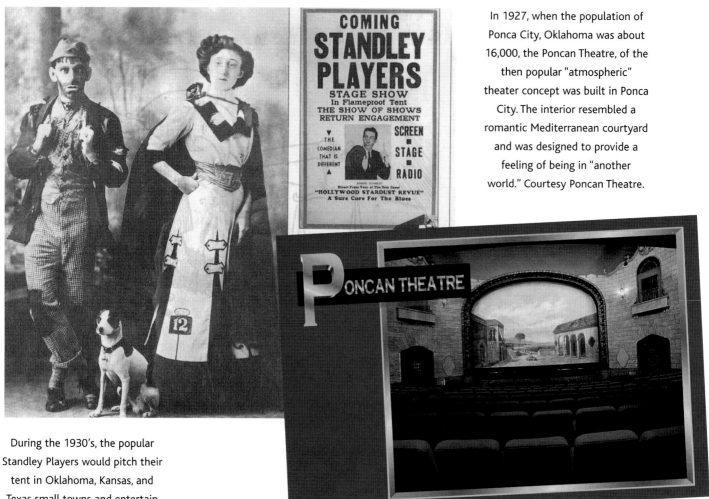

In 1927, when the population of Ponca City, Oklahoma was about 16,000, the Poncan Theatre, of the then popular "atmospheric" theater concept was built in Ponca City. The interior resembled a romantic Mediterranean courtyard and was designed to provide a feeling of being in "another world." Courtesy Poncan Theatre.

During the 1930's, the popular Standley Players would pitch their tent in Oklahoma, Kansas, and Texas small towns and entertain crowds of people. The audiences were said to enjoy tent shows in spite of sweltering summer heat. Jack Standley, a horse trainer, and his wife, Marjorie, a showgirl, founded the group in 1927. The show was advertised as "A Sure Cure for the Blues." Courtesy Oklahoma Publishing Company.

of Miami. They had come from Kansas in 1912 and purchased the Pastime Theater. They soon sold it and acquired the Airdome, added a roof, made stage improvements, and installed better seats. All 900 seats were often filled.[52]

The father, George, took care of the mechanical aspects of the theater and ran the projector for the motion pictures. His wife Lou was in charge of ticket sales and free icewater. The daughters took turns at the piano, and the son-in-law was the operator and general manager. John and Elizabeth later managed the Coleman Theater of Miami for many years.[53]

Traveling road-shows began disappearing nationwide in the early 1920s. Movies were becoming big business but burlesque and vaudeville continued for a few years.[54]

A theater called the Glory B was built in Miami. Quite grand with an excellent stage and equipment, it soon replaced the McWilliams Opera House Theater with its presentation of Vaudeville, legitimate theater, and movies. The Miami Music Club brought in famous guest artists that included Madame Schumann Heink, Ignace Paderewski, and others. *The Mikado* and similar musical and stage plays were also produced by local talent.[55]

George and Al Coleman and several other local men who had become million-aires through the lead and zinc industry continued to live in the area. George Coleman had no particular hobby, but loved good theater. He devoted much time, energy, and money to building a magnificent theater.[56]

Coleman secured the services of architects Carl and Robert Boller of Kansas City, Missouri. The Boller brothers were well known across mid-America for build-ing "atmospheric theaters" that brought their customers into another world when they entered the building. In 1927, the Boller-designed Poncan Theatre was built in Ponca City, Oklahoma.[57]

The Poncan was Spanish Colonial Revival in style. The atmosphere of the inte-rior resembled that of a romantic Mediterranean courtyard. It cost $200,000 to build, plus another $80,000 for equipment including a $22,000 Wurlitzer organ. It was planned for legitimate theater as well as film. The opening movie on September 20, 1927 was *Shanghai Bound* with Richard Dix. Ethel Barrymore, Sally Rand, John Phillip Sousa and his band, Will Rogers, and others in vaudeville and silent movies appeared there.[58]

The public reaction to the 1927 Warner Brothers first feature-length talking film *The Jazz Singer* was so favorable that soon nearly all theaters in the country were wired for sound. Stock companies, vaudeville houses, and road shows almost disap-peared, especially in the smaller cities and towns. Two years later, the Poncan Theatre was remodeled to accommodate talking pictures.[59]

In 1929, the Coleman Theater in Miami, Oklahoma, was built and opened. Designed by the Boller brothers, the magnificent structure was built by George C. Coleman at a cost of $600,000. The exterior architecture was Spanish Mission Revival with terra cotta gargoyles and other handcarved figures. The elegant Louis XV interior was declared to be "an awesome sight" when the theater and movie palace opened on April 18, 1929, to a full house.[60]

Miami's "Coleman Theater Beautiful," a magnificent structure with an opulent Louis XV interior, opened to a full house on April 19, 1929. The building was listed on the National Register of Historical Places in 1988. In 1989, the city of Miami began to restore the theater to its original grandeur. Courtesy Coleman Theater Beautiful.

Just a few months after the Coleman opened, the stock market crash struck a final blow to the legitimate theater all over the country. The people of Miami carried on with some live theater, occasional music recitals, the Lions Club Minstrels, and other community musical and theatrical events, but the great stage of the new theater had been built too late.[61]

In 1983, the Coleman Theater was listed on the National Register of Historic Places. The Coleman family gave the theater to the city of Miami in 1989. In 1996, the citizens of Miami donated $85,000 to repurchase and renovate the "Mighty Wurlitzer," the original pipe organ. Volunteer groups enthusiastically supported the restoration with their time, energy, and money. The original gold-leaf trim, stained-glass panels, crystal chandeliers, silk damask panels, carved mahogany staircases and railings, decorative moldings, and carpeting underwent careful restoration using the original colors. Elaborate backstage mechanical systems were discovered and found to be operable.[62]

As the restoration of the grand old theater proceeded, visitors from 44 states and 26 foreign countries were attracted to Miami in 1998. Japanese and German television crews prepared travel documentaries to show in their own countries. Some American network and independent companies prepared video presentations for public broadcasting. Many Route 66 tourists visited as they traveled through the Midwest. The theater became the number one tourist attraction in Miami.[63]

On October 11, 1985, the Poncan Theatre in Ponca City closed its doors. The following month it was listed on the National Register of Historic Places. In 1989, the Poncan Theatre Company was formed to purchase, restore, maintain, and operate the facility as a community-based performing arts center. After the owners, Eula and Wanda Baumert, donated the facility to the new corporation, $1 million was raised to supplement the volunteer labor needed to restore the theater. The people of Ponca City, rallying to save the theater, eagerly waited for the corporation slogan, "An Old Friend's Back," to come true.[64]

Imagine their astonishment at the sudden reappearance of the hand-painted asbestos stage curtain once installed to protect the audience from a backstage fire. The almost mythical curtain had been missing for many years. During restoration, an obscure rope was pulled, mechanical gears began to mesh, and a beautiful Mediterranean scene unfolded as the original curtain slowly lowered and fell into place.[65]

Completion of the restoration was celebrated on September 17, 1994. The Poncan Theatre became the home of the Ponca Playhouse, the Ponca City Civic Orchestra, and the Ponca City Arts and Humanities Council. Plays, concerts, movies, reunions, dance programs, musical recitals, and forums soon enlivened the 792-seat theater and reception facility.[66]

As the sometimes incomprehensible complexities of the electronic age in music came to the state, Oklahomans continued to exhibit a need for music, especially the light and lively, and to show a desire to preserve their historical roots.

5

A COMMON *Bond*

5

*The careers of scores of Oklahoma musicians of different cultural and
racial backgrounds indicated they all found a common bond in
Oklahoma's early musical environment. They were influenced by
each other and freely exchanged their styles and ideas.*[1]

An Oklahoman, Hart Wand, is recognized as having written the first published
song characteristic of blues music. Hart's father, one of the first non-Indians to arrive
in Oklahoma City, was a druggist. Hart worked for his father, played the violin, and
led a small orchestra that performed for social affairs in the area and for Indian dances
held in Wynnewood and Purcell, Oklahoma. Hart often practiced in the back room
of the drugstore. He was especially intrigued with a little tune he had made up that
had stayed in his mind. A Black porter who worked for the Wands often whistled the
tune when he heard Hart playing it. One day while listening to the melody, he leaned
on his broom and said, "That gives me the blues to go back to Dallas."[2]

Anabelle Robbins, a young pianist friend of Hart's, arranged the tune for him.
Hart named the song "The Dallas Blues" and published it himself in March of 1912.
Printed in gold on dark blue paper, the song sold out in a week. The second printing
sold almost as fast because Hart had started taking it to nearby towns. The tune was
a sensation and into its third printing before he got it copyrighted on September 12,
1912.[3]

In just a few weeks, the tune was heard up and down the Mississippi River.
Words were added in the 1920s by a Chicago lyricist. The piece became universally
identified as belonging to Black music and continued to be popular throughout the
years. It had a simple twelve-bar blues melody in three four-bar phrases, similar to
later blues patterns, with a short phrase on the sub-dominant harmony. After its publication, musicians such as Baby Seal and W.C. Handy would produce hundreds of
similar songs, but "Dallas Blues" was the only song Hart ever wrote. After he became
a businessman in New Orleans, he thought of the song as a souvenir of his youth.[4]

Barney Kessel, a self-taught musician born in Muskogee, Oklahoma, on October 17, 1923, preferred to play with Ellis Ezell's all-Black band than with one of the several white bands in the area. He found their choice of music to be more interesting, with richer melody, rhythm, and harmony than the usual stock arrangements played by the white groups.[5]

Kessel was a devoted fan and imitator of Charlie Christian. At the age of 16, he spent three days playing guitar with his hero in Oklahoma City. From Christian, Kessel learned that to grow musically he had to be true to himself and rely on the work of other musicians only as a point of departure. After Christian's early death some years later, critic Leonard Feather described Kessel as perhaps the most outstanding exponent of Christian's style. The German critic Joachim Ernst called Kessel the most rhythmically vital guitarist in modern jazz.[6]

Kessel left Muskogee in 1942 and joined Ben Pollachi's orchestra to support Chico Marx and his piano performances. In the 1940s, he worked on the soundtrack for the motion picture *Jammin' the Blues*, played with Charlie Barnet's orchestra, Hal McIntryre's band, and Artie Shaw's orchestra. In 1941, he became one of Lionel Hampton's All Stars for a Gene Norman "Just Jazz" concert in Pasadena, California. Barney once said that he had been influenced most by Charlie Christian, Maurice Ravel, Louis Armstrong, Nat "King" Cole, Claude Debussy, Lester Young, and Roy Eldridge.[7]

Variety to Kessel meant personal growth. In the 1950s, he worked as a studio musician, did radio broadcasts, served as music director for the early Bob Crosby shows, and recorded soundtracks for four Elvis Presley films. In the 1960s, he was instrumentalist on the Righteous Brothers' "You've Lost That Lovin Feelin" and the Beach Boys' "Good Vibrations." He also recorded with Marlene Dietrich, Judy Garland, Barbra Streisand, Gene Autry, Tex Ritter, Stan Kenton, Lawrence Welk, Dinah Shore, Joe Tex, and Ike and Tina Turner. He made 71 five-minute devotional programs with Mahalia Jackson in the 1960s.[8]

Bob Dunn was also involved in changing the sound of American music. He had grown up listening to his father's fiddling music near Braggs, Oklahoma, a few miles southeast of Muskogee. He became fascinated with the Hawaiian guitar when he heard performers play it at Kusa, Oklahoma, near Henryetta, in 1917. He purchased a Hawaiian guitar, learned to play it by correspondence, and later joined the Panhandle Cowboys and Indians, an Oklahoma band from 1927 to 1934. Dunn left the group for a job with Milton Brown and His Musical Brownies, who were featured on KAT Radio in Fort Worth, Texas. Brown's band, formed in 1932, played white jazz. Like Bob Wills, Brown had formerly been with the Light Crust Doughboys, a southwestern band.[9]

Dunn started to modernize his Hawaiian guitar to make it a jazz instrument. He raised and magnetized the strings of a standard flat-top guitar, attached an electrical pick-up, and plugged the altered instrument into an amplifier. He played the instrument flat like the Hawaiians did. Brown made a recording of Dunn playing his electric guitar in January 1935.[10]

Trombonist Eddie Durham was also intrigued with the guitar. He was born near San Marcos, Texas, in 1906. When Eddie was a teenager working for the Miller Brothers at the 101 Ranch near Ponca City, Oklahoma, he began to write musical arrangements. When the musicians wanted to start playing for dances after the shows, the band leader had asked how they could have a dance without a piano. Durham solved the problem by writing horn arrangements that made brass instruments sound like a piano. Saxophone players from the Wild West minstrel sideshow helped make the dance band a reality and gave Eddie Durham and the musicians a chance to play jazz.[11]

In 1926, Durham left the 101 Ranch group to play the trombone with the Oklahoma City Blue Devils. The guitar remained his hobby. Later with Bennie Moten's orchestra he experimented with the guitar. After Moten died, Durham played in the brass section of Jimmy Lunceford's band. Lunceford, who was fascinated with Durham's experiments, became determined to use the guitar as a solo instrument. Durham would play his guitar with a resonator and Lunceford would hold the microphone close to the hole in the top of the guitar to amplify the effect. Impressed, Lunceford featured Durham as a soloist for a recording of "Hittin' the Bottle" in September of 1935.[12]

Dunn, Durham, and Lunceford took the guitar from the rhythm section of jazz bands and made it suitable for solo work in an exciting way. Charlie Christian of Oklahoma City also demonstrated the capabilities of the amplified guitar to the world of music.[13]

Bob Wills, who was born in 1905 and died in 1975, was credited with fusing country music with jazz during the years he spent in Oklahoma. He came to the Cain's Ballroom in Tulsa in the 1930s and organized his Texas Playboys using techniques he had learned from Otto Gray to commercialize and preserve rural musical traditions.[14]

Wills included Black music in his repertoire. He had freely borrowed from blues music as well as jazz when he was growing up in Texas. His musicians were not real cowboys but they dressed in distinctive cowboy attire and set a new image with their music that became popularly known as "western swing" or "Okie jazz." Wills preferred to describe his music as western swing or western jazz. His fans included people of all incomes, the unschooled, the educated, preachers, characters of ill repute, oil field workers, businessmen, Indians, Anglos, Mexicans, Blacks, the old, and the young. He also blended Tin Pan Alley with his music.[15]

Wills' successful first recording session in 1935 included Black music and frontier fiddling. Hundreds of his records were sold over the next ten years. The fact that some musicians and critics had regarded his music as racist and rather crude did not seem to matter to Wills nor evidently to most Americans.[16]

By 1939 Wills had one of the largest swing bands in America. He was actually credited with having two bands, one string and one horn, in his orchestra. This gave him a larger repertoire than any other orchestra had ever managed to have before in musical history. Perhaps this accounted for his wide appeal to people of all ages and status. He once boasted that he could give the crowd western music, rumbas, or jitterbug, saying "We just lay it on like they want it."[17]

The recording of "Big Beaver" by his group in 1940 brought his music back full circle to when he had learned the tune as a boy listening to one of his Black friends, a cotton picker, hum it in the primitive form. After combining the old tune with other Black folk music, he and his orchestra recorded it. During the recording session, Wills lowered his fiddle bow and played the old music in the most up-to-date style of the day. If he had not "hollered," no one would have known they were listening to anything other than a regular swing band playing the popular music of the 1940s.[18]

By 1935, he had also made other changes. He added reeds and brasses to his string band despite predictions that such a combination would not work. When he later added drums, he moved closer to jazz and farther away from a fiddle band. His musicians who played string instruments were at times playing their fiddles, tenor banjos, guitars, and steel guitars like jazz horns. For example, Leon McAuliffe could make his steel guitar substitute for a tailgate trombone by sliding his steel bar along the strings. Jesse Ashlock could make sounds on a fiddle like jazz musicians did on a trumpet. Wills was soon drawing larger audiences than his critics who were making fun of him.[19]

Wills and his group were often invited to play for state functions. They played a variety of music and became nationally famous. In 1941, *Metronome* sent a reporter from New York City to Tulsa to interview Wills and his musicians for its publication. The writer was surprised to find that the band leader and his musicians were really top quality performers who played the best of swing music.[20]

The *New York Times* noted that Wills had not been afraid to use pop music, Tin Pan Alley, and Broadway tunes to widen his repertoire. The years Bob Wills spent in Oklahoma, 1934 to 1942, are considered the best of his musical career. In Oklahoma he had his best bands, made his first movies, and wrote and recorded some of his most successful compositions, including "New San Antonio Rose." He went into the United States Army in 1942 and moved to California at the end of World War II. In California he earned more money but he always seemed to have a nostalgia for Tulsa, especially when he sang "Take Me Back To Tulsa." During his time in Tulsa, the image of Bob Wills and his band had changed. The provincial southwestern "hillbilly" band leader had become a well-known musical figure who had one of the largest swing bands in America. The new and radical form of Wills' music continued to enjoy unprecedented popularity. When he died in 1975, he was taken back to Tulsa and buried there.[21]

Johnnie Lee Wills, who was born in 1912 and died in 1984, came to Tulsa with his brother Bob and four other band members in 1934. The Texans began to broadcast daily over radio station KVOO. When Bob went to California in 1943, he took some band members with him and left the others with Johnnie Lee in Tulsa.[22]

Johnnie Lee Wills and his band played for dances in the Tulsa, Oklahoma area. Courtesy Guy Logsdon.

Johnnie Lee and his band recorded for RCA Victor and other studios. They had national hits that included "Rag Mop" and "Milk Cow Blues." They also had their own syndicated radio show, and historian Guy Logsdon arranged a series of concerts for Johnny Lee and his group in Washington, D.C. in 1982. Johnnie Lee made Tulsa his home until he died in 1984. His son, John Thomas, often reminded people that his Uncle Bob was only in Tulsa for about eight years; therefore, many of the people who thought they had danced to Bob Wills and his band in Cain's Ballroom in the 1940s may have actually been dancing to the music of Johnnie Lee Wills and His Orchestra.[23]

In 1996, Johnnie Lee's family, friends, fans, and fellow Tulsans gathered to help dedicate a street near the Expo Square Pavillion in Tulsa to him. For more than 40 years the Johnnie Lee Wills Stampede Rodeo had been held there annually. The street was renamed the Johnnie Lee Wills Lane.[24] Speakers at the dedication ceremony noted Johnnie Lee's many outstanding contributions to the musical history of Tulsa and Western swing music as well as to the city of Tulsa. As members of the crowd came by to pay their respects to the family, Lee's widow, Irene, remarked, "Bob had his fans. But Johnnie Lee had the friends."[25]

Billy Jack Wills, who was born in 1926 and died in 1991, the youngest brother of Bob Wills, was a singer, songwriter, bassist, and played the drums and guitar. He was a member of Johnnie Lee's band in the early 1940s. He later became a bassist and drummer with Bob's Texas Playboys for six years after World War II. His "Rock-A-Bye Baby Blues" was a 1950 hit that featured his vocalizing. His most famous songs were "Faded Love" and "Lily Dale." "Faded Love" was an inverted version of Benjamin Russell Hanby's 1856 "Darling Nellie Gray," the melody of which had been used as a fiddle tune in the Wills family for several decades prior to the 1950s. In 1988, "Faded Love" became Oklahoma's official country song.[26]

Music had also flowed from generations of the Haggard family before Jim and Flossie moved from Checotah, Oklahoma, to Bakersfield, California, in 1935. Their son Merle, born in 1937, became a well-known country musician after a brief career with delinquency. Merle married Bonnie Owens, formerly the wife of Buck Owens, of Blanchard, Oklahoma. After he made several recordings, his "Okie From Muskogee" became popular nationally. His "Mama Tried" and "Hungry Eyes" were credited with presenting Oklahomans living in California in a more revealing and literate manner than had any previous song.[27]

Tommy Collins, whose given name was Leonard Raymond Sipes, was born in Bethany, Oklahoma. The former University of Central Oklahoma chemistry major wrote more than 800 songs and became recognized as one of the leading pioneers of the Bakersfield sound that propelled Buck Owens and Merle Haggard on the road to super stardom.[28] His first recording in 1953, "If You Ain't Lovin', You Ain't Livin'," became a country classic in 1988. In 1954, his "You Better Not Do That" sold over a half million copies. Most of his popular songs have been about the lighter side of romance, novelty hits like "All the Monkey's Ain't In the Zoo" and "High On A Hilltop." In 1980, Merle Haggard recorded his "Leonard," a Collins tribute song that went to Top 10.[29]

Another music figure who began to affect music in the state and in the nation in the 1930s was Woodrow Wilson "Woody" Guthrie, 1912–1967, of Okemah, Oklahoma. He became one of the most influential music figures of his time. His vital and unifying songs, "Oklahoma Hills," "Bound For Glory," and "This Land Is Your Land," continued to inspire several generations of music makers. New Yorkers and other easterners did not regard him as a "hillbilly." Rather, they regarded him as a folk singer who was sometimes quite eccentric.[30]

Guthrie wrote more than 1,000 songs over a 17-year period. He wrote songs of social protest and dwelt on the rural traditions of successful problem solving based on a frontier past that stressed pragmatism and innovation. At times he flirted with the "outlaw mentality." During the devastating economy of the 1930s in Oklahoma, outlawry and incarcerations for "noble causes" were often seen, especially in the case of bank robbery, as merely stealing from thieves. Guthrie once observed, "Some will rob you with a six-gun and some with a fountain pen." Consequently, folk heroes of questionable repute—Billy the Kid, Bonnie and Clyde—were often adulated and regarded as western Robin Hoods.[31]

Although Guthrie was known as a social critic in the best tradition of western political radicalism, he was not a critic of urban life. Rather, he was one of the first rural musicians to take his messages to big city audiences in New York and California with occasional visits to Oklahoma and trips to the South. He championed a variety of causes, both rural and urban. He castigated perceived and unpardonable wrongs as he saw them. Guthrie was a rare individual who could cross over racial lines and speak to aspects of the human condition that transcended regional or group identification.[32]

During the 1950s, Guthrie began, at times, to manifest odd behavior that was later diagnosed as a symptom of Huntington's chorea, the same illness that had afflicted his mother. The disease clouded his thinking and made it increasingly difficult for him to manage his guitar playing. Guthrie died in 1967 after a 15-year struggle with the disease.[33]

One year prior to Guthrie's death, the United States Department of the Interior awarded him a Conservation Service Award in recognition of the love and respect for the land that had characterized his work. In 1988, he was inducted into the Rock and Roll Hall of Fame. Nine years later, he became one of the first inducted into the Oklahoma Music Hall of Fame in ceremonies held in Muskogee, Oklahoma, on April 18, 1997.[34]

Guthrie, who had his own share of bad fortune, is remembered for saying:

> I hate a song that makes you think that you are not any good, . . . I
> am out to sing songs that will prove to you that this is your world and
> that if it has hit you pretty hard and knocked you for a dozen loops, no
> matter what color, what size you are, how you are built, I am out to sing
> the songs that make you take pride in yourself and in your work. And
> the songs that I sing are made up for the most by all sorts of folks just
> about like you . . . [35]

A new generation of songwriters and singers were influenced by Guthrie's music. Robert Zimmerman, a young Minnesota folk singer and songwriter, idolized Woody Guthrie. He imitated his hero's dress, posture, and musical style. Zimmerman hitched rides to New York City during the winter of 1960-1961 to visit Guthrie when he was hospitalized there.[36]

Zimmerman changed his name to Bob Dylan and began performing in the Greenwich Village folk clubs. He is considered the first song poet to have emerged from the folk scene and a musician who revitalized folk music and songwriting.

Woodrow Wilson Guthrie (1912-1967), American folk-singer, song-writer, poet, novelist, and news columnist, was born in Okemah, Oklahoma. Courtesy Guy Logsdon.

On July 14, 1997, Lieutenant Governor Mary Fallin presented a proclamation to Woody Guthrie's sister, Mary Jo Edgmon, that proclaimed the date "Woody Guthrie Day" in the state of Oklahoma. Courtesy *Okemah News Leader*.

Although it was not generally recognized, Bob Dylan's harmonica playing was more typical of the blues scene than of the folk scene. Signed to Columbia Records by agent John Hammond, Dylan launched a career featuring anti-war songs and made the transition from traditional folk to socially conscious protest music. Youth protest groups adopted his songs and considered him a spokesman for their generation.[37]

Tom Paxton, a songwriter from Bristow, Oklahoma, is another musician greatly influenced by Guthrie. Paxton studied drama at the University of Oklahoma. His protest and anti-war songs, more "wry than angry," are directed at what Paxton perceives to be hypocrisy in America.[38]

When Guthrie died on October 7, 1967, Paxton was performing at London's Albert Hall. The audience was stunned when they heard the news because many of Guthrie's songs had come into the repertoire of the British Skiffle musicians in the late 1950s and were popular in Britian. When Paxton began to lead theater-goers in singing "This Land Is Your Land," they sang with one voice, not with tears, but with joy, because that was the effect that Guthrie and his songs often had on those who listened to his music. Many people respected him as the first country singer with a conscience. Paxton remembers that Guthrie "above all, gave us courage, and taught us that honesty required that, at times, songwriters had to stand up and say, 'Whoa, we've run far enough.' "[39]

Okemah's native son, Dan Brook, a nationally recognized sculptor, and Arlo Guthrie unveiled Brook's bronze bust of Arlo's father during the 1998 three-day Woody Guthrie Free Folk Arts Festival held in Okemah, Oklahoma, Woody's hometown. The bust was later completed to form a life-sized statue of Woody. The finished statuary has been placed in Okemah's downtown park. Courtesy *Okemah News Leader.*

Twelve years later, Paxton sang a "clever but chilling" song at a Woody Guthrie festival in Oklahoma. The song was about the recent Three Mile Island nuclear accident. Neither the song nor the program was well received in Oklahoma at the time, but three years later a movement had gathered momentum in Okemah, Oklahoma, to honor Woody Guthrie, its native son.[40]

Okemah's first Woody Guthrie Day was celebrated on July 14, 1997. Lt. Governor Mary Fallin presented a proclamation to Guthrie's sister, Mary Jo Edgmon, that proclaimed July 14 Woody Guthrie Day in the state of Oklahoma. The Woody Guthrie Memorial Group expanded its program for providing scholarships to high school seniors to also include contributions to burn centers and to research for a cure for Huntington's disease in recognition of afflictions that Guthrie, his mother, and other family members had endured. They also worked to support the completion of a bronze sculpture of Guthrie by Okemah's Dan Brook and to install it in a downtown site, as well as placing markers at Woody Guthrie points of interest in Okemah.[41]

Memorabilia owned by Woody's sister and a collection of scrapbooks in the Ofuskee County Historical Museum in Okemah reflected the relationship between genius and simplicity that was apparent in his lyrics. Newspaper clippings revealed a wealth of information about his life and achievements.[42]

Jack Guthrie, 1915–1948, was born in Olive, Oklahoma, and became a singer, songwriter, guitar, and bass fiddle player, but his short career was troubled with bad health. For a few years in the 1940s he was regarded as one of the most influential country singers. His 1945 recording of "Oklahoma Hills" became one of the top songs of the decade and a country standard still heard in the 1990s. He was Woody's cousin.[43]

Ernie Marrs, from Bristow, wrote civil rights songs. Elton Britt, 1917–1972, was born in Arkansas and grew up in eastern Oklahoma. He developed a style that incorporated and popularized the rural Oklahoma traditions of dances, parties, and family song fests. His style and repertoire impressed out-of-state talent scouts and led to radio contracts that totaled about 56 albums and 672 single releases over 22 years. Britt's recorded version of Bob Miller's "There a Star Spangled Banner Waving Somewhere" in 1942 sold more than a million and a half copies and the same amount of sheet music. His live shows featured his high falsetto, his breath-taking triple yodels, and his talent for holding a note for five choruses of a song.[44]

Johnny Bond, 1915–1978, a singer, songwriter, and guitarist, had recordings on Columbia and later Starday that became popular and demonstrated his flair for country, western, and novelty entertainment. He wrote "Cimarron (Roll On)," which became a western classic, and "I Wonder Where You Are Tonight," a bluegrass standard. He was born in Enville and grew up in south-central Oklahoma.[45]

Noel Edwin Boggs, 1917–1974, one of the country's finest steel guitarists, was born in Oklahoma City. While still in high school, he worked for local radio stations. He joined Hank Penny's Radio Cowboys and toured in the East and South. He later started recording and formed his own band. He also played with Jimmy Wakely. As a member of Bob Wills' Texas Playboys, he met guitarists Jimmy Wyble and Cameron Hill. The musical input of the three musicians helped to develop the distinctive sound of western swing.[46]

Noel appeared on about 2,000 commercial recordings as a soloist with Bob Wills, Spade Cooley, Jimmy Wakely, Hank Penny, Bill Boyd, Sheb Wooley, Les

Anderson, Merle Travis, and the Cass County Boys. He made television appearances with Spade Cooley and Jimmy Wakely. He also worked on radio with Rex Allen, Roy Rogers, Gene Autry, and The Sons of the Pioneers. He did USO tours, appeared in many nightspots in Reno, Las Vegas, and Lake Tahoe, Nevada, and worked in Paramount and Columbia movies, where he created special sound effects and did solo work.[47]

One of the most multi-faceted performers in country music, Sheb Wooley, became widely known for his achievements as an actor, comedian, and writer, as himself, and his alter-ego, Ben Colder. He was born near Erick, Oklahoma, in 1921. By the age of four, he was a proficient horseman and he worked as a rodeo rider during his teens. He also formed his own band during his high school days at Plainview, Oklahoma.[48] After appearing in Nashville and on the Calumet Radio Network, fulfilling a recording contract with MGM, and acting in the movies *Rocky Mountain* and *High Noon,* Wooley entered television. In 1959, he began a seven-year run as Pete Nolan on the television series *Rawhide* after appearing on *Cheyenne, Lassie, Range Rider,* and *The Lone Ranger.* He debuted on the Pop Chart with "Are You Satisfied?" His novelty hit "The Purple People Eater" gained international popularity and stayed at the top of the Pop Chart for six weeks, becoming number 12 in the United Kingdom. His "That's My Pa" became a number one Country hit. As Ben Colder, his alter-ego, he scored with several comedy hits that included "Don't Go Near the Eskimos," "Hello Wall," "Almost Persuaded," "Harper Valley P.T.A. (Later That Same Day)," and "Fifteen Beers Ago." "Blue Guitar" and "Tie A Tiger" were hits under his own name.[49]

Cash Box gave Wooley a special award in 1964 for his contributions to country and popular music as a singer, recording artist, entertainer, and songwriter. In 1968, he was chosen the Country Music Association Comedian of the Year as Ben Colder. Wooley brought Ben Colder to television's *Hee Haw* and began to write theme music for the show.[50]

Stoney Edwards, born in Seminole, Oklahoma, in 1929, became one of the few Black performers in country music. His first song, "A Two Dollar Toy," led to an appearance with Bob Wills in California where he sang "Mama's Hungry Eyes." His first album, *Stoney Edwards, A Country Singer,* was released in 1971. His "A Two Dollar Toy" made the Top 70. "She's My Rock" went into the Top 20 and stayed there almost four months. "Mississippi, You're On My Mind" reached the top regions of the charts in 1975. In 1978, his "If I Had To Do It All Over Again" became a minor hit. In 1981, he appeared on *Music America* with the album *No Way To Drown A Memory* that led to a Top 60 single of the same name.[51]

The Willis Brothers, also known as the Oklahoma Wranglers, were one of the foremost country groups and a mainstay of the *Grand Ole Opry* for years. Joe, Guy, and Skeeter Willis left the family farm in 1932 to work at a Shawnee radio station. When Joe married in 1939, his younger brother Vic replaced him. After the younger brothers saw active service in World War II, they joined the *Grand Ole Opry* and started recording in 1946. They left the *Grand Ole Opry* in 1949 and became an integral part of Eddy Arnold's touring show and his radio show. They made two movies, *Feuding Rhythm* and *Hoedown,* in 1949.[52]

After leaving the Arnold show in 1953, they toured the country with Springfield, Missouri's Ozark Jubilee. They were televised on *Midwestern Hayride* and appeared over WRCP-TV in Chattanooga, Tennessee, in 1956-1957. The brothers rejoined the *Grand Ole Opry* in 1960 and remained until Guy's death in 1981. Their popularity extended beyond the United States. They had fans throughout Europe and Central America where they had entertained on USO tours.[53]

By the end of the 1940s, Oklahomans had contributed many creative works to the American music scene and industry. Songs by Oklahomans had captured the imagination not only of America but of the world.[54]

Woody Guthrie's "Oklahoma Hills," written in the 1930s, described the history, culture, and mood of the Depression years. Albert Brumley, who was born in Missouri, grew up on a farm near McAlester, Oklahoma, where he chopped cotton and observed the state penitentiary. His song "I'll Fly Away" set a country gospel standard. Brumley also brought together thoughts on rural electrification, the growth of radio, and the popularity of gospel programs among rural audiences in "Turn Your Radio On," published in 1938. During his lifetime, 1905 to 1977, he wrote more than 800 hymns and country music that he called "memory songs."[55]

Pinky Tomlin, who was born in Arkansas and grew up in Durant, Oklahoma, appeared in twelve movies in the 1930s and wrote songs that captured another aspect of the hard times in America that portrayed a cinematic response. His "The Love Bug Will Bite You If You Don't Watch Out" was sung by Darla Hood of Leedy, Oklahoma, in a Hal Roach comedy, *Our Gang*. His "Object of My Affections" and "What's the Reason I'm Not Pleasin' You?" were especially popular. His unforgettable kiddie productions were said to be "cute, telling, and altogether fantastic."[56]

Meanwhile, changes were going on in the emerging music industry. A movement away from marketing for specific audiences, such as hillbilly for rural European-Americans and Cajun for the people of the Louisiana bayous, had begun in the eastern recording and publishing houses. By the 1930s, marketing was designed to appeal to larger audiences in order to promote cultural homogenization and to increase profits.[57] Country music played on the radio became more sophisticated and the hillbilly image was confined to *The Grand Ole Opry* in Nashville and to the South. The cowboy image became harsher and more realistic. Adultery, alcoholism, blood, dirt, and insanity began to be reflected in music for radio and the movies. Traditional rural music became known as "old time" and categorized as "blue-grass."[58] Later, as record companies tried to adapt country music to urban tastes, Nashville became the center for musical conservatism. Austin, Texas, became the unofficial center for the dissatisfied. Their music was not particularly different, but they tended to dress in an "earthy" manner and wore long hair. Some country musicians called themselves "outlaws" and displayed contempt for audiences, the movie business, and society in general. Some singers who were ex-convicts, exploited their convictions to increase record sales and their popularity. Those efforts led country music away from rural values except for music played for smaller audiences in both urban and rural areas.[59]

Oklahoma's country music remained conservative and did not usually take part in "outlaw music." It adapted to Nashville and the *Grand Ole Opry*. Oklahomans who migrated to the West Coast, especially to Bakersfield, California, during the 1930s, and others stationed on military bases during World War II, had caused an upsurge in the popularity of country music in other areas. Some researchers observed that in the 1920s the use of written arrangements led to a larger proportion of musicians who had studied music and had become capable readers. Many also began to recognize the relationship of jazz and country music to the musical history of America and included material about Oklahoma's musicians in musical histories.[60]

Making a living from music alone in Oklahoma became almost impossible for musicians, songwriters, and vocalists. Competition for jobs was great because there were many musically talented people in the state. Some superb classical, popular, country, and western musicians worked at part-time jobs and waited for opportunities to drive long distances on weekends to play five or six hours for meager pay. Consequently, many musicians, after they became accomplished, left the state to find larger paying audiences and more opportunities.[61]

Radio recording equipment, and later television, affected the music industry and Oklahomans. On the national scene, the electronic media led the way. Copying and overdubbing became common as the increasingly powerful entertainment industry reacted to the exigencies of popularity polls and other commercial factors.[62]

Musical moods and attitudes were also changing. The so-called new music was not always really new, but rather white musicians performing rhythm and blues the way they had watched Black artists perform it while they were growing up. The new younger audiences were embracing old Black music with the images projected by white performers on television and in the movies.[63]

By the end of the 1950s, rock and roll had also appeared on the music scene. In 1955 Bill Haley and the Comets had reached the top position on *Billboard*'s pop chart, and in April of 1956 Elvis Presley had followed with "Heartbreak Hotel," changing the face of American music.[64]

An Oklahoma high school journalism teacher, Mae Boren Axton, later known as the "Queen Mother of Country Music," played an important role in the change. Her collaboration with Elvis Presley to co-write "Heartbreak Hotel" has been called the turning point in the evolution of rock and roll.[65]

Mae Axton's son, Hoyt, was born in Duncan, Oklahoma. He composed songs that rock musicians liked to sing. His "Eve of Destruction" dealt seriously with the drug problem and his "Snowball Friend" was about the causes and consequences of cocaine use. His "Seven Came" was an apocalyptic vision of the end of the world and God's sorrow over the self-destruction of the human race.[66]

When Axton began to compose happier and more optimistic songs, his music was performed by Three Dog Night. They reached the top of the charts with Axton's "Joy to the World" about a bullfrog named Jeremiah. A year later, the band reached the top again with Axton's "Never Been to Spain."[67]

Axton and Roger Miller have also written lyrics classified as "nonsense songs" about the impossibility of roller-skating in a buffalo herd, about Axton's wine-sipping bullfrog, and about other whimsical notions and fancies.[68]

The work of Oklahoma's musicians and composers of country or country-inspired music frequently reached into the pop field, either by their own performances or by non-Oklahomans who had no country background. Although rural life and such terms as "hillbilly" were sometimes rejected by musicians who had fled from the isolation, privation, and hard work of the farm, they tended to look back through the rose-colored glasses of memory. While rural life was put down, it was also sentimentalized as America's fascination with country living was revealed in its music and continued to attract loyal urban and rural audiences.[69]

After the early hard years of poverty and dust, Oklahoma parents wanted a better life for their children. Consequently, they encouraged them, especially their daughters, to practice and develop their musical talents. George Carney's research found that at least 23 Oklahoma female musicians had been born in the twentieth century. More than 90 percent had been born prior to 1950 and 77 percent had been born in a rural area of the state. The selections made by Carney were based on inclusions in leading encyclopedias and biographical dictionaries covering American music. Research data from other sources was also used.[70]

Laura Rucker was born in Oklahoma in 1908. Little is recorded of her family history. She was an African-American jazz singer, pianist, and bandleader who moved to Kansas City. Ed Lewis, another Oklahoma musician, joined her there in 1926. Her noted recordings are "Little Joe," "St. Louis Blues," "Fancy Tricks," "Something's Wrong," "Swing My Rhythm," and "I'm the Lonesome One."[71]

Agnes "Sis" Cunningham was born near Watonga, Oklahoma, in 1909. While a child, she played piano with her father, an old time fiddler who knew more than 500 fiddle tunes. The two co-authored "There Are Strange Things Happening in This Land." After attending Southwestern Oklahoma State University in Weatherford and Commonwealth College in Mena, Arkansas, Sis became a vocalist, composer, and pianist in the folk style. In 1937, she taught music at the Southern Labor School for Women in North Carolina, where she directed the singing of labor songs.[72] In 1941, she joined the Almanac Singers and sang with Woody Guthrie. Cunningham's folk composition "Belt Line Girls" was one of her first women's era songs. Some of her later compositions included "Mister Congressman," "Song of the Evicted Tenant," "My Oklahoma Home (It Blowed Away)," "How Can You Keep on Movin," and "Oil Derrick Out By Tulsa." She performed with the Red Dust Players in Oklahoma from 1939 to 1941 presenting skits and songs for sharecroppers and union workers. Some of her works were recorded by Smithsonian Folkways Recordings. From 1962 to 1988, she edited *Broadside,* a folk music magazine she founded in New York City. The popular magazine recorded political viewpoints reflected in the folk song explosion of the 1960s and introduced the legendary folk-artists Malvina Reynolds, Bob Dylan, and Peter Seeger. Sis was the first successful woman entrepreneur in the music industry.[73]

Rosa "Rose" Lee Carter, 1914–1997, of Snyder, Oklahoma, and two of her siblings, Anna and Jim, were original members of the Chuck Wagon Gang led by their father. Rose was a vocalist for the group, singing the high-soprano lead in a four-part harmony quartet with a country-gospel style. The group's first recording for Columbia Records in 1936 stayed on the roster for the next 40 years.[74]

Carter organized a radio show called *The Carter Quartet* that aired over KFYO in Lubbock, Texas. She continued to work on radio on Fort Worth's WBAP on a weekly program called *The Roundup* in 1936. The group toured the United States and played to large crowds at the Hollywood Bowl, Carnegie Hall, and *The Grand Ole Opry.* Later, she hosted a television show called *Gospel-Roundup.* Her *Chuck Wagon Favorites* songbook influenced the southern gospel style of the 1940s. In the 1950s, her group was the first to have an album of gospel songs issued.[75]

In 1987, her group received a gold record from SESAC to commemorate 50 years of recording gospel music. In 1988, country music fans voted it the top gospel singing group in America. Sales of the group's records exceeded $30 million. Rose sang with the Chuck Wagon Gang from 1935 until 1966. The group became a radio institution in the Southwest by singing songs from shape-note hymnals using four-part harmony led by Carter's high soprano. Bill C. Malone wrote in 1981 that their recording of "Jesus Hold My Hand" illustrated "the plain unadorned style of gentle and restrained harmony for which they were always famous."[76]

Billy Lee Tipton, whose real name was Dorothy Lucille Tipton, was born in Oklahoma City in 1914. She moved to Kansas City when she was 14 years old and was enrolled in the Concannon School of Music, where she studied piano, violin, and saxophone. She also attended three years of high school at Southwest High in Kansas City and played the saxophone with the school's orchestra. Her senior year was completed at Muskogee, Oklahoma, and at Conner State College High School in Warner, Oklahoma. She played saxophone with the school band at Conner High.[77]

At a time when female musicians were not well accepted in public entertainments, Tipton began to cross-dress as a male named Billy Tipton. Her first paying job was as a male with the Banner Cavaliers from 1935 to 1937, playing piano and saxophone. She also performed with the group on radio stations WKY, KTOK, and KFXR in Oklahoma City.[78]

Later, still dressing as a male, she played and sang with George Mayer and His Music So Rare Band at the Cotton Club in Joplin, Missouri, from 1940 to 1943, and the Palmero Club in Corpus Christi in 1944. During 1947-1950, she played with George Mayer's Sophisticated Swing Trio in Oregon and later with Mayer's Quartet in Spokane, Washington.[79]

After forming the Billy Tipton Trio and the Billy Tipton Quartet, the jazz musician and her group played clubs in the Pacific Northwest in the early 1950s. Her "Sweet Georgia Brown" and "Billy Tipton Plays Hi Fi on the Piano" were recorded by Doshay Records in 1956.[80]

Lee Wiley, 1915-1975, was born in Fort Gibson, Oklahoma. In her teens, she ran away from home, was temporarily blinded in a riding accident, sang on Tulsa radio, and, when she was about 15 years old, went to New York City. By age 17, she was singing with the Lee Reisman Orchestra in the Central Park Casino. Soon, the jazz, Dixieland, and Swing singer and composer became a vocalist for the Leo Reisman, Victor Young, Eddie Condon, Paul Whiteman, and Jess Stacy ensembles. She co-composed "Got the South in My Soul," "Anytime, Anyday, Anywhere," and "Eerie Moan." From 1936 to 1938, she had a successful television career as the star of the CBS show *Saturday Night Swing.* She performed with Eddie Condon at Town Hall and Famous Door.[81]

Wiley was the first singer to do albums devoted to the works of just one composer. She did individual albums of Irving Berlin, Cole Porter, and George Gershwin in 1939-1940. A 1983 television drama, *Something About Lee Wiley,* was based on her life story. Her discography listed more than 50 records and included "I've Got a Crush on You," "It's Only a Paper Moon," "George Gershwin Songs," and many others. Historian Stanley Green wrote, "Lee Wiley's elegant delivery. . . .was rightfully described as insightful, perceptive, intimate, and intelligent; warm and wistful; sweet and sensual." George Frazier stated, "Lee Wiley has class. . . . the best we have."[82]

Kay Starr was born Kathryn La Verne Starks in 1922 in Dougherty, Oklahoma, to American Indian and Irish parents. Raised in Dallas, Texas, and Memphis, Tennessee, she began her career as a hillbilly singer when she won a contest on WRR radio in Dallas. The station gave her a 15-minute weekly radio program. She also sang country music on *Saturday Night Jamboree* on WMPS radio in Memphis and popular music on her own weekly program.[83] During her high school years, 1937 to 1939, Starr performed with the big band of jazz violinist Joe Venuti. She soon became recognized as a jazz singer. She recorded her first disc, "Baby Me" and "Love

With a Capital You," in 1939 with the Glenn Miller Band. She also performed with Bob Crosby in Camel Caravan and sang with Glenn Miller in 1939. She had her own television show and recorded with Ben Webster and Count Basie. She was a vocalist with several big bands. Her hit "Wheel of Fortune" stayed at number one for ten weeks in 1952. In 1955, her "Rock and Roll Waltz" stayed for six weeks at the number one spot and was a million copy seller. In 1959, she recorded "Lazy River," "Foolin Around," and "Crazy," with Capitol Records. Later, she recorded several jazz and country albums on independent labels.[84] A story is told about how during a visit to her hometown of Dougherty, Starr heard Pee Wee King's fiddle tune, "Bonaparte's Retreat," for the first time as it played on a jukebox. She immediately called Roy Acuff's publishing house and asked permission to record the song herself. She received permission to do so with lyrics provided by Acuff. The recording was a hit and sold almost one million copies.[85]

Leonard Feather wrote that Kay Starr had been exposed to big-voiced blues singers of the past in her early years and always retained some jazz qualities in her music, but, in her later years, her work increasingly emphasized the pop-music culture. Scott Shea commented, "Only a broad palette could contain the many colors in the music of Kay Starr."[86]

Berta Leah "Lea" Mathews was born in McAlester, Oklahoma, in 1925. She performed as a singer in the jazz style during the 1950s. She won an amateur contest in Washington, D.C., in 1945, was a soloist at Café Society in New York City in 1950, performed concerts at Willis Conover's House of Sounds from 1951 to 1952, and sang with Woody Herman from 1954 to 1955. She was listed in Feather's *The Encyclopedia of Jazz* but not many details of her musical career have been recorded.[87]

Patti Page, a country singer and actress born Clara Ann Fowler in Claremore, Oklahoma, in 1927, first sang in church with her seven sisters. Later Page and her sister Rena formed the Fowler Sisters. In 1947, she became a regular on Don McNeil's *Breakfast Club* on ABC radio. She overdubbed her own voice to make it sound like a vocal group in 1948. The record "Confess" became her first hit. In 1949, Page used the same overdubbing techniques while making her first million seller, "With My Eyes Wide Open, I'm Dreaming."[88] Page charted 39 hits from 1948 to 1951. Four number one hits included "I Went to Your Wedding," "The Tennessee Waltz," "All My Love," and "How Much Is That Doggie In the Window." "Allegheny Moon" was a number two hit and "Old Cape Cod" became a number three. "Mama From the Train," a top 15, followed, and in 1951, she was the first female musician to reach top five in both country and pop music. In the 1950s, Page was the first woman to use multi-track recording, a technological breakthrough. Her crossover version of "The Tennessee Waltz" also made musical history when it stayed number one on the pop charts for 13 weeks in 1951. Then it crossed to country top three, was certified gold, and more than three million copies of it were sold. Her "Mockin' Bird Hill" was another very popular song. Her total sale of albums is said to have exceeded $60 million.[89] Page preferred to use a pitch pipe to work out her own recordings. She and Kay Starr, along with Rosemary Clooney and Jo Stafford, were recognized as the best female vocal stars of the 1950s. Patti received an honorary arts degree from the University of Oklahoma in 1981 and was inducted into the Oklahoma Hall of Fame in Oklahoma City in 1983 and the Music Hall of Fame in Muskogee, Oklahoma, in 1997.[90]

At least 15 more female musicians were born in Oklahoma before the early 1950s. They included Marilyn Moore, Bonnie Owens, Jean Shepard, Pat Moran, Wanda Jackson, Norma Jean, Molly Bee, Anita Bryant, Lorrie Collins, Gus Hardin, Mary Kay Place, Gail Davies, Cassie Gaines, Becky Hobbs, and Reba McEntire.[91]

The lack of recording studios and jobs caused many Oklahoma musicians to migrate if they wanted to continue their careers. Marilyn Moore, who had broken into her parents' vaudeville act when she was three years old, sang with local bands during her high school years, and later the jazz singer went to Chicago. She sang with Woody Herman and Charlie Barnet. After her recording debut in 1957 with *O Captain* and *Moody Marilyn Moore*, she was compared to Billie Holiday of the 1930s. She returned to Oklahoma City in the 1950s.[92]

Country singer Bonnie Owens was born Bonnie Campbell in Blanchard, Oklahoma, and she sometimes picked cotton near there as a child. In the evenings, she would go outside and try her best to sing loud enough for a special little neighbor boy to hear her. After moving to Arizona with her family, she was recognized as the best yodeler in the state, and in the eighth grade she began to sing for school assemblies. In the 1950s, Owens became recognized as the first major female artist to appear from Bakersfield, California, a center of country music. She and Merle Haggard received Academy of Country Music Best Vocal Duo awards in 1965, 1966, and 1967. Bonnie also received the Top Female Vocalist award from the Academy of Country Music in 1965. Her major hits included "Don't Take Advantage of Me," "Just Between the Two of Us" with Merle Haggard in 1964, "Number One Heel," "Why Don't Daddy Live Here Anymore," and "Consider the Children."[93]

Ollie Imogene "Jean" Shepard was born in Pauls Valley, Oklahoma. Her family moved to nearby Hugo in 1936 when she was three years old. She learned to sing by listening to Jimmie Rodgers records played on an old wind-up Victrola, Tulsa's KVOO radio broadcasts of *The Grand Ole Opry*, and the Bob Wills Orchestra, and by singing in church with her nine siblings.[94]

In 1946, the family moved to Visalia, California, where the 14-year-old high school student organized an all-girl western swing band that performed regularly at Pismo Beach near San Luis Obispo. Shepard also performed on radio station KNGS weekly during her high school years.[95] A fellow musician, Hank Thompson, was so impressed with Jean's talents that he introduced her to several record executives, and Shepard signed with Capitol Records in 1953. The same year, she recorded her number one country hit, "A Dear John Letter," a Korean War song with narration from Terlin Husky, which crossed over to Top Five pop charts. Her 1956 LP, *Songs Of A Love Affair*, was the first concept album to be recorded by a female country singer. One side of the recordings revealed the perspective from a single woman's point of view, and the other side presented the wife's view of the situation. Between 1953 and 1978, she charted 45 hits. She was an original member of the Ozark Jubilee between 1955 and 1957 and also joined *The Grand Ole Opry* in 1955 after Top Five country hits that included "A Satisfied Mind" and "Beautiful Lies."[96]

In the 1970s, Shepard helped found the Association of Country Music Entertainers to preserve the genre and keep it "country." She was the first female in country music to sell one million records and to overdub her voice on record, and the first country singer to remain with the *Grand Ole Opry* for more than 35 years. She also appeared at Wembly music festivals in England, enjoying popularity there.[97]

Pat Moran was born Helen Mudgett in Enid, Oklahoma, in 1931 to a musical family. She became a pianist and bandleader. After studying classical music at Phillips University in Enid in the early 1940s and at the Cincinnati Conservatory of Music, she switched to jazz and formed her own jazz quartet. She went to New York City in the mid-1940s. *This Is Pat Moran* was listed on her discography.[98]

Wanda Lavonne Jackson was born in Maud, Oklahoma. Her father taught her to play the guitar when she was three. He helped her to read music and to pick out melodies on the piano keyboard when she was nine years old.[99] While she attended Capitol Hill High School in Oklahoma City from 1953 to 1955, she won a talent contest at local radio station KLPR and gained a 15-minute daily program of her own. Later expanded to a 30-minute program, it became one of the most popular country music broadcasts in the Oklahoma City area.[100]

At one time, Jackson was called the "Queen of Rock and Roll" and the female answer to Elvis Presley. She was with the Ozark Jubilee from 1955 to 1957. With the help of Hank Thompson, she signed with Decca Records in 1954 and recorded 15 country tracks. Her "You Can't Have My Love," a duet with Billy Gray, reached the Top 10. In 1956, she signed a contract with agent Jim Halsey. Her first release with Capitol Records was "I Gotta Know," and the next was "Hot Dog! That Made Him Mad." She was voted Most Promising Female Vocalist in 1956. Her "Fujiyama Mama" and "Let's Have a Party" became major hits. "Right or Wrong" and "In the Middle of a Heartache" went Top 10 in 1961. She charted 30 country hits between 1954 and 1974, and her recordings became Capitol Record's best sellers in the German language. From the mid-1950s to early 1970s, she remained a favorite in Las Vegas. She toured New Zealand, the Philippines, Korea, the Middle East, Canada, Europe, and Scandinavia, recorded in Sweden, and was especially popular in Germany, Holland, and Japan. She also played the fair and rodeo circuits and the Trianon ballroom in Oklahoma City.[101]

Norma Jean, born in Webster, Oklahoma, in 1938, was the first woman musician to record a woman-oriented truck-driving song in country music with her "Truck Drivin' Woman" in 1968. Her best known song was "Let's Go All the Way." Her "Go Cat Go" was a 1964 Top 10 hit, and in 1965 she had another Top 10 hit, "I Wouldn't Buy a Used Car From Him." In 1966, her "The Game of Triangles" was a Top Five Hit. One of her best albums reflecting the life of the poor, *I Guess That Comes From Being Poor,* recorded in 1972, included "Hundred Dollar Funeral," "There Won't Be Any Patches in Heaven," and "The Lord Must Have Loved the Poor/He made So Many of Them."[102]

Molly Bee, born Molly Beachboard in Oklahoma City in 1939, was a country vocalist, dancer, and actress who said that she spent her early years singing, yodeling, and riding a mule around the family farm. Her family moved to Tucson, Arizona, while she was still a child. She performed on the Rex Allen Show when she was ten years old. A year later, she appeared with Cliffie Stone's *Hometown Jamboree,* a television show in Hollywood, California, and with the *Pinky Lee TV Show,* when she was 13. While she was still 13, she signed with Capitol Records for duets with Tennessee Ernie Ford entitled "I Saw Mommy Kissing Santa Claus" and "Don't Start Courtin' in a Hot Rod Ford."[103] She became a member of the *Tennessee Ernie TV Show* and later debuted as an actress in *The Boy Friend, Finian's Rainbow,* and *Paint Your Wagon* with notable actors like Alan Young and Buddy Ebsen. She also acted in *Chartreuse Caboose* and *The Young Swingers.* She recorded with Liberty Records beteeen 1962 and 1964, with MGM Records the following two years, then with Granite Records and Accord Records. She also performed concerts, USO Tours with Bob Hope, fairs, rodeos, and summer stock.[104]

Anita Bryant, a country and gospel vocalist, first sang "Jesus Loves Me," in public at the age of two years in a Southern Baptist Church in Barnsdall, Oklahoma, where she was born. Six years later, she became a professional singer on radio, and when she was 12, she had her own TV show in Oklahoma City on WKY. Bryant won the *Arthur Godfrey's Talent Scouts* contest in 1957 and was named Miss Tulsa and Miss Oklahoma in 1958 when she was 18. The same year, she signed with Carlton Records.[105] Her first successful songs were "Till There Was You," "Six Boys and Seven Girls," "Promise Me a Rose," "Do-Re-Mi," "Paper Roses," and "My Little Corner of the World." From 1960 to 1967, she was a regular with Bob Hope's Christmas Tours of Vietnam. She performed at the White House and sang on the Billy Graham Crusades. In 1968, she sang at both the Democratic and Republican conventions. Her songs were less in the pop genre and increasingly religious or patriotic from the 1960s on.[106]

Lorrie Collins, a country and rockabilly vocalist, songwriter, and guitarist, was born in 1942 near Tahlequah, grew up on a dairy farm, and went to a one-room country school. Her mother sang country and gospel songs. Her younger brother Larry was well known as the co-writer of "Delta Dawn" in 1972 and the composer of "You're the Reason God Made Oklahoma" in 1981.[107] When Lorrie was eight years old, she won a Tulsa talent contest hosted by Leon Mcauliffe, a western swing star with Bob Wills' Texas Playboys. Three years later, she performed on television in *Town Hall Party,* hosted by Tex Ritter. She later appeared on *Ozark Jubilee, The Steve Allen Show, Grand Ole Opry,* and *The Johnny Cash Road Show.* She signed with Columbia Records in 1951.[108] Lorrie and Larry's music appealed to fans of all ages. Tex Ritter said that "on recordings and fairs and rodeos here at *Ranch Party,* they just bring down the house every time." The hopped-up hillbilly style of Lorrie's rocka-ballad "Rock Boppin' Baby" and Larry's "Whistle Bait" predated Elvis Presley, but songs like "Soda Poppin' Around" and "Hot Rod" seemed to speak directly to teenagers. Their work has held up better than the recordings of other juveniles of that period.[109]

Gus Hardin, a country singer born Carolyn Ann Blankenship, performed in Tulsa night clubs for 15 years. She later moved to Alabama to record with Fame Studios, returning to Tulsa in the late 1980s to perform again in nightclubs. Her albums include *Gus Hardin, Fallen Angel,* and *Wall of Tears.* She was legally blind from 1979 to 1984. Musician Leon Russell described Hardin's voice as "a combination of Tammy Wynette, Otis Redding, and a truck driver."[110]

Mary Kay Place, a country vocalist and composer born in Tulsa in 1947, sang both pop and country songs in school and for local events. After graduating from the University of Tulsa she moved to Hollywood to find employment in the entertainment industry. She appeared on the television series *Mary Hartman, Mary Hartman* from 1976 to 1978 and made her singing debut on *All in the Family* with the song "If Communism Comes Knockin' at Your Door, Don't Answer It."[111] Place's best known songs are "Don't Make Love to a Country Music Singer," "Baby Boy," "Cattle Kate," "Aimin' To Please," "Marlboro Man," "Vitamin L," and "Dolly's Dive." Her *Tonite! At the Capri Lounge* was one of five finalists for the Grammy Awards for best

Popular singer and entertainer Anita Bryant Green was claimed by both Oklahoma City and Tulsa. She was inducted into the Oklahoma Hall of Fame in 1966. Courtesy Oklahoma Heritage Association.

country music album in 1976, and she was nominated for the Top New Female Country and Western singer by *Record World* in 1977.[112]

Country singer, composer, and guitarist Gail Davies was born Patricia Gail Dickerson in Broken Bow in 1948 to a musically talented family. Her father was a pioneer performer on *Louisiana Hayride* and a guitarist. Her mother played guitar and her grandmother sang folk tunes. At five, she moved to the Seattle, Washington, area with her mother and two brothers.[113] Davies began singing at clubs with her brother Ron when she was 14 years old. During her high school years she switched to the music of the Beatles. After high school, she toured with a rock band in the Los Angeles area for nine years. She signed as a songwriter with Beechwood Music Publishing in 1973 and became the first woman in country music to write, arrange, and produce her own recordings with Warner Brothers from 1980 to 1984.[114]

In 1982, Davies decided not to marry the father of her unborn child. Her struggle with societal attitudes toward single motherhood and her consequent maturing gave rise to two feminist-oriented albums, *Givin' Herself Away* and *Where Is a Woman to Go?* She was quoted as stating, "I guess what the ladies in the songs are saying is that they can use all the love and affection they can get . . . but a lot of women are finding out that they can supply the other things themselves. They can put bread on their own tables. The image of women in country music has changed. Country music has always been a reflection of what's going on in a society. Now, the new independence that women have found and the confidence that women are finding in themselves are going to be reflected in their music."[115]

By 1984, Davies had ten Top 20 country music hits. In 1986, she organized the first women songwriters in the round on *Austin City Limits.* She moved to Capitol Records in 1990 and released *The Other Side of Love* and *The Best of Gail Davies.* She was hired by Liberty Records as its first female staff producer in 1991. In 1994, Gail formed her own record label, called Little Chickadee Records. In 1995 Ed Morris of *Billboard* Magazine wrote, "Gail Davies has returned to reclaim her ranking as one of the most creative figures in the music industry. And, since she wrote all the songs, produced the album and issued it on her own label, she's clearly the most industrious as well."[116]

Rock singer Cassie LaRue Gaines was born in Miami, Oklahoma, in 1948 and graduated from Miami High School in 1966. She attended Northeastern A&M College in Miami and graduated from Memphis State University with a degree in physical education. In 1976 she became one of Lynyrd Skynyrd's three backup singers and introduced her younger brother Steve to the band. He joined it the same year, replacing Ed King on guitar. She was the vocalist on *One More from the Road,* a Top 10 album, and *Street Survivors.* Sadly, Cassie and Steve Gaines were killed in a plane crash near Gillsburg, Mississippi, on October 20, 1977, just as their musical careers were starting.[117]

Becky Hobbs, a country vocalist, composer, pianist, accordionist, and guitarist born in 1950 in Bartlesville, was often called "rockabilly." She was the daughter of a violinist who loved big band music and a mother who preferred country. Hobbs played her own compositions on the piano from the age of nine. By the time she was 14, she was writing protest songs influenced by Bob Dylan. At 15, she formed her own first all-female band, The Four Faces of Eve. While a student at the University of Tulsa in the late 1960s she performed in mini-skirts and go-go boots in her second all-female rock band named Sir Prize Package.[118]

In 1971, Hobbs worked in Baton Rouge, Louisiana, with a bar band called Swamp Fox. Two years later, she moved to the Los Angeles area with the band. Her biggest hit was a 1983 duet, "Let's Get Over Them Together," with Moe Bandy. In 1985, she debuted on *The Grand Ole Opry.* Her "I Can't Say Goodbye to You" received first place at the American Song Festival. "I Want to Know You Before We Make Love" gained a BMI Performance Award, and "Most Promising Act" received an award in the British Academy of Country Music's international section in 1989. Her recordings included "Angels Among Us," "A Little Hunk of Heaven," "Talk Back Trembling Lips," and "Jones on the Jukebox."[119] Hobbs traveled to Africa in 1992 with her group, the Hearthrobs, for the government's Arts America. She performed in nine countries and in 1989 took part in the Grantham Festival in England. She was showcased in Music City as a Jerry Lee Lewis-style piano pounder and as a blonde whirlwind. She tried to write strong, pro-female compositions on subjects that had not been written about before.[120]

Reba McEntire, country singer, composer, guitarist, pianist, drummer, and fiddler born in Chockie in 1954, was the daughter of a gifted single mother who was a schoolteacher. McEntire began singing for local events and winning awards at an early age. She was a member of the Chorvettes, a singing group, while she attended Southeastern Oklahoma State University in Durant. She sang the national anthem at the National Finals Rodeo in Oklahoma City in 1974. She signed her first recording contract in 1975 with Phonogram Records and recorded her first chart song, "I Don't Want to Be a One Night Stand," in 1976.[121]

McEntire's "How Blue" was a number one hit in 1984. Over the following nine years she had one number one hit after another for a total of 16, including "Somebody Should Leave," "Whoever's in New England," "Little Rock," and "What Am I Gonna' Do About You." Reba became the Country Music Association's Female Vocalist of the Year for 1984, 1985, 1986, 1987, 1990, and 1991. She first appeared on *Grand Ole Opry* in 1977 and became a member in 1986. Reba received many other awards and performed at Carnegie Hall, New York, in 1986. Her tour with Brooks and Dunn in 1998 was the highest grossing tour in the history of country music. By 1999, more than 40 million of her records had been sold. Her "Rumor Has It" was a double platinum recording. *Reba McEntire's Greatest Hits, For My Broken Heart, It's Your Call,* and *Read My Mind* were all triple platinum recordings. *Greatest Hits Vol. II* became a quintuple recording.[122]

With the support of her mother, Reba resisted efforts by producers to take her distinctive country sound into the pop-music genre, feeling that country music was slipping away. She said, "The old Ray Price-type songs are something I'll never get away from. Western Swing, that's my roots and my heritage. . . I'm just trying to find a balance and not get too far one way or the other," during a *Country Music Magazine* interview in 1987.[123]

McEntire also tried to sing songs for women and to express for them the things they were unable to say for themselves. Onstage, she evoked emotions from laughter to tears, shock, and surprise, leaving her audiences with a new sense of themselves as they walked out the door. Her "I Heard Her Crying" addressed the social issue of abused children. "The Stairs" referred to battered women, and "All Dressed Up" spoke about nursing homes for the elderly. She also has looked for songs by female songwriters as she tried to break the power of the male-dominated music business. Meanwhile, she has been supported by millions of female fans of all ages.[124]

Many Oklahoma musicians, male and female, left the state to further their careers and achieved extraordinary successes, but they reflect only a minority of the musical talent in the state. Many diverse peoples who came to Oklahoma voluntarily, or under force, set the roots of the state's musical history. The lyrics of the early music were usually set to simple tunes and rhythms for everyone to enjoy. Music alleviated loneliness and hardship as people herded cattle, tended their families, and guided hand plows through the virgin prairie sod. Both settlers and travelers passing through brought variations of music that coalesced into new genres as the population blended. By mid-twentieth century, new technologies began to forge other new sounds, but characteristics of early Oklahoma music could still be heard in the fast-moving modern world.

6

Classical

HYECHKA

6

Classical music developed at a remarkable rate after the Indian and non-Indian cultures were joined together by statehood in 1907. Oklahoma women were generally recognized as the primary force behind the development of operatic and symphonic music that occurred while their men were devoting their energies to oil, the economy, and to power. [1]

One of those pioneer women was 17-year-old Anna Murphy. Her father, Samuel Murphy, had established a law practice before she came to Oklahoma City by train on June 31, 1889. Four months later she married Henry Overholser, a businessman who became known as "the father of Oklahoma City." Anna became a prominent hostess and civic leader. She and other socialites sponsored many social events to benefit the needy and to organize and later support libraries, schools, community projects, music, and the arts.[2]

The cast of a theatrical production at the Becker Stage Theater in Shawnee, Oklahoma Territory, ca. 1904. Jessie McKee Whitson and Ina Salmon Rieves are among the cast members. Courtesy Santa Fe Depot Museum.

In 1890, Overholser established a theater in a large building he built on the southeast corner of Grand Boulevard and Robinson Avenue. Productions of *Hamlet, Trilby, Uncle Tom's Cabin, The Drunkard,* and various popular melodramas were presented by different groups of touring performers that staged plays and musicals in Oklahoma Territory during the late 1800s. Traveling entertainers from New York City and from London also entertained audiences by candlelight or oil lamplight in rented halls or crudely improvised facilities.[3]

Traveling performers had become available in the territories. Before the Civil War, the Indian nations had a fairly good system of transportation by boat, stagecoach, and ox-drawn freight wagon using rivers and public and military roads. Meanwhile, the railroads had engaged in extensive rail construction between 1865 and 1890 to bring in settlers and also to tap the vast coal reserves of Indian Territory as well as the expanding lead, zinc, oil, lumbering, and tobacco industries. Effective year-round transportation also permitted entertainers and musicians to travel throughout the area and made it possible for local talent to leave in search of education and better job opportunities.[4]

People in the Indian and Oklahoma territories enjoyed the general pattern of theater entertainments that existed east of the Mississippi River until the outbreak of World War I. Traveling road companies flourished. The opera house became the center of attraction for all people interested in the theater. In 1902, Henry Overholser and his wife built their second Overholser Opera House at 217 West Grand

The Overholser Opera House, built in 1890, occupied the second floor of a barn-like structure. The first floor of the building housed a general store. Kerosene lamps hung from the ceiling of the entertainment area. A bright red calico curtain hung from a wire, and was operated by two men who pulled at its front edges while they walked forward and backward. At times, the chairs were removed to make space for dancing. Some early arrivals for a charity ball included Ben Miller, Ledrue Guthrie and his brother Ralph, Mrs. Nettie Wheeler Chappall, Mrs. Miller, and Mrs. Henry Overholser. Courtesy Oklahoma Publishing Company Library.

The Busby Theater in McAlester, Oklahoma opened to the public in 1908. Courtesy Archives of the McAlester Building Museum.

In 1900, the membership of the Twentieth Century Club included, Top Row: Mrs. Whit M. Grant, Mrs. Horace Wilson, Mrs. Frank Wardell, Mrs. G.W. Carrico, Mrs. T.M. Richardson, Mrs. R.B. Ragon; Second Row: Mrs. Henry Overholser, Mrs. W.M. Eicholtz, Mrs. J.W. Hall, Mrs. Charles Gilpin, Mrs. Nelson Darling, Mrs. G.G. Schlberg, Mrs. D.C. Lewis; Third Row: Mrs. W.G. Jonte, Mrs. J.B. Harrell, Mrs. J. G. Street, Mrs. S.M. Gloyd, Mrs. O.S. Russell, Mrs. R.T. Edwards, Mrs. J.W. Grant; Fourth Row: Mrs. L.M. Keyes, Mrs. Allen Hall, Mrs. Claude Richardson, Mrs. T.M. Upshaw, Mrs. Lee Van Winkle, and Mrs. A.B. Tucker. Courtesy Oklahoma Publishing Company Library.

(CLASSICAL HYECHKA)

Boulevard, about one half block to the west of their first building. The ornate accommodations included 16 luxurious boxes, 1,800 leather chairs, 720 electric lights, and what was at the time the largest stage in the West. After a grand opening on November 30, 1903, the new theater hosted local and out-of-town performers playing to enthusiastic audiences. Oklahoma's statehood celebration in 1907 included a performance of William Shakespeare's *Taming of the Shrew* at the new opera house. Sara Bernhardt and Lillian Russell, two of the world's greatest actresses, also appeared on the Overholser stage that same year.[5]

Local amateur theatrical productions were popular throughout Oklahoma Territory, and road companies followed the circuits established by opera houses. Consequently, the latest entertainments were readily available in Oklahoma during the late 1800s and early 1900s.[6]

In 1907, William P. Busby built an opera house in McAlester, an Oklahoma town settled predominantly by Italian miners and cowboys. The structure was as high as an average five-story building and was appreciated for its almost perfect acoustics, seating capacity for more than 1,300, and huge stage that permitted the currently popular *Ben Hur* to be performed without leaving out any scenes. People traveled long distances to see *Ben Hur* and its exciting chariot race staged with live horses and a complicated treadmill. Many big-name entertainers were featured until musical tastes changed and patronage declined drastically. The structure that had cost an estimated $240,000 when built, was sold in 1931 or 1932 for about $2,500. After sev-

Nearly all of its 1,350 seats at the Busby were filled and there were standees in the balcony to see Marguerite Clark and Dewolf Hopper in his successful Broadway show *Happyland* on opening night, March 13, 1908. Courtesy Archives of the McAlester Building Museum.

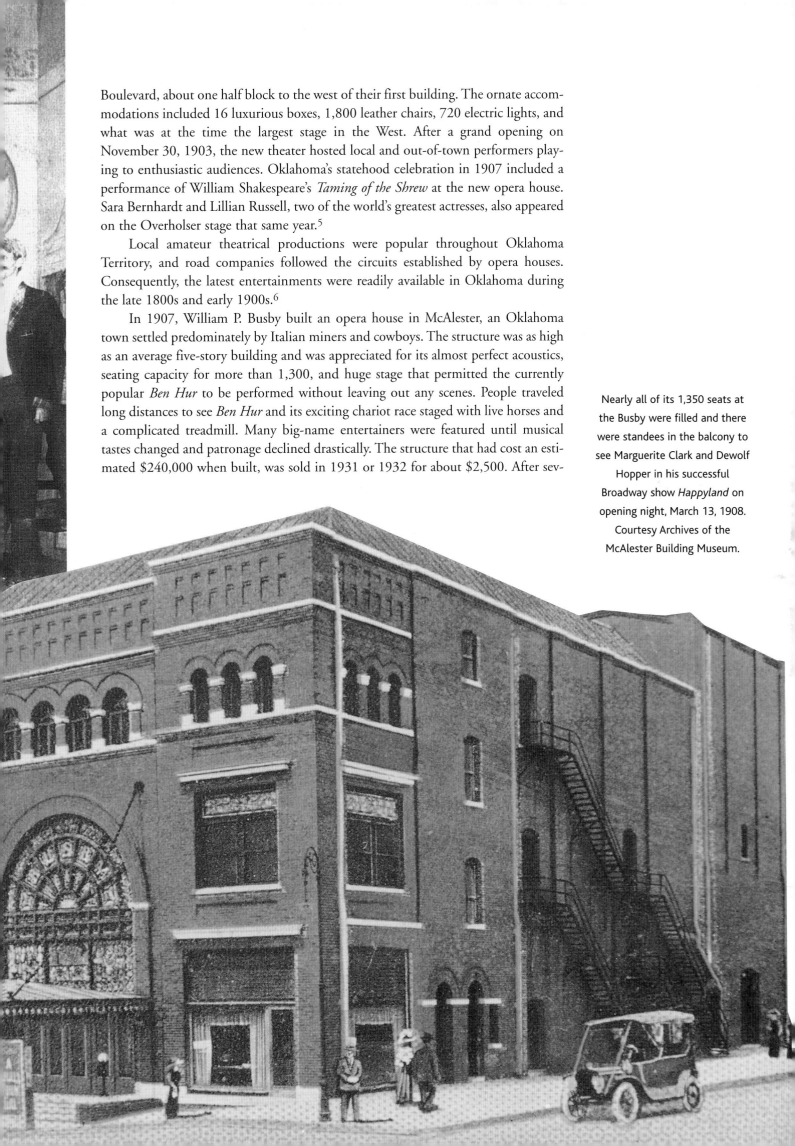

eral remodelings, it served as a commodious and beautiful house of worship for the McAlester Church of Christ. Eventually, the building was torn down to make room for a parking lot.[7]

Public education received considerable attention by the First Territorial Legislature after statehood. The teaching of music was sanctioned by law in public schools, and most school boards provided for music supervisors. Graduates of state schools often went to eastern universities or to Europe for more study. Many musicians and vocalists returned to Oklahoma to teach music. Literary and music clubs that had existed before statehood flourished. Local choirs became choral societies, glee clubs, and music study clubs. Federations were formed as the number of music clubs increased. Old-time "singing schools" rapidly disappeared. By 1937, more than 150 musical clubs were in the state federation. Outstanding musical and literary groups such as the San Souci Club, the En Avant and the Twentieth Century were organized in Oklahoma City by the beginning of the twentieth century. The Apollo Club, a male chorus, was founded in Oklahoma City in 1899 and in Tulsa in 1913. Businessmen began to finance Grand Opera Tours.[8]

Several "Entertainment and Recreation" organizations were popular on the University of Oklahoma campus. Miss Neele Goodrich (standing), sang for the Mandolin Club, ca. 1900. The Emma A. Coleman Collection. Courtesy Western History Collections, University of Oklahoma Libraries.

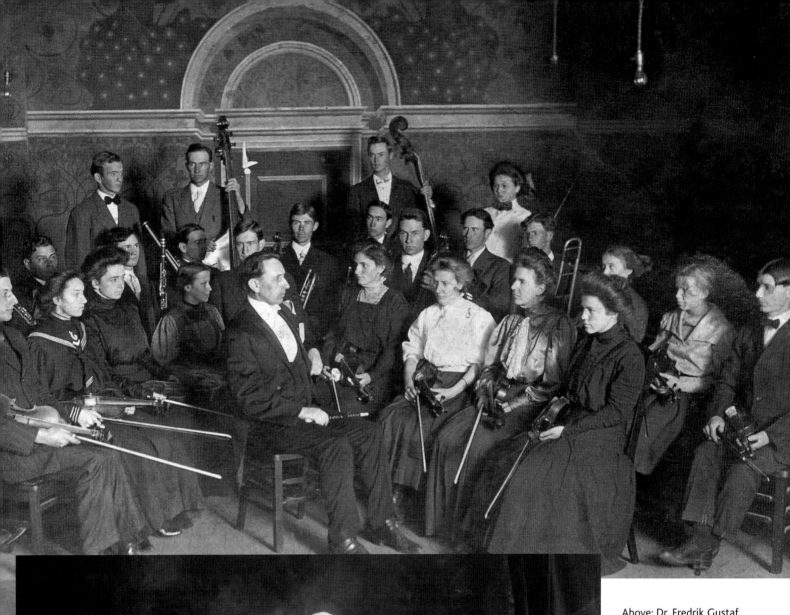

Above: Dr. Fredrik Gustaf Holmberg and the University of Oklahoma Orchestra, ca. 1903 or 1904. Courtesy Western History Collections, University of Oklahoma Libraries.

Left: The University of Oklahoma Band entertained students and the Norman community. Richard A. Conkling Collection. Courtesy Western History Collections, University of Oklahoma Libraries.

The Perkins Ladies Band. First Row: Blanche Wagner, Grace Mathias, Madeline Harding, Vera Sutherland. Second Row: Nina Stansbury, Edith Williams, Mattie Stansbury, Dr. Furrow (director), Maude Vail, Laura Jones, Stella Fulvider. Back Row: Elsie Williams, Ola Johns, Mable Ratliff, Bess Carpenter, Leona Wagner, Beulah Hoffman, Bertha Carpenter, Grace Sellix, Rose Williams. The R.E. Cunningham Collection. Courtesy Western History Collections, University of Oklahoma Libraries.

Musical groups were being organized by the students and faculty at the University of Oklahoma. By 1904, the university had an orchestra. In 1905, they organized a band. The Ladies Band of Perkins, which included members from Stillwater and Cushing as well as Perkins, played for the inauguration of Governor Frank Frantz in Guthrie in 1905, and Oklahomans all over the state continued to show considerable interest in music.[9]

Groups of businessmen in Tulsa and in Oklahoma City also financed Grand Opera Tours to their areas. Hathaway Harper, a businessman and attorney who came to Oklahoma Territory in 1895 from Indiana, became known as Oklahoma City's first impresario when he brought the popular eastern soprano Ellen Beach Yaw to the city. She was well known for her ability to reach a higher note than any other vocalist of the period. She entertained an overflow crowd at the first Overholser Theater in 1896. In 1903, Harper staged one of the largest musical events in the history of the territory when he brought Madame Lillian Nordica, a soprano, and eastern orchestras to perform in a three-day musical affair at Oklahoma City's Delmar Garden. The festival attracted "swarms of music lovers" from all over the area.[10]

In 1909, Harper built the Metropolitan Theater Building, later known as the Palace Theater, on the south side of West Grand Boulevard, across from the Terminal Building in Oklahoma City. Under Harper's management, the theater had its own stock company. For one year, the city enjoyed good stock-company plays, and the popular Chicago Ladies Orchestra furnished music at times.[11]

When the Metropolitan Theater proved to be a failing financial endeavor, Harper went into the insurance business. Some of the Metropolitan performers later became successful on Broadway and in the movies. One stagehand, Lon Chaney, headed for Hollywood and earned a world-wide reputation for his acting abilities. He was known as the "Man of a Thousand Faces" because he could distort his face and body under layers of disguise. Chaney was quoted as having said "My whole career has been devoted to keeping people from knowing me."[12]

Harper was also interested in aviation. In 1909, he sponsored the first air show in Oklahoma, "an inglorious affair." After the crowd waited all afternoon for the wind to die down, the pilot managed to fly his strange looking craft over a nearby fence and land safely. No one asked to be refunded their one dollar admission fee and Harper was able to satisfy the flier and his manager with less than the $2,000 he had contracted to pay them. He later owned the first airplane in Oklahoma City. However, he was more interested in providing classical music and first-rate entertainment for the people of Oklahoma. He soon devoted all of his time to those enterprises.[13]

The 1910-1911 music program in Oklahoma City included Guiseppe Verdi's *Il Trovatore,* Michael Balfe's *Bohemian Girl,* Georges Bizet's *Carmen,* and Gounod's *Faust.* Soprano Geraldine Farrar was heard in 1916 and again in 1918. Pianist Ignace Paderewski appeared in 1916. In 1918, the popular Scotsman Henry Lauder made a memorable appearance at the Overholser Theater in his farewell American tour. Although, his heart was heavy over the loss of his only son, who had died recently on a battlefield in France, he sang and strutted through his acts with his usual "bouncy gaiety."[14]

Productions and artists that Harper brought to the city during the early 1900s included *The Auctioneer* with David Warfield, Guy Bates Post in *The Masquerador,* coloratura soprano Amelita Gulli-Curci (twice), coloratura Louisa Tetrazzini (twice), the operetta *Chu Chin Chow,* violinist Erika Morini, soprano Emma Calve, contralto Ernestine Schumann-Heink, violinist Fritz Kreisler, dancer Anna Pavlova, lyric tenor John McCormack (on three occasions), and others. Anna Pavlova (1881-1931) was especially well received. The Russian dancer, the most famous ballet dancer of her generation, was a small, delicate woman who often traveled to remote areas to acquaint people with the beauty and living art of ballet. She was famous for the pronounced spiritual quality of her graceful, poetic dancing.[15]

Irene Bowers Sells, a reporter for the *Daily Advertiser,* wrote that the 1919 entertainment season in Oklahoma City was outstanding. Soprano Alma Gluck sang the lead in the Chicago Opera's fall presentation of Giacomo Puccini's *La Boheme.* Two night performances and one matinee were presented at the fairgrounds auditorium. Soprano Rosa Raisa and Sophie Braslau were heard in Verdi's *Aida* and Romaki Miera in Puccini's *Madame Butterfly.* The Scotti Grand Opera Company presented Pietro Mascagni's *Cavalleria Rusticana* in May and featured the famous Antonio Scotti artists, chorus, and orchestra with principals from the Metropolitan Opera. Reinald Werrenrath, the popular baritone, and Galli Curci added to the excellence of the season. The San Carlo Grand Opera rendered a double December billing with a matinee performance of Friedrich von Flotow's *Martha* at the Overholser Opera House.[16]

Anna Pavlova, "The Incomparable," and the Ballet Russe brought many talented performers in Oklahoma City. She has been remembered as "one of the unforgettable memories of the Overholser Theater days." Courtesy Oklahoma Publishing Company Library.

Pianist Ignace Paderewski played at the Overholser Opera House in 1916. Courtesy Oklahoma Publishing Company Library.

In 1921, Mary Garden, the famous soprano, appeared at the Overholser Opera House with the Chicago Grand Opera Company. She was at the height of her career. Later, in 1949, at the age of 72, she came out of retirement at Banchory, Scotland, not to sing, but to talk about opera on another tour of the United States. Courtesy Oklahoma Publishing Company Library.

Years later, Harper's niece, Winifred Harper King, reminisced that Amelita Galli-Curci had to have water with ice floating in it even on the coldest evenings. She also recalled that soprano Mary Garden's dress of a thousand mirrors had to be rearranged before each of her numbers. Winifred had seen and heard Enrico Caruso and many other famous artists perform in Oklahoma City before the advent of motion pictures. She declared that Ignacey Paderewski was "the greatest of them all."[17]

After Harper died, Sells suggested that music lovers in Oklahoma should erect a memorial to him because he had provided "rare musical feasts when no one else had the courage to do it." She wondered how he could have done it, as it was a rare year that he did not lose money. When he did make a profit it was usually lost on his next venture. Sells wrote that in spite of financial hardship, Harper never seemed discouraged, always appeared well dressed, managed to eat regularly, and continued to bring good music to Oklahoma City until his death in 1933. Harper had often said that "Broadway doesn't make productions too good or too big for Oklahoma City!"[18]

Theaters and entertainment areas in Oklahoma City during the early 1900s included the Folly Theater, the Delmar Garden, the Blossom Heath and others. The Folly Theater, built in 1907 at 125 West Grand Boulevard, functioned first as a vaudeville theater. When the popularity of vaudeville declined, burlesque shows with occasional motion pictures were presented. Midwest Enterprises later owned the building, which then housed a movie theater, until the structure was destroyed by fire in 1947.[19]

The Delmar Garden was a spectacular entertainment complex in Oklahoma City from 1902 to 1910. The facility was reported to have been the victim of too much water, from the flooding Canadian River, and too little beer as prohibition passed after the complex opened. The establishment included a theater, dancing

Oklahoma's Delmar Garden served as an amusement park, a theater, race track, hotel, restaurant, beer garden, baseball park, and as a convention center (1902-1910). The sunken ballroom and public dining room were in the Blossom Heath Restaurant, owned by Mr. and Mrs. Billy Gragg, on West Thirty-Ninth near Grand Boulevard. The music of the big bands, Glenn Miller, Fats Waller, and Spike Jones was heard there during the Depression years. The restaurant's "fabulous" chicken dinners were available for 25 cents. Courtesy Wayne Mackey Post Card Collection, Oklahoma Heritage Association.

MANUFACTURED BY CURT TEICH & CO., CHICAGO, ILL.

3609 DELMAR PARK, OKLAHOMA CITY, OKLA.

pavilion, baseball park, beer garden, amusement park, rides, race track, hotel, and restaurant. It hosted large meetings and conventions that included the State Constitutional Convention in 1905.[20]

Oklahoma businessman Charles Colcord had provided the 140-acre site for the Delmar Garden and also funds to build the facilities. Ten streetcars brought customers from the downtown area to multi-story loading and unloading platforms. The grand structures and the entire park were considered to be a sight worth seeing.[21]

The theater presented musical and stage presentations featuring local and out-of-state talents such as the actor Lon Chaney, prize fighter John L Sullivan, and legendary pacing horse Dan Patch. Music heard at the Delmar Garden was considered to have been "bright, catchy, or charming." Young men escorted their lady friends to the dance pavilion to dance a two-step, a novelette, and intermezzo two-step, or perhaps a rag. One often remembered tune was "I'd Rather Two-Step Than Waltz, Bill."[22]

Orchestras and street bands were popular in the early 1900s. Finley's Orchestra was enjoyed for about the first decade at the turn of the century. It entertained at the Folly Theater, the Delmar Garden, and the Lee-Huckins Hotel in Oklahoma City. The Oklahoma Coliseum, also called the Stockyards Coliseum, opened in 1922 with a three-day showing of the road show *The Merry Widow*. Later, Al Jolson, Jack Dempsey, John Phillip Sousa's Band, and Al Smith also appeared there. After the building was destroyed by fire in 1930, it was rebuilt without a stage.[23]

Tulsa's first city band was organized on June 15, 1902, by Clarence E. Eaton, a realtor who had come to Tulsa from Illinois. Eaton played the snare drum and Joe Sisson directed the group. The band was an important attraction in many celebrations and parades. It performed for the first Fourth of July celebration held in Tulsa. The musicians were seated on two connected lumber wagons pulled along the parade route by a team of nine oxen that were driven and handled by Jack Wimberly.[24]

The band's original ten members soon grew to 25. They included A.E. Bradshaw, who later became vice president of the First National Bank of Tulsa, and Charles Steele, who became a member of the Tulsa County Bar. Henry Perryman, the son of the Chief of the Creek Indian Nation, played the baritone horn.[25]

At first, businessmen in Tulsa paid for the band instruments and uniforms in return for concerts played two or three times a week on the corners of First Street and Main Street, Second Street and Main Street, and First Street and Boston Avenue in downtown Tulsa. In 1904, the group accepted the offer of the newly organized Tulsa Commercial Club to provide new instruments and uniforms, and the use of a private area in the Commercial Club in return for their services.[26]

A special permit enabled the musicians to play at the St. Louis World's Fair in 1904. They played at intervals for about a week in the Indian Territory Building and attracted much attention. Later, they participated in various booster trips sponsored by the Tulsa Commercial Club. The group also was received by President Theodore Roosevelt in the East Room of the White House when they made a trip to Washington, D.C., in 1908.[27]

Early directors of the band included Dr. Will Marshall, Dr. F. E. Kreyer, George Maxey, and Vernon Knauss. The name of the group, Commercial Club Band, was dropped about 1910 when the Tulsa Chamber of Commerce was organized. Dr. Kreyer, an accomplished musician and the first salaried director of the band, had also organized an orchestra that played for parties, balls, and performances at the Grand Theater, the only playhouse in Tulsa at the time. After Knauss left the band, various skilled musicians directed the group. By 1921, a guild of 275 trained musicians had evolved and were carrying on the musical programs that the founders of the original band had envisioned when they organized the group in 1902.[28]

Another group of Tulsans concerned about the quality of life in their city—which for them demanded the presence of music—were the ten women called together by Mrs. W. N. Robinson on October 20, 1904, to organize a music club. The purpose of the club was to promote interest in music in Tulsa and to provide mutual musical education for the club members.[29]

When Mrs. Strouvelle was given the privilege of suggesting a name for the club, she suggested "Hyechka," the Creek word for music. She wanted to perpetuate the name and legends of her own people, the Creek Indians, whom she considered to be the real pioneers of Oklahoma. The club approved the idea of linking the organization with the people whose lives had "meant most to the best development in the new state."[30]

Mrs. Fred Clinton was the first president of the Hyechka Club. She was unanimously reelected each year until she was elected president for life in 1921. Such an honor was the first in the history of federated clubs. An almost unprecedented spirit of cooperation existed among the members from its beginning. Many of the club members received honors at home and abroad. The club's bimonthly programs, always held on Saturdays to accommodate schoolteachers, were well attended. The club was honored when its district, which included Louisiana, Arkansas, Missouri, and Oklahoma, was named the Hyechka District. The distinction was a tribute to Tulsa member Mrs. O. L. Frost for her leadership abilities.[31]

The Hyechka Club gave most of its proceeds from annual concerts and entertainments to charity each year along with one tenth of its other annual income. Members assisted young artists and entertained at local and county schools to foster a love of good music in students. They sponsored "sings" and gave prizes for memory and musical contests. The group cooperated with school instructors who often were valued members of the club. The organization tried to demonstrate to the public that civic work went hand in hand with artistic endeavors.[32]

One of the active club members, Mrs. Robert Fox, headed an effort that acquired a pipe organ for the Convention Hall. In 1915, the organ was dedicated under the patronage of the Hyechka Club. Dr. Fred Clinton also served the organization well. He began an effort to bring world-famous artists to Tulsa. When Madame Schumann-Heink, a famous contralto, doubted the ability of "tiny Tulsa" to pay for her services, Dr. Clinton went to Muskogee and gave her $1,000 to come to Tulsa and perform in the second musical festival that was sponsored by the Hyechka Club in 1908.[33]

By 1934, Bentonelli had become one of the most popular tenors in Europe. He had sung 512 performances of 51 operas throughout Europe and North Africa. The list included two world premieres plus command performances for Benito Mussolini and most of the crowned heads of Europe. However, the homesick Oklahoman returned to the United States to sign a contract as leading tenor for the Chicago Opera Company. In 1936, he became the first Oklahoman to sing major roles with the Metropolitan Opera Company in New York City. In Chicago and New York City, he sang with Lily Pons, Ezio Pinza, and soprano Vina Bovy.[45]

He later returned to the University of Oklahoma in Norman in 1940 and earned a master's degree in modern languages followed by further work at Yale University. He accepted a position as professor of music and advisor to the Department of Voice at the University of Oklahoma and became chairman of the department in 1944. Benton was inducted into the Oklahoma Hall of Fame in 1951.[46]

One of Benton's students at the university was Laven Sowell, who won a voice contest sponsored by Charles Wagner and his touring opera company. After he graduated, Sowell toured with Wagner's company for a few years. He later became active with the Tulsa Opera.[47]

Wagner, a well-known music teacher, had been instrumental in bringing chautauquas to Oklahoma. When Will Rogers toured with the Wagner Opera Company as a trick-roper and humorist, he was encouraged to change his performances to solo acts. Later, Rogers gained much national and international fame when he appeared on Broadway in the Ziegfield Follies of 1916. A statue of Rogers stands in the United States Capitol in Washington, D. C. Another statue of him was placed at the Will Rogers Memorial in Claremore, Oklahoma.[48]

After World War II ended, interest in having an opera company again picked up in Tulsa. Bess Gowans, a well-known Tulsa piano teacher and accompanist, became the project's catalyst. The nucleus of the original group included Ralph Sassano, a successful New York City opera singer; his wife, Ione Sanger, an Oklahoman who had gained prominence as a singer in New York City; Mary Helen Markham, who had been an opera singer with the San Francisco Opera Company and whose mother lived in Tulsa; Beryl Bliss, an opera singer who was married to Charles Bliss, a local hotel owner; and Bess Gowans.[49]

Maud Lorton, a powerful and controversial figure known as the "Patron of Art," was considered to have had more impact on the successful development of the organization than anyone else. She and her husband Eugene owned the *Tulsa World* newspaper. After Lorton died, she married Barton Myers and became known as Maud Lorton Myers, or "Lady Maud," a title she seemed to enjoy. She was known to be gracious and congenial to everyone but made surprise moves and always stood firm. She also engaged in theatrics of her own, usually making a grand entrance on opening nights, accompanied by a spotlight, after the audience was seated. When the move to grand opera needed considerable financial support, Lady Maud replaced nearly every opera board member with a Tulsan who could offer financial support from private resources or was influential enough to bring in more patrons. She died in the spring of 1962.[50]

Gerald Whitney, the first conductor of the Tulsa Opera, also was director of music in Tulsa Public Schools. Although he had no experience as a conductor, he was an excellent musician and Bess Gowans had strongly recommended him. He organized and rehearsed the orchestra, and was a natural for the position of conductor. He

From left to right, John Alexander, Maralin Niska, and Linda Roark. Roark was a former Tulsa University student who had a powerful soprano voice. She sang starring roles with the New York City Opera and later returned to Tulsa in 1973 as a guest artist. Courtesy Jack A. Williams and Laven Sowell.

was often praised by visiting guest artists for his work. In spite of union and non-union problems, he assembled and prepared a 31-piece orchestra with excellent cooperation from Paul Crimisky, a well-known Tulsa band director who headed up the local musician's union. Their first production was a "rousing success." Whitney remained with the group as conductor until 1957. He then served on the board for a few years.[51]

The Tulsa Opera Club was incorporated December 1, 1948. In 1951, the name "Tulsa Opera Club" was changed to "Tulsa Opera, Inc." By 1953, the community was agitating for grand opera. After financial success was assured, the Tulsa Opera made a successful transition to grand opera and national prominence with a production of Giacomo Puccini's *Madame Butterfly* on November 19 and 21 in 1953. Imported professional vocalists sang the major roles. No deficit was incurred and the company began its history of profitability.[52]

The Opera Guild was formed in 1955 for educational and fundraising purposes. Because of the foresight and efforts of early Tulsans to make available opportunities for learning about opera and to bring outstanding guest artists to Tulsa, several young people chose careers in opera. The guild members encouraged and helped young operatic talent. Ed Purrington, general manager of Tulsa Opera, Inc. from 1975 to 1987, was remembered for "uncanny" ability to evaluate young singers and to present them in the way that best revealed their vocal and dramatic talents. Purrington praised Laven Sowell for the all-volunteer chorus that Sowell developed after he became permanent chorus master in 1966. Sowell was credited with "making musical unity out of a widely divergent group of individuals of varying musical discipline."[53]

Ed Purrington, the General Manager and Artistic Director of the Tulsa Opera, 1975-1987, received a Governor's Proclamation as the Oklahoma Federation of Music Club's "Musician of the Year" from Betty Price, the Executive Director of the Oklahoma State Arts Council. Courtesy Jack A. Williams and Laven Sowell.

Linda Roark, a powerful soprano, made her debut as a chorus member with the Tulsa Opera while still a student at Tulsa University. Later, she starred as Minnie in Giacomo Puccini's *The Girl of the Golden West* with the New York City Opera. She returned to Tulsa as Linda Roark-Strummer to perform the same role in the Oklahoma premiere of the same opera in 1991.[54]

Tulsa native David Hamilton performed with the Tulsa Opera Chorus while he was a high school student in 1975. He returned to Tulsa in 1983 for his local debut as Yamadori in Puccini's *Madame Butterfly*. He later appeared regularly with the Metropolitan Opera and frequently on the Met's *Saturday Matinee* broadcasts.[55]

William Lewis, the high school senior who had appeared in the first Tulsa Opera production in 1948, returned to Tulsa in 1975 to sing the role of Cavardosi in Puccini's *Tosca*. He had become a star performer at the Metropolitan Opera and other major opera houses in the country.[56]

The first Wagnerian opera given in Oklahoma in its entirety was *Die Walkure* with Simon Estes as Wotan. The performance led to an engagement for Estes with the Metropolitian Opera Company. He later starred as Porgy in the 1986 Tulsa production of George Gershwin's *Porgy and Bess*. Estes and Tulsan Jayne Reed founded the Simon Estes Educational Foundation to provide funding for promising high school seniors.[57]

In the 1980s, world-renowned native Oklahomans Leona Mitchell and William Johns appeared in Verdi's *Il Trovatore*. Mitchell also sang the title role of *Aida* in 1985 in Tulsa.[58]

Burch Mayo, a local high school senior and the son of a Tulsa hotel owner, had reportedly promised his father that if he was permitted to perform the role of Germont in the first Tulsa opera club performance of *La Traviata* during the fall of 1948 he would never again try for a career in opera. His father agreed. After a repeat performance the following spring, Burch kept his part of the bargain. He later became prominent in Tulsa for his support of the Tulsa Philharmonic Orchestra.[59]

Early attempts to organize a symphony orchestra in Tulsa failed. A group called the Tulsa Philharmonic Society was started in 1914 but soon dispersed. In 1924, another Tulsa symphony orchestra was formed and disbanded. Later, in the 1930s, the Works Progress Administration, or WPA, helped found an orchestra that was short-lived.[60]

William Lewis appeared in the first Tulsa Opera production in 1948. He became a star performer in the Metropolitan Opera and other major opera houses. He returned to Tulsa as a guest artist in 1975. Courtesy Jack A. Williams and Laven Sowell.

Finally, in 1948, during the days of oil prosperity, a group of visionaries that included Burch Mayo and Herbert Gussman met for the purpose of bringing art and culture to Tulsa. The Tulsa Philharmonic Orchestra was organized by music-loving citizens and was incorporated as a not-for-profit group in November, 1948.[61]

Over the years, the orchestra presented a mixture of classical repertoire, popular music, and light classics. Internationally acclaimed guest conductors, classical guest artists, and popular guest artists performed for northeastern Oklahomans.[62]

H. Arthur Brown served as the first conductor of the new part-time symphony orchestra. The Tulsa Philharmonic began to be recognized as one of the country's leading orchestras during his ten-year tenure. Future conductors were Valdimire Golschmann, 1958 to 1961; Franco Autori, 1961 to 1971; Skitch Henderson, 1971 to 1974; Thomas Lewis, 1974 to 1978; Murray Sidlin, 1978 to 1980; Joel Lazar, 1980 to 1983; and Bernard Rubenstein 1984 to 1996. The 1997-98 season began with Kenneth Jean as music director.[63]

The Tulsa Performing Arts Center became the main performance site for the Tulsa Philharmonic. The orchestra also contracted to play for the Tulsa Opera productions, some performances for the Tulsa Ballet, and for other regular concerts at the Philbrook Museum, the Walter Arts Center at Holland Hall, the PACE Theater, Cain's Ballroom, the Brady Theater, and the Bernsen Center in Tulsa. The Tulsa musicians enriched the community by teaching at local universities, and by coaching talented students of all age groups. They also traveled in Oklahoma to other areas to present concerts made possible through the statewide touring program of the Oklahoma Arts Council.[67]

The musicians and dedicated Philharmonic volunteers believed that music was not only entertaining for children but also encouraged development of their emotional and intellectual well-being. Brown, the first conductor, started several programs that included pop series and children's concerts featuring local students as soloists. The later "Our Lollipops Series" at Holland Hall's Walter Arts Center, for children ages four to nine and their families, was designed to develop creativity while introducing children to the magical world of music. Yearly educational events also included Young Person's Concerts at Chapman Music Hall for third- through eighth-graders.[68]

By the end of the 1990s, the Tulsa Philharmonic Orchestra had expanded its learning program to include all ages. The Ambassador Program and the Tulsa Youth Symphony provided opportunities for talented junior and senior high school students to play in a full student orchestra and also to represent Tulsa on tours to England and to locations in the United States. Some of those students have gone on to musical careers but the majority have chosen non-musical opportunities. The real purpose of the youth program has been to foster a lifelong appreciation of music.[69]

Several generations of Tulsans have been introduced to classical music since the annual Young Person's Concerts began in 1949. More than 60 chamber music assemblies have also given concerts in area schools, nursing homes, and other locations.[70]

Among the board of directors, staff, musicians, and volunteers of the Tulsa Philharmonic, no two people appeared to be more dedicated than Burch Mayo and Herb Gussman. Art critic James D. Watts of the *Tulsa World* wrote that "they, more than anyone, dragged the Tulsa Philharmonic into existence. They were the thinkers and doers and music lovers and Tulsa's bagmen for culture."[71]

Mayo and Gussman were the first vice presidents of the early organization. In 1950, Mayo was elected president of the Philharmonic Board of Directors, and

Gussman became executive vice president. They held those positions for 20 years and each remained active as a director emeritus. Betty Clark, a later director emeritus of the board, declared, "These two gentlemen are the reason the Tulsa Philharmonic exists today. They knew and loved, lived and breathed music, and they managed to share that passion for music with many other people."[72]

The two men were innovative, inventive, fun-loving, and tireless money raisers. Their services often went beyond those vital roles. Richard Minshall, a Philharmonic board member, called them "Pipes" and "Fingers," especially when they offered memberships in the "Hundred Dollar Turn-Down Club." Fingers, an accomplished guitarist, cheerfully explained that the pair "knew a lot of people were just giving us money to shut us up, get us out of their offices, or off the phone." "But," added Pipes, a former opera singer, "that was fine with us. Just as long as we got something out of 'em."[73]

Consequently, some of Tulsa's leading citizens and top business executives decided it was better to pay club dues on time and be spared visits from Fingers and Pipes. In fact, they seemed to happily agree that joining the club was well worth the price to be rid of the two characters.[74]

The history of classical music in Tulsa has been a testament to Tulsans' dedication, hard work, and also to the early contributions of composers and musicians. Franklin Sonnakolb, born in Amsterdam, Netherlands, was a composer, pianist, and lecturer in Tulsa for 18 years. He had been a pupil of world-famous masters and had composed more than 180 compositions that included *Osage Indian Opera*. Other early contributors were Clarence Burg, Lemuel J. Childers, Lucile Crist Carson, E. Edwin Crerie, Milton Dietrich, Charles F. Giard, Marie Hine, Galen Holcomb, Claude Lapman, Johnny Marvin, Gerald J. Mraz, Hugh McAmis, Edwin Vail McIntyre, Samuel McReynolds, Paul Wesley Thomas, and Joseph Wynne. Another list compiled by WPA writers included Mayme Rabinowitz, the Reverend Father Ignatius Groll, Robert W. Wolfe, Wynn York, and Spencer Norton.[75]

Paolo Conte, an early dean of music at Oklahoma Baptist University in Shawnee, Oklahoma, was born and educated in Palermo, Italy. He composed more than 200 works that were published in New York City. Oscar J. Lehrer, who was born in Transylvania, came to America in 1889. He organized the First Infantry Regiment Band of the Oklahoma National Guard with Tom Mix as his drum major. In 1916, he became professor of music and instructor of the band at the University of Oklahoma. His compositions included band music, sacred music, cantatas, operettas, and music for violin. Composer James Neilsen, the conductor of a band and orchestra at Oklahoma City University, was born in Scotland. He composed 200 works for orchestra, band, chorus, and voice.[77]

Samuel A. McReynolds was perhaps Oklahoma's first recognized composer of classical music. He came to Oklahoma Territory with his parents in 1893 when he was nine years old. By 1905, he had composed an award-winning composition called *Romanza* for mandolin and orchestra. His work placed first in a competition sponsored by the Genoa Musical Society in Italy. Emile Francia, a Tulsan, recommended McReynolds for a scholarship at the Verdi Institute in Genoa, Italy. The young composer received the grant and while studying in Europe he gained much recognition for five concertos for mandolin with orchestra accompaniment which he composed while living there. Noted mandolinists performed the works in European centers.[78]

Roy Harris, the son of Oklahoma pioneers, became one of the outstanding composers of the twentieth century and contributed much to the world of classical music.

His father and grandfather had traveled to Oklahoma with only an ox cart, a gun, and basic provisions. Harris was born in a log cabin in Lincoln County on February 12, 1898, President Abraham Lincoln's birthday. The family moved to Gabriel Valley, California, when Roy was five years old.[79]

Harris learned to play the clarinet and the piano as a child but did not consider music for a career until after he had served in World War I. He then completed studies at the University of California, became a private pupil of Arthur Farwel, and in 1926 went to Paris to study with Nadia Boulanger.[80]

A man of irrepressible energy, Harris developed a style that was his own and considered to be distinctly American. He looked to his own cultural background for inspiration. The vast prairies and wide open spaces of the West were suggested at times in his music. Cowboys, African-Americans, the American Civil War, minstrel shows, mountain and folk songs were all to be heard in his music.[81]

Symphony No. 3 was one of Harris's earliest symphonies and one of his most powerful works. During the London blitz of World War II when a Britisher wanted to bury a collection of the world's best classical music underground for a future civilization to uncover, he included one of Harris's symphonies. The selection, Symphony No. 3, was the only American work chosen.[82]

Symphony No. 4, "Folk Song," was considered genuinely American in both atmosphere and spirit. It cleverly interwove the cowboy melodies "Oh Bury Me Not On The Lone Prairie" and "The Streets of Laredo," western fiddle ditties "Jump Up My Lady" and "The Blackbird and the Crow," the romantic "The Gal I Left Behind" and "I'm Going Away For To Stay a Little While," a Black spiritual, "De Trumpet Sound In My Soul," and a Civil War tune, "When Johnny Comes Marching Home."[83]

During World War II when the Allies became optimistic that the Soviet Union's fierce resistance of the Nazi invasion would be effective, Harris, excited by the turn of events, composed his powerful and rhythmic Symphony No. 5 and dedicated it to the Soviet Union. The work was introduced by the Boston Symphony Orchestra under the baton of Serge Koussevitsky on February 24, 1943, and was transmitted by short-wave to the Soviet Union. It was also sent 11 times to American forces around the world.[84]

Because Harris had been born on President Lincoln's birthday and under similar circumstances in a log cabin, he often felt a closeness to the former president. Harris's Symphony No. 6 reflected the composer's admiration and spiritual affinity

(CLASSICAL HYECHKA)

7

After statehood in 1907, some pioneer women dreamed of having symphony orchestras in their hometowns. A small group of women in Oklahoma City began to work toward that actuality by first organizing the Ladies Music Club for the advancement of musical culture in the city and in the state.[1]

In 1908, to get their plan started, Mrs. Edwin L. Dunn invited nine women to her home at 109 West Park Avenue. The club grew steadily until, at one time, it had 800 associate members and a limited number of professionally active musicians. Although men were added to the membership rolls, the name of the club was never changed.[2]

A brief history of the association was written by Mrs. Dunn in 1913. She included her thoughts about the future of music. She wrote about the recent inventions that included self-playing pianos, pipe organs, and voice recorders. A voice recording of Mrs. Charles Ames, the first president of the Ladies Music Club, and the original copy of the history were placed in a time capsule and buried in a cornerstone somewhere in downtown Oklahoma City.[3]

Mrs. Ames remained president of the club for 26 years. While she lived in New York, she selected many of the guest artists that appeared in Oklahoma City under the sponsorship of the Ladies Music Club. Mrs. Edmond Ferguson and Mrs. Jules Bloch served as presidents of the group when Mrs. Ames was out of town.

In the following decades a multitude of musical presentations were sponsored by the Ladies Music Club. Among the performers were pianists Frank LaForge, Josef Lhevinne, Joseph Hoffman, Ernest Hutcheson, and Mischa Levitski and violinists Maude Powell, Eridia Morini, Emil Telmanyi, and Albert Spalding. Numerous sopranos appeared, including Maggie Leyte, Frances Alda, Olive Klein, Alma Gluck, Grace Wagner, Louis Hubbard, Lucille Chalfant, and Laura Townsley McCoy. Among the others were Enrico ArReoni, Lambert Murphy, Frederick Jagel, and Marie Chamlee, tenors, and Reinald Werrenrath and Renato Zanelli, baritones. In addition, there were ballets, lectures, and orchestral performances, and events featuring Russian dancers, cellists, quartets, and other artists.[4]

In 1921, Mrs. Frank Buttram, an accomplished musician and a member of the Ladies Music Club, asked Dr. Fredrik Gustaf Holmberg, dean of the Fine Arts Department at the University of Oklahoma in Norman, to help her organize a string choir for the club. Male musicians were soon included. After some brass and reed instruments were added to the string instruments, the Ladies Music Club announced that they had a 54-piece orchestra.[5]

In 1903, Holmberg accepted a position at the University of Oklahoma because the idea of living in a growing territory appealed to him. He was named associate professor in 1905, director of the School of Fine Arts in 1908, and dean of the school in 1910.[6]

Holmberg, born in Joenkolping, Sweden, on August 18, 1872, had emigrated to America when he was 15 years old. He attended Bethany College at Lindsborg, Kansas, where he also worked summers in the Kansas wheatfields and played with dance orchestras in the winter months. He earned his undergraduate degree in music with major study in violin and composition and went on to Chicago for four more years of study in music to become an individual master.[7]

Holmberg played with several show orchestras in Chicago before he got his first opportunity to conduct a symphony orchestra. When he raised his baton and gave the cue for the props man to raise the curtain for his debut with a Chicago Symphony Orchestra, the audience began to clap and laugh uproariously because his coattails caught in the stage curtain and were pulled over his shoulders before he could get himself untangled. A rewarding concert followed.[8]

A concert held by Dean Holmberg and the Ladies Music Club on February 23, 1924, showed a complement of 24 violins, 14 violas, four cellos, two flutes, one clarinet, one oboe, and one bassoon, with Jeanette True at the piano. They presented Wolfgang Mozart's Symphony No. 40, Puccini's *Vissi d'Arte,* the first movement of Ludwig van Beethoven's Piano Concerto No. 1 in C Minor, Peter Tchaikovsky's *Arabian Dance,* and Alexandre Luigini's *Ballet Eqyptien.* Soprano E. E. Cornelius, accompanied by J.S. Frank, sang Walter Kramer's "Old English Dance," Rudolph Frimi's "Adieu," and Ernst Gillet's "Precieuse."[9]

Two months later, on April 24, 1924, the Ladies Music Club Orchestra gave its first public concert on a Sunday afternoon in the Central High School auditorium. The program was well presented with an interesting contrast in numbers. Richard Wagner's Prelude from *Lohengrin,* Tchaikovsky's *Andante Cantabile,* Percy Grainger's *Mock Morris Dance,* and two movements from Antonio Vivaldi's Concert in A Minor were favored by the audience. Gillet's *Passe Pied,* Beethoven's *Adagio Cantabile* from Menuet G, Victor Herbert's *Air de Ballet,* Carl Dusch's *American Indian Melody,* and Theodore Moses Tobani's *Wedding Serenade* were all played with good musicianship.[10]

Ade Davis wore a quaint costume and sang the aria "They Call Me Mimi" from Puccini's *La Boheme* and "Springs Awakening" by Wilford Sanderson. After persistent applause, she also sang "Ma Lindy Lou." Ira T. Parker, a tenor, sang a melody from Puccini's *Tosca.* Parker's encore was "Passing By." A solo by Mildred Nelson and a duet by Mr. and Mrs. Earl Verden were also well received. "Parade of the Wooden Soldiers" was played a second time after an insistent round of applause.[11]

The musicians donated their services for the first concert and they played to a packed auditorium. A local newspaper headline read, "Symphony for the City Is a Vision of Music Club." Another periodical reported the performance to have been an inspiration to those who saw the possibilities of a future municipal symphony of ability and merit.[12] Encouraged by the good public reaction to their orchestra, the Ladies Music Club asked Dean Holmberg to develop full instrumentation. Holmberg was determined to make classical music permanent and popular in Oklahoma. Mrs. Frederick Owen, the president of the musical group at that time, declared the ensemble to be the "nucleus" of a symphony orchestra for Oklahoma City. The Chamber of Commerce, although dubious at first about the economic value of the orchestra, soon became supportive. George Frederickson, president of the Frederickson-Kroh Music Company, pointed out that, in the past, businessmen in the city had underwritten grand operas for as much as $30,000 for each performance which indicated that money was available for good music. Furthermore, he added that all the money spent on an orchestra would remain in the city.[13]

When the sponsors for the symphony began to raise money for the first year's budget, nearly half was raised the first day. Businessman John A. Brown, the first president of the new 12-member orchestra committee, reported that they expected to sell 1,200 season tickets. He said the guarantors had subscribed from $50 to $750 each. Merle Buttram was vice president and T. E. Braniff chairman of the group. Symphonic concerts for children began under the baton of Dean Holmberg with the sponsorship of the first board of directors.[14]

Mrs. Frank Buttram, ca. 1938. Mrs. Buttram was called "The Mother of the first Oklahoma City Symphony Orchestra." She was inducted into the Oklahoma Hall of Fame in 1964. Courtesy Oklahoma Publishing Company Library.

(PIONEER WOMEN WHO DARED TO DREAM)

Dr. Fredrik Gustaf Holmberg, who was born August 17, 1872, and died January, 1936, was the music director of the first symphony orchestra in Oklahoma City. Courtesy Archives of Contemporary History, Oklahoma Christian University.

A local correspondent wrote that the news that Oklahoma City had an orchestra that qualified as a symphony was like a "bolt out of a clear sky," and wondered if any other city no older than 30 some years could make such a claim. Another writer looked forward to the union of the past and the present when Dean Holmberg would direct a group of 50 professional musicians. Not only would the audience hear good music, but they would also see the results of all that had gone on before during the past years. The columnist pointed out that "upon the sturdy foundation erected by pioneers, we are building our house and we add every stone with the hope of making the complete project as perfect as their dreams."[15]

When members of the Ladies Music Club were interviewed by the media, they not only expressed their social and cultural pleasure in having a symphony orchestra but also noted the value of classical music to the state. They listed the educational, mental, and physical benefits to the community, especially to the children of Oklahoma. They pointed to the music appreciation, independence of thought, and self-expression gained by children through the practical playing of an instrument by themselves and with others. All of these factors they saw as strengthening children by giving them confidence in "their own powers."[16]

MRS. GEORGE ADE DAVIS
Soprano Soloist

Assisting Artists

First Concert

Monday Evening

October 27

MR. Wm. C. SHULL
Baritone Soloist

What a Symphony Orchestra Means to Oklahoma City

THE announcement of a series of Symphony Concerts marks a big step forward in the marvelous growth and history of our city. Perhaps no city of such a few years growth has ever achieved a like accomplishment. Cities which have Symphonies regard them as their very best, highest grade civic advertisement.

We believe the people of Oklahoma City will agree, at the close of this concert, that the organization IS a symphony orchestra, in every sense of the word, and capable of taking a leading rank among similar organizations elsewhere in America.

Those who have labored to bring this orchestra into being sincerely hope that it meets with the fondest expectations of tonight's audience. And we trust that it will continue to receive the patronage its merit deserves, for it is only by continous support that it can render to Oklahoma City the service it is destined to give.

One citizen said she would not take a million dollars for the Theo. Thomas Orchestra Concerts she heard when a child. No one can measure the worth of these concerts to our twenty-five thousand school children, offering to them many hours of real pleasure and inspiration.

It may be mentioned that the Philadelphia Symphony Orchestra is giving 80 concerts this season, and that seats for the entire series are already sold out. The Oklahoma City Symphony Orchestra deserves, and undoubtedly will receive, similar support.

Oklahoma City
Symphony Orchestra

DEAN FREDRIK HOLMBERG, Director

Personnel

Violin
Genevieve Bradley
Anna Shapiro
Marjorie Watkins
Emmett Anderson
Genet Byfield
Argyle B. Shero
Epaphra Staton
Mazo Pickle
T. B. Pedigo
Florence McClure
Nadine Duck
Kathleen Williams
Nina Gill
G. H. Parkhurst
C. E. Whitney
Dearsley Babcock
Milton McCullough
Lucrezia Cook
Laura Kendall
Harry Steinberg
G. A. McFall

Viola
E. H. Frey
Oscar J. Lehrer
Irma Stott
George Ketcham

Violoncello
G. M. Dieterich
Gertrude Veal
Martha Watkins
S. A. McReynolds
Howard Boyer

Bass Viol
Joe Shwadlenak
R. S. Witzel
O. J. Pishney

Flute
Raymond E. Selders
Ernest R. Chamberlain

Oboe
Marjorie Scott
O. W. Exendine

Clarinet
George L. Emery
V. O. Eslick
George Bradley
Virgil Sprankle

Bassoon
Joseph Turinger
Ralph Cook

French Horn
S. B. White
J. M. Perry

Trumpet
Ruhl Potts
Charles H. McClain

Trombone
John Moore
R. G. Kelchner

Tuba
Frank Apelt

Tympani and Traps
O. H. Zimmerman
Claire Williams

Piano
Jeanette True

Librarian
T. B. Pedigo

Reporter Edith Johnson also stressed that music exerted power. She called it "a strange and ineffable power," too great to be expressed in words, that helps to reveal us to ourselves and others to us, binds together the past, the present and the future; blends our present joys and sorrows, utters the unutterable, and "finds the deep instinct which is in all of us to express through the medium of the senses, the spiritual realities that underlie them and it is this quality in music that makes it akin to love." She further observed that the practical and commercial importance of having a symphony orchestra in the city had not yet been fully realized in Oklahoma City. She remarked that Lindsborg, Kansas, and Bethlehem, Pennsylvania, might have remained obscure little towns but for their music which had been drawing thousands of visitors each year.[17]

The vision for a symphony orchestra in Oklahoma City was realized on the evening of October 27, 1924, in the Shrine Auditorium at Northwest Sixth Street and North Robinson. An audience of about 1,500 people was treated to a series of surprises as the 58-member symphony orchestra of the Ladies Music Club, under the direction of Maestro Holmberg, played "steadily, politely, and forcefully with assurance like one great instrument."[18]

Mozart's Symphony in C (Jupiter) was played in perfect unison with good tone gradation and depth of feeling. The listeners had enjoyed the variations and majestic swells of the theme which wound through many phases. Antonin Dvorak's *Indian Lament* offered interesting differences between tribal music under an open sky and the same thought reproduced by a master of music into a modern frame. A reviewer observed that "the orchestra unveiled the shaded meanings without losing the primitive element." The audience was "delighted."[19]

Meyer-Helmud's *Rococco Serenade* followed. It was a direct contrast to the Dvorak presentation as it introduced new thoughts to the listeners. Georges Bizet's stately Adagietto of the *L'Arlesienne Suite* was considered to have been the greatest accomplishment of the evening. The simplicity and majesty of the piece had appealed immediately as it was delivered with almost a touch of sorrow. Under Holmberg's direction, just the right feel of woodwind was placed on the strings. The concluding popular numbers, Latan's *Parade of the Wooden Soldiers* and the *Waltz* by Charles Waldteufel relaxed the audience. Mrs. George Ade Davis, the soloist, received much praise and a standing ovation. She then sang the "Mad Scene" from Gaetano Donizetti's *Lucia de Lammermoor* and was remembered for not "missing a note."[20]

Reaction to the concert was dramatic. The event would be remembered as a "night of realization," and as an expression of appreciation and desire for classical music. Thomas E. Braniff, the founder of Braniff Airlines, stated that cultural facilities, like the symphony, should be regarded on the same level as educational facilities. Ed Overholser, the president of the Oklahoma Chamber of Commerce, expected the symphony would be a commercial asset to the community. A local newspaper observed that only those who had done the work really understood what it took to make the symphony a reality and to keep it functioning. The news media praised the musicians and also gave much credit to the Ladies Music Club.[21]

Early musicians included violinists Genevieve Bradley, Anna Shapiro, Marjorie Watkins, Emmett Anderson, Genet Byfield, Argyle B. Shero, Epaphra Staton, Mazo Pickle, T. B. Pedigo, Florence McClure, Nadine Duck, Kathleen Williams, Nina Gill, G. H. Parkhurst, C. E. Whitney, Dearsley Babock, Milton McCullough, Lucrezia Cook, Laura Kendall, Harry Steinberg, and G. A. McFali; violists E.H. Frey, Oscar J. Lehrer, Irma Stott, and George Ketcham; violoncellists G. M Dieterich, Gertrude

Veal, Martha Watkins, S. A. Reynolds, and Howard Boyer; bass violists Joe Shwadlenak, R. S. Wetzel, and O. J. Pishney; flutists Raymond E. Selders and Ernest R. Chamberlain; oboists Marjorie Scott and O.W. Exendine; clarinetists George L. Emery, V. O. Eslik, George Bradley, and Virgil Sprankle; bassoonists Joseph Truinger and Ralph Cook; french horn players S. B. White and J.M. Perry; trumpeters Ruhl Potts and Charles H. McClain; trombonists John Moore and R. G. Kelchner; tuba player Frank Apelt; tympanists and traps players O.H. Zimmerman and Claire Williams; pianist Jeanette True; and librarian T.B. Pedigo.[22]

Six concerts were given during the 1924-25 season. Attendance increased with each. One newspaper predicted a great future for symphonic music in Oklahoma. The concerts were noted for "understandable music" without any of the so-called "high brow" in the programs. A critic wrote that all tastes usually found something pleasing in each concert. Holmberg was praised for his professionalism, stature, lack of pretense, and the "exaggerated impatience" that he displayed until all were seated and he could offer "one of his bits of drollery." The maestro was considered to be a strict disciplinarian, who always maintained his personal dignity, and exhibited a good sense of humor. One time, when asked, "Why don't you play 'Yes Sir, that's My Baby'?," Holmberg replied, "Maybe we should try it sometime."[23]

The program for the January 17, 1927 concert included:

Festival Overture..Keler Bela

Keler Bela cannot be given a place among great composers. This composition has, however, had much to do with improving the taste for better music with the general public. His music has served as a "stepping-stone" from poor music to really great music. His many overtures have been and are very popular with amateurs as well as semi-professional bands and orchestras.

The spirit of the overture on this program is festive as the title indicates. It opens with an Andante Maestoso, religious in character. This is followed by a rather agitated movement in rapid tempo. After this, the first slow movement is repeated with a somewhat different orchestration. This slow movement is followed by a repetition of the Agitato. This Agitato is followed by a Coda in march style. The march has something of a patriotic, religious character.

Symphony No. 4 in F Minor (Second, Third and Fourth Movements)
....Tschaikowsky

This Symphony, esteemed by its composer as his finest work, is one of the grandest, most impassioned works in the entire realm of modern orchestral music.

The Second Movement (Andantiono in style of a song) is meditative, reflective and reminiscent in temperament. The music seems to say: "How sad that so many things have been and have ceased to be; and yet it is pleasant to look into a possible future of hope and joy. We think of joyous hours that have passed. We think of sadder moments and irreparable losses. It is sad and yet sweet to delve into the past."

The exquisite opening theme in this movement is given out by the oboe, accompanied by the strings. After this the cellos and violins intone a more courageous theme and after some development, a third theme is introduced by the clarinets. This is followed by fragmentary repetitions of earlier materials and the movement ends with the original oboe theme broken into fragments, growing quieter and softer until it dies away entirely.

The Third Movement (Scherzo) opens with a rollicking theme scored pizzicato for the strings. Mr. Walter Damrosch suggests that it portrays milling-around clatter, a chatter of the people at a Russian Country Fair. The next theme in slower tempo and written principally for the Wood-wind is a Russian peasant dance at the same country Fair. The third theme scored to begin with the brass choir is a kind of clown march. Soon the wood-wind introduces the dance theme and the march and dance are cleverly combined to form a very complicated but interesting conglomoration. Fragments of the first theme (pizzicato for strings) is also in evidence at this time. In other words, the three principal themes, all strongly contrasted are performed at the same time creating the atmosphere of a Fair sure enough. From this part of the movement there are repetitions and developments of the three themes mentioned above, the movement ending with a flutter of fragments of the various themes.

The Fourth Movement (Allegro con fuoco) is a wild rondo (round), consisting of three chief themes. The first robust and breezy, the second a fold tune "In the field there stood a birch-tree," the third theme appearing after a return of the first is a joyous, march-like theme. Towards the end the so-called Fate theme from the first movement is proclaimed double fortissimo by all the wood and brass instruments. The character of the music in this last movement is best described by the composer himself in a letter to his patroness, Nadeshda von Meck, as follows: "If you find no pleasure in yourself, look about you. Mix with the people. Note how the multitudes understand how to be merry and happy. Imagine a picture of a popular festival. You are alone and a stranger to all this, but have partly forgotten yourself in the joy and happiness of the crowd when unwearying fate again announces its presence. But the multitude does not concern itself with you. How it enjoys itself! How happy it is! There is such a thing as simple joy, vigorous and primitive. Rejoice in the joy of others and it is still possible to live. That is all I can tell you about my Symphony No. 4, my dear friend. Naturally words cannot describe,--instrumental music does not admit of a satisfactory analysis"

INTERMISSION (10 MINUTES)

Symphonic Espagnole (Allegro non troppo)...............Edouard Lalo
    Anna Shapiro
    Josef Noll, Accompanist

Slavonic Dance No. 6...Dvorak
    This is an artistically idealized Bohemian country dance. Notice the strong accents. The dance steps are part springing and tripping and part stamping.

Midsummer Nights Serenade..Albenis
    This music is very romantic and an expression of sentimental love.

Les Preludes (Symphonic Poem)..................................Liszt
    A Symphonic Poem may be said to be a kind of Symphony merged into one large movement. Franz Liszt composed several symphonic poems of which the one on the program is perhaps the best known.

The first theme, in slow tempo, is introduced by the strings. The answer is scored for the wood-wind. There is a considerable development of this theme and changes rhythm several times. The next theme which is used prominently throughout the composition is introduced by the violas and French horns. A great development of this last mentioned theme follows and part of the two first motifts are also used in this development and a massive grandure is the result. The next part of the composition is a little Allegretto in pastoral style—graceful, light, simple and innocent. Towards the end of this rural picture the main theme of the piece is again heard with on Climax piled on top of another. Next we hear a new theme in march tempo very firey and heroic in character. The music then changes to Andante Maestoso for full orchestra and the composition comes to and end in a tremendous tableau of grandure.[24]

The symphony was soon accepted as a permanent organization in the city. The concert field was extended to other cities in Oklahoma and to neighboring states. One program writer pondered, "What does the symphony mean to Oklahoma City? No one can say. As well try to place a financial value on the sunrise or a dollar mark on the song of a bird." One concert included *Desert Suite,* an American composition by Homer Grunn, who attempted to convey the abstract emotions evoked by the Great American Desert. The writer explained that the composer used music to portray a landscape that attracts as it repels, and the strange grandeur of vast distances, with the loneliness that provides the independence to enjoy nature without interference. The writer also observed that the music "leads us to the edge of the infinite and almost impels us to gaze into it." The titles of the movements were "At Sunrise," "Choya Dance," "On the Mesa," and "Oasis."[25]

A writer in a 1925-26 Concert Program observed that the orchestra set a goal for young people and strove to implant ambition as it tried to stimulate their desire to learn more about music. Twenty-five hundred Oklahoma fifth- and sixth-graders had listened to the orchestra during the 1924-25 season. The commentator reflected that good music aroused high ideals, motives, and inspirations in young people, while light music encouraged less purpose, and cheap music led to cheap behavior.[26]

Mrs. Charles Fischer, an internationally known opera singer, attended an Oklahoma City Symphony concert with Mrs. Frank Buttram in May of 1925. Mrs. Fischer confessed that she had not expected to hear anything like the performance that she had enjoyed in Oklahoma City. She declared, "You can only hear such music as this in the leading musical centers in the East."[27]

On the afternoon of March 15, 1926, the orchestra played a program for fourth- through sixth-grade students in the Central High School auditorium. The evening performance on that date honored Conductor Holmberg with a special concert called the "Alumni Special." The program opened with Beethoven's Symphony No. 2. A local music critic wrote that the first movement showed contrast with difficult antiphonal work. The symphony's interpretation of Beethoven's playful Scherzo was praised. Raymond Selders, flautist, and Arthur Nave, oboist, were considered to have been outstanding. When an enormous bouquet was presented to Maestro Holmberg, he walked nonchalantly down the steps of the Shrine Auditorium stage and proceeded along until he located Mrs. Holmberg. Unaffectedly, and with grace, he gave the flowers to his wife.[28]

The alumni of the University of Oklahoma considered the symphony to be a tribute to Dean Holmberg and thanked him for building a "musical organization in

Oklahoma of a type that is very rare west of the Mississippi." Businessman John A. Brown stated that the orchestra was a monument to Dean Holmberg who had done more than any one person or group to promote the growth of classical music in Oklahoma. Brown added that the symphony, from the standpoint of cultural education, had placed Oklahoma "in the front rank among the states of the Union."[29]

The orchestra patrons generally agreed that the work Fredrik Holmberg and the musicians were doing was not just "a flash-in-the-pan." They considered it to be "a foundation down on bedrock," which would last.[30]

About three weeks later, public school students were invited to attend a free concert in the Shrine Auditorium. Young people streamed in with enthusiasm and with pencils in hand. Before the concert was over, the programs had been well marked. All the seats had been taken, aisle steps had been used for additional seating, all standing room was filled, and Maestro Holmberg had won over his audience.[31]

Franz Schubet's Symphony No. 8 and Bizet's *L'Arlesienne Suite* had brought sincere resoponses and the *Blue Danube Waltz* presented Johann Strauss in tempos that rivaled the Viennese. Grieg's *March of the Dwarfs* and Peter Tchaikovsky's *March Slave* were also played. Ten numbers did not seem to make for too long a program. The youthful audience sat until the last encore became a demand. Maestro Holmberg seemed to leave the students with a feeling of being one with the orchestra as they quietly left the auditorium.[32]

The Ladies Music Club devoted much time to promoting appreciation for classical music and for the Oklahoma City Symphony Orchestra. They formed groups in six nearby cities as well as in Oklahoma City. The state-wide musical contests that Holmberg had initiated in 1919 to occur at the same time as the athletic meets at the University of Oklahoma were continuing. Each additional year had seen more contestants. By 1923, 80 students vied for honors in the voice contest, 80 in piano, 30 in violin, 45 in Girls Glee Club, and 25 in Boys Glee Club. Twenty bands and 15 orchestras were also included. By the spring of 1925, 1,700 contestants took part in the competitions. When the public began to ask for Sunday afternoon concerts by the symphony, they were started on February 20, 1926. The performances were well attended and endorsed.[33]

The *New World Symphony* was one of the principal numbers on the opening program for the 1926-27 season. Dvorak had introduced American Indian and Black melodies as themes in the work. The *Peer Gynt Suites* by Edvard Grieg and Richard Wagner's march from *Tannhauser* were also included. At that time, the 65-piece orchestra had only six professional musicians and no full-time players. Anna Shapiro, who had studied violin in Europe for the past year, was the concertmaster of the group.[34]

The December, 1926 concert featured the *Egmont Overture* by Beethoven, the Reverie *Voice of the Bells* by Alexandre Luigini and "Baccchanale" from the opera *Natomi* by Victor Herbert. The *Indian Invocation* idealized the spirit of prayer as an inherent belief of certain Native American tribes. *Finlandia* by Jan Sibelius used melody to depict the struggle in Finland's revolution and ended with an exultant climax.[35]

By the end of the fourth season, Oklahomans were expressing pride in their symphonic orchestra, its music director, and in individual musicians. A University of Oklahoma professor played a bassoon. A local fireman, who was also chief of the Delaware Indian tribe, played a clarinet. Alfred Nave, an oboist, had performed with a symphony orchestra in Paris, France. The tuba musician had played professionally in the East before coming to Oklahoma. At this time, Oklahoma City was one of 49 cities that had supported a symphony orchestra for at least five years. New York's symphony began in 1842 and was considered to have been the first in the United States. The Boston Symphony began about 40 years later in 1881. The Chicago Symphony was organized in 1890. Several other symphonies had been started but had failed to succeed. The Oklahoma City Symphony Orchestra's annual operating expenses of $12,000 in 1928-29 were also lower than the expenditures of any other recognized symphony group in the country.[36]

A music critic wrote that during a December, 1930 concert, Conductor Holmberg and his 60 players reveled in Grieg and followed their usual method of authentically defining his suite *Sigurd Jorsalfar* and the *Crusader*. Writers Milton Cross and David Ewen noted that few composers linked the land and music like Grieg did. They wrote that to listen to Grieg's music was like being brought into the world of Norwegian people, customs, sagas, geography, fjords, and mountain streams. The local critic observed, "Whatever else our symphony may or may not do, Grieg is above technical or musical reproach, a boast many more famous symphony orchestras may justly envy."[37]

The seventh season opened with a planned cut to five concerts because the Oklahoma economy was steadily deteriorating The concert programs for the year were varied with considerable American music. Guest soloists included Mrs. Frank Buttram and other local artists. The final concert was performed on May 12, 1931. Tchaikovsky's *March Slave,* Grieg's *Peer Gynt Suite,* and the first movement of Dvorak's *New World Symphony* were played.[38]

Meanwhile, the extended drought, dust storms, the stock market crash in 1929, the depressed national economy, the 25 percent unemployment rate, and many bank failures were devastating the state of Oklahoma. The state government was facing bankruptcy. Families and other hungry people were forming long lines at the public soup kitchens. Many desperate people left Oklahoma to find work, and competition for elective positions was intense.[39]

In 1930, Republicans were not very popular in Oklahoma because President Herbert Hoover was generally blamed for the Great Depression. Frank Buttram, a wealthy oil man and businessman, who had always been a booster of the Oklahoma City Symphony, was one of the leading Republican candidates for governor and was supported by *The Daily Oklahoman*. His opponent was William H. "Alfalfa Bill" Murray, a Democrat, who claimed to be a champion of the unemployed city workers and farmers. He condemned the "metropolitan press"— Oklahoma City and Tulsa newspapers—as well as musical education and the arts. Murray's supporters purchased a newspaper, *The Blue Valley Farmer*, in Roff, Oklahoma, that became known as "The Mouthpiece of Alfalfa Bill."[40]

After Murray became governor, he ordered a cut in the number of state employees, harried institutions of higher learning, considered cutting college faculties by 30 percent, and insisted that higher education was making "high-toned" bums of college students. Letters in the Holmberg Collection at the University of Oklahoma revealed that the new state administration was expected to cut educational appropriations for the university and "conflicts of interest" criticisms were being voiced that Holmberg, a full-time university employee, was too involved with a private orchestra sponsored by Buttram. Consequently, the adverse political climate plus the depressed economy in the state led to a decision to disband the Oklahoma City Symphony in the spring of 1931.[41]

When Dean Holmberg was later asked by Mrs. Frank Buttram to get together a group of about 40 musicians to present summer concerts, he declined. He pointed out that most of the players would need an "enormous" amount of drilling or they would ruin the reputation of the former Oklahoma City Symphony Orchestra. He mentioned that he had suggested to someone else that if another symphony orchestra was organized it should perhaps be named something like the "Oklahoma Park Orchestra." He doubted however, that such a group would get much support from the community. He further explained to Mrs. Buttram:

> . . . of course, as you know I am forbidden to conduct the orchestra, or perhaps I should say the University authorities have been forbidden to allow me to conduct the orchestra. That, however, does not say that I could not help organize it and get it started... I shall, of course, do everything I can, without getting into trouble, to help the orchestra on its feet, but unless it is taken up with the Governor of the State and he can be convinced that it is not just a "Buttram Orchestra" I shall be unable to do much and you had better start now to arrange for someone else to conduct.[42]

When asked about his most valuable contributions to the University of Oklahoma, Holmberg listed the establishment of interscholastic fine arts contests and the system he had set up for the certification of music teachers as his most rewarding work at the university. Also, in spite of the fact that the professor in charge of the history department had once told the faculty that music did not have any history, Holmberg had proved to him and the rest of the men involved that the history of music was worthy of consideration. Subjects that Holmberg recommended were soon given elective credit toward an A.B. degree at the university. By 1931, Holmberg had stimulated much interest in classical music throughout Oklahoma with his creative ideas for high school and college students.[43]

The Holmberg Collection at the University of Oklahoma shows that the music director had favored having music appreciation courses for credit in high schools, a circulating library of good music records, neighborhood singing clubs, a civic symphony giving popular concerts, and Sunday School union singing clubs. He also saw a need for a city to engage a city music supervisor and pointed out that the expense would be more than repaid in better morals and in the general pride of the citizens.[44]

Holmberg placed much emphasis on good community music. He stressed that although many people cannot understand music, all can appreciate it. He believed that folk songs of all nations would be more popular if community music was in vogue. He regarded folk songs to be the "mother and father" of modern music. He considered it had been a great musical discovery when composers had realized that folk songs of different nations could be fused into one composition and still retain their own unity. Holmberg saw the new art as "absolute music" such as found in the works of Bach, Hayden, Mozart, and Beethoven and he considered that the acceptance of folk songs into classical music had caused a revolution that was still going on. He noted that the best composers strove to idealize the folk songs of nations. He wrote an article entitled "Folk Songs Give Insight Into Souls of Nations." It was published locally in *The Daily Oklahoman*.[45]

Oklahoma received much recognition outside its state borders for Holmberg's innovative ideas in musical education and for the outstanding Oklahoma City

Symphony Orchestra, which the maestro had organized with the help of Mrs. Frank Buttram. Under his direction, the symphony became recognized as one of the 49 professional groups in the United States as early as 1927. After the orchestra was disbanded in 1931, the Ladies Music Club presented a series of concerts, frequently with famous guest artists, and an occasional opera.[46]

The Ladies Music Club and other Oklahomans did not give up their dreams for another symphony orchestra. They began to experience new hopes for symphonic music to be heard again when the Federal Music Project (FMP) was started in Oklahoma with a symphony orchestra in Tulsa during 1936.[47]

Twenty-six year-old Ralph Rose became the first musical director of the Oklahoma Federal Symphony Orchestra in 1937. Rose, from Oklahoma City, had been acclaimed as a child prodigy and his career had flourished until the Great Depression. Courtesy Archives of Contemporary History, Oklahoma Christian University Library.

Dean Richardson, director of the FMP for the State of Oklahoma, began to organize a symphony in Oklahoma City during the same year. The Oklahoma Sinfonia that had been organized by Bruce Blakenay and his wife Alice under the sponsorship of the Oklahoma Chamber Music Society, was the only active musical group in Oklahoma City that qualified for a federal grant from the Works Progress Administration. Democratic subsidy programs were resented in the state, but when the opposition was faced with the reality of what the $50,000 in federal grant money would do for the area, the protests diminished.[48]

The new symphony was licensed in 1937 to be the orchestra for the entire state, not just Oklahoma City. Ralph Rose, a child prodigy who had studied music in Kansas City and at the Curtis Institute in Philadelphia, became musical director of the group. In 1927, Rose had made his debut as a soloist with the American Orchestra Society. His career had flourished until the depressed economy created funding problems. Rose returned to Oklahoma City and worked with his father in the family's candy-making business until he became the conductor of the Tulsa Junior Symphony. He later accepted the assistant directorship of the Tulsa WPA Orchestra. He was just 26 years old when he came back to Oklahoma City to be the musical director of the Oklahoma Federal Symphony.[49]

When the Tulsa symphony management hired 15 players away from the Oklahoma Federal Symphony by offering the musicians a $25 a month pay raise, Richardson made no changes in his schedule. Consequently, Rose coaxed, instructed, and cajoled his group of young and mostly inexperienced musicians into shape. All day, every day, the Shrine Auditorium was filled with the sounds of the musicians practicing.[50]

Meanwhile, a privately funded orchestra foundation had been set up to support the Tulsa WPA Orchestra organized by Richardson. Many Tulsans did not support the New Deal and were anxious to end the federal support and control of their symphony. They failed to raise sufficient operating funds and their orchestra ceased to function by the end of 1937. Tulsa did not activate another symphony until 1948.[51]

About 250 Jefferson grade school students in Oklahoma City heard the first public concert of the new symphony in their school on Western Avenue in September of 1937. The group received high marks in *The Daily Oklahoman* and *The Black Dispatch* noted their approval of the orchestra.[52]

The first formal concert on January 3, 1938, was preceded by an affair for special guests who gathered to honor Guy Mair, who was also the assistant to the national director of the Federal Music Project. Mair, who had practiced with the musicians, said that "Oklahoma is very advanced musically." He also declared:

> Ralph, here, is just a baby in years, but he is one of two or three
> conductors, throughout the nation, who has that certain something
> which makes a great Conductor. A man has to be more than an instru-
> mentalist to lead. He has to draw that music out of every man in the
> orchestra with his very life's blood, and Ralph can do this.[53]

The following evening, some 3,000 people heard Tchaikovsky's Symphony in B Minor and his *Capriccio Italien* and Franz Lizt's Concerto No. 1 for Piano and Orchestra in E Flat Major, with Guy Mair as soloist. Many curtain calls and encores followed the performance.[54]

Local reviewers praised Conductor Rose for his true musicianship and his excellent understanding of classical style. He was credited with achieving remarkable tone quality, particularly from the string section in such a short time. Dean Richardson, the state director of the WPA, pronounced the concert to be "Marvelous, wonderful, thrilling, and exciting." He wrote, "The concert should go down in the annals as the beginning of a new era in Oklahoma City music . . . for this orchestra belongs to the entire Southwest, Oklahoma City being merely the center of operations." Another newspaper critic was impressed with the "musical skills" shown by the musicians. The orchestra became popular overnight. *The Oklahoma City Times* noted that music lovers exhausted their repertoire of glowing adjectives to praise the new orchestra. Other newspapers were also generous with their compliments. This first concert which was dedicated to Dean Holmberg, was considered to have been a fitting tribute to the director of Oklahoma City's first symphony orchestra.[55]

When a reporter asked Rose what was needed to be a successful musician, Rose listed hard work combined with natural talent, sincerity, and honesty. He said that symphonic music must be considered like a book in fine print that tells a story. He stressed that the ability to see images, pictures, and to understand the music could be developed by taking some time each day to sit back and listen to classical music.[56]

Edith Johnson wrote in her *Daily Oklahoman* column that the second concert of the orchestra was

> a cause for pride in Oklahoma and Oklahomans. It was an occasion for gratitude to the works progress administration for producing such a program . . . . It was an opportunity to discover how much talent has sprung from the soil of Oklahoma, less than 50 years ago pioneer territory. Genius lives in our midst even though many of us have not realized that.[57]

Johnson credited Ralph Rose and Melvin Tinsley of Tulsa with genius. Tinsley's *Pastel Poem* and one more of his compositions had been included in the program. *Silhouette,* composed by Wynn York of Claremore was judged to have been a special favorite with the audience. She said that Conductor Rose and the orchestra "spellbound" the listeners with the *Water Music Suite* by James Handel-Harty and Dvorak's *New World Symphony.* The audience was praised in local papers for allowing the orchestra to play the entire symphony before applauding. Johnson also questioned the "righteousness of that by-law of rugged individualism, 'let genius starve if it must'." She pointed to the little country of Finland that had granted a life subsidy to Jan Sibelius. She believed that no Finn would ever say that Sibelius would have been a more productive man if he had been told to work or starve. She observed that Sibelius had made life richer even for hundreds of Americans, who have felt better for hearing his music but continue to be reluctant, even suspicious, of giving any material aid to musical talent. She noted that the richest nation on earth had never subsidized a musician nor an artist. She concluded by writing that someday soon

> . . . it may be, the creative artist will be held in as high esteem as the business man. The great conductor will be on par with the president of a bank or a railroad or a great poet will rank with the head of a oil company . . . or a politician.[58]

The 1,800-seat Shrine Auditorium had been regarded as a perfect setting for symphony concerts. However, when the owners of the building became involved in financial problems that ended in bankruptcy, the managers of the symphony began to rent space in the new Municipal Auditorium.[59]

The Municipal Auditorium was in a huge all-purpose facility that was used as a concert hall, a boxing ring, basketball court, and for other events such as conventions, trade shows, dances, and plays. The auditorium was part of the Civic Center which had been built as a Public Works Administration (PWA) Project. The edifice was erected on land that originally had been the tract that William L. Couch, the leader of the Boomer Movement and the first provisional mayor of Oklahoma City,

The top balcony of the Municipal Auditorium was almost a full block from the stage. Courtesy Archives of Contemporary History, Oklahoma Christian University.

(PIONEER WOMEN WHO DARED TO DREAM)

had staked his claim at noon on April 22, 1889, the opening day of the historic Land Run into Oklahoma Territory. The railroads and other individuals contested Couch's claim because Couch had not actually taken part in the run. An employee of the Chicago, Rock Island and Pacific Railroad, Couch had merely walked over and claimed a site west of the Santa Fe Depot as the opening time arrived.[60]

Later, the Couch family lost their claim and the city purchased the land in 1928 when the municipality bought up the Rock Island and Santa Fe railroad right-of-ways in the business district. During the leadership of City Manager Red Mosier and the Oklahoma City Chamber of Commerce, the voters approved a $1.8 million bond issue to qualify for a PWA municipal building grant. The federal government paid 45

percent of the total building costs of the Civic Center, which also housed the Municipal Auditorium. The art deco structure was built in 1935-1936, officially opened October, 1937, and was one of 620 projects cited for its architectural significance out of 26,474 federal and non-federal projects in the United States at that time. The edifice occupied one city block in length and three-fourths of a city block in width. The top balcony was almost a full block from the stage. Six thousand people could be seated on folding chairs that had to be taken down and set up again between the different activities.[61]

The Municipal Auditorium became culturally and historically vital to the city and to the entire state as it housed performing arts, art galleries, radio and television communications, entertainment, social and business functions as well as city offices. After a remodeling in 1967, it became known as the Civic Center Music Hall.[62]

Municipal Auditorium manager Ralph Hemphill featured many superior artists. Nino Martini, the leading lyric tenor of the Metropolitan Opera Company performed on the stage of the new facility on October 22, 1937. This attractive singer from historic Verona, Italy, was wholeheartedly received. He had a world-wide reputation for winning over an audience before he even sang a note. On the first of November, the Don Cossack male chorus of 36 "singing horsemen" entertained. The program writer noted that the intense feeling of their voices raised in the sacred music of Russia, the pathos of their folk songs, and the boisterous shouts, whistling, and frantic dancing during their war songs made the Don Cossack concert a thrilling and unforgettable experience. The Oklahoma audience heard 21-year-old Yehudi Menuhin who was known as the "American boy genius of the violin" on November 16. He had made his debut in Carnegie Hall at the age of ten. This appearance was his first in the Southwest. Lily Pons, the tiny prima donna who was said to have the largest and sturdiest vocal chords of anyone except Caruso, appeared in November, 1937. The voice of this lovely coloratura carried to the farthest corners of the large auditorium. A reviewer declared that trying to praise this remarkable singer was like "painting the lily." The Danish Joos European Ballet came to the auditorium on January 19, 1938. The all-star cast and company traveled with three baggage cars of costumes and scenery. They also brought along their own orchestra.[63]

A local newspaper recognized individual musicians in the WPA orchestra. Harpist Gail Laughton, barely old enough to play in the orchestra, had made front-page news when he had played his harp for Henry Ford. He was also recognized as one of the best harpists in the symphony. He played a harp that had been made by his father in the family's harp-making shop in Oklahoma. Laughton later went to Hollywood where he dubbed the sound track for some of Harpo Marx's films. Other musicians were principal bassoonist Betty Sullivan Johnson, Annette Burford, Steele Hutto, Madeline Morsteller in the bass fiddle section, bass trombone player Harold Wiles, tuba player Virgil Estes, and Billy Jordan, who played the marimba.[64]

Another local newspaper noted the diversity of nationalities among the members of the symphony. A native Belgian French hornist had played with the Paris Symphony, the Washington D.C. National Symphony, and the John Phillip Sousa Band. Native American Edward Twist played the bass viol as if it were its smaller brother, the cello. Ingram Cleveland had incorporated melodies of his Cherokee people into his symphonic composition, *Spavinaw Moonlight.* Adrian Primo, the first concertmaster of the local group, was of French heritage and had performed in Vienna and Paris. Other nations were represented by violinist Leatha Sparlin and Horace Thornburg from Scandinavia; cellist Samuel McReynolds from Scotland; Conductor Rose, violinist Myere Bello, Don Frankel, and Walter Kessler from Israel; tuba and double bass player John Hugh Kaurfman, cellist Eugen Raheger, cellist Don Garlick, violinist George Unger and timpanist Robert Rigsbee from Germany; and clarinetist Garth Cashion and trumper player Ross Bour, Jr. from France. [65]

A strange violin proved to be no handicap to Conductor Rose when his violin was stolen the night before a concert. He played "fit to shame a thief" as he delivered his own arrangement of Arcangelo Corelli's *La Folia* on a borrowed violin. The same month, Victor Alessandro, Jr. made a guest appearance with the symphony. Youthful Mickey Rooney took the baton from Alessandro and directed the musicians through a rehearsal of the Prelude of Act 3 from Wagner's *Lohengrin.* The players said that Rooney was a "pretty good conductor."[66]

After the acoustics in the auditorium had been tested satisfactorily, the orchestra began to hold their rehearsals and concerts there in February, 1938. The success of the orchestra was now evident, but Richardson was having administrative problems. Ron Stephens, the state WPA director, complained Richardson was becoming too independent and neglecting his administrative duties. Artists, who considered themselves to be professionals, were questioning Richardson's policy of using his limited resources to hire only those musicians that "he" considered to the "best qualified." Richardson also often clashed with his superior in Washington, D.C.[67]

The Daily Oklahoman reported that Sokoloff came to Oklahoma City in May of 1938. After hearing a rehearsal by the Oklahoma Federal Symphony he said he was "agreeably surprised." He expressed his approval of the work Rose was doing. He asked that Julia Smith's *Episodic Suite,* a composition that included "Waltz for Little Lulu," be played. A local critic noted that Sokoloff seemed to enjoy the work. Tulsa composer Lemuel Childers' *Spaces* was also performed and well received by the audience. The national director gave a brief talk at the concert. He urged the public and the musicians to understand that the Federal Music Project was not a relief program but a works program. The aim of the program, he said, was to provide a permanent intelligent effort toward improvement and progress in musical activities.[68]

Before a children's concert in the Oklahoma City Auditorium on Saturday afternoon, January 15, 1947, conductor Victor Alessandro explained how the music went round and round to finally come out of the big horn. The concert was sponsored by the Junior League. From left to right, Alessandro, Denver Cox, Patricia Gilliand, Ronald Mitchel, Claudia Lee. Courtesy Oklahoma Publishing Company Library.

VICTOR ALESSANDRO
Conductor

CLYDE ROLLER
Assistant Conductor

HERE'S WHAT THE PRESS IS SAYING!

ALTUS: "Finest musical ever to come to Altus . . . large crowd, intense interest, spontaneous applause . . . Altus audiences have reached a turning point in supporting highest type of music . . ."

ELK CITY: "Concerts complete success . . . packed houses with all standing room used . . . Alessandro triumph . . . "

CHICKASHA: " . . . clapped loud and long for encores . . . "

ANADARKO: " . . . was an all-round success . . . packed house held in rapt attention."

LAWTON: " . . . spontaneous applause for five minutes . . . "

SHAWNEE: " . . . orchestra has large crowds . . . music patrons thrilled."

WEATHERFORD: " . . . crowded to capacity . . . from towns within a radius of a hundred miles . . . "

OKLAHOMA CITY: " . . . the beginning of a new era in Oklahoma City music . . . under his (Alessandro's) experienced hand a world of dynamic life comes into musical being . . . "

" . . . the orchestra sings a surer lovelier song. Victor Alessandro holds them spellbound at the tip of his baton . . . "

" . . . a performance to stir the listener to his inner depths . . . "

" . . . Yes, it made you glad and happy to realize that Oklahoma which has imported 99 percent of its music can produce it within its own borders, not with borrowed talent, but with talent as indigeous to it as its red soil. You were thankful, too, that this series of concerts given by the orchestra may be heard within the purchasing power of the not-too-well-filled purse. Those who love music for its own sake may hear it . . . "

" . . . The hardest thing to find among Oklahoma City music lovers Tuesday morning was a fresh adjective . . . 'Marvelous' 'thrilling', 'wonderful', 'exciting,' strung from mouth to mouth . . . "

" . . . Curtain calls for orchestra mount to ten . . . Public enthusiasm reaches its peak ., . "

" . . . Children clapped and howled and demanded four encores . . . exhilarating in their power . . . "

ADRIAN PRIMO
Concertmaster

Oklahomans continued to support the Oklahoma Federal Symphony Orchestra under the direction of its second conductor, Victor Alessandro (1938-1951). Courtesy Archives of Contemporary History, Oklahoma Christian University.

THE OKLAHOMA FEDERAL SYMPHONY ORCHESTRA

presented by
Works Progress Admistration
FEDERAL MUSIC PROJECT

Nikolai Sokoloff
National Director

Dean Richardson
State Director

Municipal Auditorium
Oklahoma City, Oklahoma

DEAN RICHARDSON
State Director

The August 22, 1938, issue of *Time* Magazine reported on the music debut of *Little Lulu* in three-quarter time. The announcement read:

> It happened March twenty-first. That evening at Altus, Oklahoma, the Oklahoma Federal Symphony Orchestra presented a program of Wagner, Dvorak, Debussy and Tchaikovsky. Also, *Episodic Suite,* by a modern American composer, Julia Smith.

Julia Smith was from Denton, Texas. Her sister, Mrs. Emory Smith, played with the Oklahoma Federal Symphony. The *Episodic Suite* enjoyed nationwide publicity because the third movement, "Waltz for Little Lulu," had been written for the Little Lulu of cartoon fame.[69]

Rupert described the Federal Music Project as a nationwide cultural reclamation project that embraced instrumentalists, vocalists, composers, teachers, librarians, copyists, arrangers, tuners, and music binders. He wrote that many of them, after long periods of unemployment or working at non-music jobs, needed months of practice and retraining to regain their former skills. The Oklahoma project offered 1,500 classes per week and had an average attendance of 25 students. The local leaders organized radio broadcasts, entertainments, and community sings, and conducted special programs for orphans, the elderly, and the sick. A 17-piece Federal Music Orchestra at the Methodist Orphan's Home in Britton, Oklahoma, had gained statewide recognition. He noted that Mrs. Walter Ferguson in her column, "A Woman's Viewpoint," referred to adult classes as the "fulfillment of a life-long dream for many." As of March 31, 1937, more than 4,000 adults and 15,432 children in Oklahoma were studying music history, music appreciation, theory, harmony, voice, and instrument in the classes. By April, 1938, the orchestra had played four formal concerts and 47 elementary school concerts.

Hundreds of city and county schoolchildren came to Mitchel Hall at the University of Central Oklahoma to hear the 65-piece Federal Symphony in April, 1938. Mildred Kidd, head of the Piano Department, was the featured soloist. She played Camille Saint-Saens' Concerto in G Minor. By this time the works of 13 Oklahoma composers had been presented to the public by the Federal Music Project. The composers included Samuel McReynolds, Paul W. Thomas, Lemuel J. Childers, Robert W. Wofe, Ingram Cleveland, Wynn Weeks, James Neilson, Theodore Dreher, Glen Holcomb, and Truman Tomlin. Symphony concerts had been given in Altus, Anadarko, Chickasha, Collinsville, Edmond, El Reno, Lawton, Muskogee, Norman, Oklahoma City, Shawnee, and Tulsa.[70]

An effort was made to determine how much money had been spent in Oklahoma's music industry by the Federal Music Project between 1935 and 1938, but the task was considered to be impossible. More than 1,600 musical instruments had been purchased in the state in addition to a large quantity of published music and other supplies. Expenditures of $96,000 could be accounted for over the two-year period. The opportunity to learn music had been eagerly grasped and, little by little, people had accumulated more equipment and musical materials. As of August 1, 1938, the project employed 94 orchestra personnel, 90 music teachers, and had a general administrative staff of six people.[71]

When the existence of the orchestra was threatened with an anticipated cut in the project, Richardson tried to insure a continued federal subsidy for the Oklahoma Federal Orchestra by securing substantial public and private support. Intent on saving the program, Richardson published much favorable material and asked Oklahoma civic leaders to pressure congressional delegations. He sent many letters to teachers, Parent Teacher Organizations, newspapers, and businessmen asking for support for the orchestra and encouraged the Ad Club to investigate the advantages of the symphony as a civic asset. He asked newspaper editors to advise the public that the orchestra was available to come to their communities and present concerts. He made it known that the only requirement was for a local symphony association to be formed to arrange for the appearance of the orchestra. He began to pressure local sponsors to launch elaborate fundraising drives. Sokoloff and Stephens cautioned Richardson to be discreet.[72]

After a successful season of playing for about 55,000 people, the symphony presented Under the Stars concerts in the Lincoln Park Amphitheater, the Taft Stadium, and Oklahoma's Hollywood Bowl. Johnson reported in September, 1938 that 6,000 people attended the closing concert at Taft Stadium. She noted that people of all ages and social groups attended the concert and joined in the applause. She overheard one man who was leaving Taft Stadium after the evening performance say, "I'm against the New Deal but Roosevelt or no Roosevelt, I'm for this symphony." Another man said, "I don't know what this is all about, but I like it, and I'm coming again."[73]

The final concert of the summer season ended Rose's time as conductor. He left his hometown to become musical director of the Texas Broadcasting Company, and later moved to Hollywood, California, to write music and scripts for radio.[74]

Many guest conductors, including Victor Alessandro, Jr., took the podium during the fall of 1938. Alessandro later accepted the permanent position. Oklahoma City's new 22-year-old director became known as the youngest conductor of a major orchestra in the United States. Alessandro's career had begun at the age of three-and-one-half when he started to lead a group of young musicians called the "Baby Band" that traveled and performed throughout the Southwest. The oldest player was 17. Later, the child prodigy trained in composition at the Eastman School of Music in Rochester, New York, and the Mozarteum Academy in Salzburg, Austria. He also studied in Rome, Italy. Unlike Rose, who had never aspired to conduct, Alessandro had always been confident that one day he would direct a symphony orchestra.[75]

Alessandro debuted with the Federal Symphony on October 25, 1938. The first Pops Concert in November included soloist Kathryn Newman singing familiar tunes from classical and light opera. In honor of a medical association meeting being held in the city and keeping with the conductor's plan to include the work of one American composer in each program, the orchestra played *Four Incapacitated Preludes* by Byron Arnold. The first composition was dedicated to a deaf man. The musicians first mimed the piece soundlessly before actually performing the music. The second Prelude was devoted to a blind person, the third to a lame individual, and the fourth to a one-armed man.[76]

On November 13, 1938, Alessandro shared the podium with his former teacher, Paul White. The program opened with the *Euryanthe Overture* by Carl Weber, followed by Beethoven's Symphony No. 5. Veteran composer Charles Wakefield Cadman, a noted pianist, played his popular work *In the Land of the Sky Blue Waters,* an Indian love song, and *Dark Corners of the Mardi Gras,* which portrayed Black participation in the New Orleans festival. White directed his composition *Five Minatures.* The concert concluded with the *Overture to Tannheuser* by Wagner.[77]

In 1939, the Oklahoma City Chamber of Commerce celebrated the golden anniversary of the Oklahoma Land Run of 1889 with a gala dinner in January. The music presented was a work known as a musical history of Mississippi, composed by Samuel McReynolds, one of Oklahoma's pioneer musicians and a cellist with the orchestra. Later that month, a concert included Johannes Brahms' Fourth Symphony and the Overture to Bedrich Smetana's opera *The Bartered Bride.* Adrian Primo, the orchestra's concertmaster, was guest soloist. He played Mozart's A Major Violin Concerto. In February, Alessandro returned to Rochester, New York, to conduct the Rochester Philharmonic on an NBC radio concert while Jose Iturbi, conductor of the Rochester orchestra, directed the Oklahoma Symphony. Pianist Jacques Abrams appeared as soloist in March and again in April when the orchestra took part in another land run celebration. They played George Enesco's *Rumanian Rhapsody No.1* and Modest Mussorgsky's *Kovantchina.*[78]

Although legislation to extend the work program had been delayed in the summer of 1939, the musicians played the July 4, 1939, concert without pay. Many Oklahomans enjoyed a Fourth of July celebration with real cannon fire and fireworks. The orchestra played Tchaikovsky's *1812 Overture,* and Alessandro used an old taxi horn to accentuate the performance of *An American in Paris.* He had advertised and searched until he found just the right type of horn.[79]

The closing concerts of the Starlight Series at Taft Stadium revealed the favorites of the audiences to be Maurice Ravel's *Bolero,* Tchaikovsky's fifth symphony, Wagner's Prelude to Act III of the opera *Lohengrin,* Johann Strauss's *Blue Danube Waltz,* Franz Schubert's Symphony No. 8 in B Minor (Unfinished), Sibelius's *Finlandia,* and Tchaikovsky's overture-fantasy *Romeo and Juliet.* After the summer season finished, Alessandro went to Texas for a six-week vacation. He returned minus his mustache, admitting that he had only worn it to make himself look older.[80]

All federal arts projects were required to have local sponsors as of September 1, 1939. The Oklahoma State Symphony Society was filling this role in Oklahoma City. It received its certificate of incorporation on December 9, 1938. Meanwhile, the state WPA director was concerned that Richardson was becoming too difficult, too autonomous, and was almost ignoring the WPA support given to the project. He also questioned Richardson's close connections with the Oklahoma State Symphony Society.[81]

Actually the Symphony Society was making generous donations to the orchestra, but it did seem reluctant to make known that federal money was being used. The developing pattern was much like the earlier Tulsa experience. Support from both federal and private sources was considered necessary to keep the symphony functioning. Stephens, the state director, believed that both Richardson and the Symphony Society were afraid of pressure or interference from local anti-New Deal groups led by *The Daily Oklahoman.*[82]

A record 4,000 people attended the November 24, 1939, concert that featured Alex Templeton as guest soloist. About 2,000 people heard violinist Albert Spalding play Beethoven's Violin Concerto in D in December. Spalding, when interviewed, remarked that radio and recordings had the same effect on music as the invention of printing had on literature. He believed that music would have a more democratic appeal as more good music became available to the public through radio and recordings. Ralph Rose, who had come back to Oklahoma City to hear Albert Spalding play, said that the Oklahoma Federal Symphony Orchestra was becoming very favorably recognized in eastern musical circles. Rose considered the orchestra to be the best symphony between Chicago, Illinois, and Los Angeles, California.[83]

In mid-1940, Mrs. Roland Wright met privately with Stephens and Carl Held, his publicity supervisor. She told them that the Oklahoma Symphony Society had no objections to giving full credit to the WPA for its support of the orchestra. She warned that the society would withdraw all its support if Richardson was removed from the project. She reiterated these statements later to the national director, Earl Moore.[84] However, in spite of the lessening of the WPA administrative and political squabbles and the obvious success of many of the music projects, the Federal Music Program declined rapidly after 1940 because of World War II. Federal monies were redirected toward national defense. The need for make-work projects almost disappeared. Virgil Estes, the tuba player, left to help make bombers. Orley Jones and all of the horn section went into the army. The Navy Band gained a flutist and two trumpeters. A second flautist became a military policeman. The Oklahoma orchestra was being "raided" by other symphony orchestras in the country.[85]

A music war with Tulsa began again in February of 1941. The Tulsans were accused of trying to steal the Oklahoma City Symphony Orchestra. Apparently the $8,000 monthly payroll was a factor. Mrs. Wright was quoted as declaring

This orchestra has been built up into one of the finest such groups in the country, and we have no intention whatsoever of handing over the finished product to another city. Although it might be possible for two cities to share the orchestra, Tulsa is not going to get the symphony as long as I am president of the society.

Richardson pointed out that the Oklahoma Orchestra Society was fulfilling its obligation to pay 25 percent of the operating costs of the orchestra. The controversy soon settled down.[86]

G. W. Baster, writing in the *Tulsa World* in March 1941, called Alessandro a virtuoso conductor who electrified his audience and imbued the orchestra with excitement. He considered Alessandro a genius at programs. When Alessandro was asked to compare classical music with swing, he reflected that no comparison could really be made between the two kinds of music. He observed that both had a place in the "scheme of things" though each had a different purpose. Swing music, he said, was for relaxation, while symphonic music was meant to be listened to and to broaden the intellect. He compared swing music to a light novel that was easy to read and said that classical music was more profound and more difficult to understand.[87] Arthur Johnson, one of the players, characterized Alessandro as having a "heart like a hotel—with room for everyone." An early polio victim, the young conductor had eleven operations on one of his legs during his childhood. He believed that if he was going to make it in the world, he "would have to learn to get along with everyone." Veteran players recalled that Alessandro got along well with the symphony directors as well as the players and audiences. One of the violin players remembered that he was once stopped on the street and told that because he sat in the back of the violin section, he must not be as good as the players that sat on the front row. Alessaandro explained, in a letter to the editor of a local newspaper, that although it was the practice to seat the best players in the front row in amateur musical groups, this did not hold true in groups of the caliber of the Oklahoma City Symphony Orchestra where the strongest players were carefully dispersed throughout the sections.[88]

Many Oklahomans were disappointed when the seven-year-old Federal Music

Project ended in 1943. They believed that the program should have become a permanent federal service. Others pointed to a series of flaws that they did not expect could ever be corrected. Many states, especially in the rural areas, had experienced administrative difficulties and serious disputes involving project administrators, various patrons of the arts, and the performers. WPA officials were apt to have little concern for the needs of artists and white-collar workers. Therefore, they themselves were sources of difficulty. Local attitudes toward culture and the arts varied dramatically in different communities. Limited budgets were always a problem. The federal government had never entertained an adequate commitment to set up a fully developed arts program. Some administrators, such as Dean Richardson, who had supportive communities had achieved much success because they used the program to secure both excellence and appreciation for the arts. The Federal Music Program had been started as a work-relief program and was meant to be terminated when that need no longer existed. When all federal funding was finally lost, the Oklahoma Symphony was the only orchestra in the nation that was privately supported on a statewide basis. The Oklahoma Symphony Society was ready to take over the financial and administrative responsibilities for the orchestra and Conductor Alessandro agreed to continue on as its musical director.[89]

However, the orchestra had a difficult time surviving World War II. The symphony board voted to liquidate the group in July of 1945. The action shocked the city and aroused sufficient financial support to continue the orchestra. The 1945-46 season opened with a double theme of victory to celebrate world peace and the survival of the symphony.[90]

Two changes were made in the Symphony Society's charter during the 1945-46 season. The name Symphony Society became Oklahoma State Symphony Orchestra, and the membership on the board was limited to 36 members.[91]

Financial problems were a continuing concern for the orchestra. Alessandro, the members of the symphony board, various women's groups, civic leaders, and many other volunteers worked diligently to keep the organization solvent. Arthur Judson, manager of the New York Philharmonic Symphony Orchestra and president of Columbia Artists, was quoted by Eugene Hills as saying

> Musically, Oklahoma City has accomplished more in its short span of
> existence than any other city in the nation . . . Your art gallery has some
> of the finest paintings I have ever seen, and you have an orchestra here
> that plays with precision and a wonderful tone the world's greatest music
> . . . this orchestra should play to more and greater audiences and with a
> larger budget. Sooner or later Oklahoma citizens must realize that if they
> want good music they will have to foot the bill.[92]

Meanwhile, a non-profit organization was started with Mrs. Frank Buttram as chairperson of its advisory board. The group was in accord with the board of directors of the symphony, and membership was open to all who were interested in supporting the Oklahoma State Symphony Orchestra.[93]

When Arthur Judson visited Oklahoma, he encouraged Mrs. E. Gordon Ferguson to start a women's committee. The purpose of the group would be to educate the public about classical music and explain the benefits of a symphony to the community, as well as to create an awareness of the continuing need for financial support of the orchestra. He later sent helpful materials to Mrs. Ferguson from other cities that already had such groups. She promptly started to contact women who might head the new organization. When she received only rejections, she finally decided to take the job herself. By October 1948, she had organized a group of 25 women, over which she presided for the next three years.[94]

The group had numerous luncheons and meetings the first year. Many women came, had a good time, and then disappeared until the next social event sponsored by the Oklahoma City Symphony Orchestra Women's Committee. The first serious meeting was held in the home of Mrs. John Kirkpatrick. Dues were set at two dollars a year. Members did make some out-of-town trips to try to create interest in the symphony, but poor road conditions discouraged travel.[95]

Mrs. Ferguson often praised Rose Karchner for her dedication and said that "She pounded the pavement in all kinds of weather going door-to-door collecting money." Mrs. Ferguson also recognized Mrs. Jules Bloch as a very hard worker. Mrs. Frank Buttram and Mrs. Robert Sherman were appreciated for generously opening their homes for many of the meetings.[96]

Early in 1949, the Women's Committee was told that it was responsible for raising $6,000. The astonished women remarked that it might as well be $600,000. Mrs. Boone Jenkins and Mrs. Vivian Head accepted the job of raising the funds and then proceeded to do so.[97]

When Stanley C. Draper, manager of the Oklahoma City Chamber of Commerce, became a member of the symphony board in 1950 and actively supported the Women's Committee. About that time, Mrs. Robert Harris, known as "Zee," became the treasurer of the Women's Committee. She was to serve in that position for many years to come. A good working relationship continued between the Symphony Board of Directors and the Women's Committee. Eunice Jenkins, Mrs. Vivian Head, Mrs. Paul Dudley, Mrs. Hugh Johnson, Mrs. Boone Jenkins, and Mrs. Rose Karchner were among those present. Mrs. David Delana and her daughter-in-law also became active in the group. Mrs. J. M. Wilk, Mrs. Charles B. Lutz, Mrs. Carl Taggert, Mrs. Joseph Rooms, Mrs. Harvey Everest, Mrs. Winston Eason, Mrs. Oscar Monrad, Mrs. William H. Taft, Miss Edith Johnson, Mrs. Florence O. Wilson, Mrs. Richard E. Swan, Miss Bernice Lemon, Mrs. Marguerite Engle, Mrs. Mary Bordeaux, Mrs. Charles A. Vose, Mrs. Charles C. Anderson, Mrs. F. Cooper, and Mrs. Don Dow served on the Women's Committee. [98]

Members of the Women's Committee went to the symphony office to do volunteer work. They helped to organize and type membership lists, address mail, and do telephone calling. Whenever they were asked if they imposed on their friends, the reply was always, "Yes, we do."[99]

The women met and entertained many artists, such as Jascha Heifetz and Arthur Rubenstein, who appeared as guests with the orchestra. When Rubenstein attended a small party that turned into a large gathering, he was rated as "very nice," but he sat quietly in a corner and said to one of the ladies, "Let's just sit here and flirt."[100]

Mrs. Ferguson always stressed that the purpose of the Women's Committee was to stimulate interest in classical music through the Oklahoma Symphony Orchestra and to assist the orchestra in every way possible. The group began to organize the radio project, children's concerts, and classes in music appreciation. They were involved in fundraising, ticket sales, program advertising, and the Young People's Concerts. The committee began a close relationship with its orchestra members. They also served coffee and treats to them on rehearsal nights.[101]

The famous tenor Mario Lanzo drew a large crowd when he appeared in Oklahoma City as guest soloist. Serge Kousevitsky, conductor of the Boston Symphony Orchestra, had discovered Lanza, a furniture mover, when the singer helped move a piano into the Academy of Music in Philadelphia when Kousevitsky performed there. Antal Dorati, conductor of the Dallas Symphony, also brought in a large audience when he conducted a concert benefit for polio research. More than $12,000 was raised as a tribute to Alessandro, who had poliomyelitis as a child.[102]

In June of 1948, Alessandro performed as guest conductor of the Boston Pops Orchestra before a crowd of 30,000 at the Charles River Explanade. While there, he met Serge Kousevitsky and Herbert Rousell, a columnist for the *Washington Post.* Later Rousell wrote that Victor Alessandro had become a definite feature in the nation's musical picture. The columnist noted that the young conductor had a "rich Americanism" and an instinctive understanding of the Southwest. Rousell also said, "Every conductor knows the musical score but Alessandro knows the score, which isn't precisely the same thing."[103]

Alessandro did not receive especially good reviews from critics Felix Borowski and Charles Buckley when he directed the Chicago Grant Park Symphony, but he received an excellent review from critic Gloria Cassidy, who was known for caustic criticism. She wrote that Alessandro had a "clear beat, a musician's point of view, and the ability to make an orchestra play well." She also stated that he made "music a living language, not a dead one."[104]

The *Houston Post* praised Alessandro for a new idea in the musical world when he brought music closer to the audience in his new Symphony-in-the-Round. A dream of Alessandro's had been realized when he conducted the orchestra in the Mirror Room of the Oklahoma Municipal Auditorium, where oval risers had been installed. Seats were placed in a tiered circle around the performers. Three hundred spectators had been expected. Six hundred came.[105]

Maestro Alessandro led the Oklahoma Symphony in a new venture when the group began to send its music out over the air waves to the entire world. Oklahoma's United States Senator Robert Kerr observed that music was an international language that did not have to be translated. He saw the broadcasts taking messages of goodwill and friendliness from Oklahoma City to the world in a form that people would understand and like.[106]

Frank White, president of the Mutual Broadcasting System, attended the first broadcast. City officials, businessmen, and local newspaper editors all cooperated to make the effort a success. Walter Harrison, managing editor of a local newspaper and a city councilman, led a drive to cut down noise while the broadcasts were in session. The city government sent traffic policemen to block off traffic on the streets near the First Christian Church at Northwest Tenth Street and Robinson Avenue, where the music was being sent out by radio to other cities and communities all over the United States. Councilman Earl Miller also wholeheartedly supported the new venture. He commented that the symphony broadcasts would offset Oklahoma's image as only a place of cowboys, wild Indians, and six-guns. Edith Johnson compared the first broadcast with the opening of the meat-packing industry in 1909 and the 1928 discovery of oil in the city. She called the event one of Oklahoma's "Red Letter Days." Critic John Rosenfield of the *Dallas Morning News* announced the Mutual Broadcasting Series from Oklahoma City and noted, "This is really a plum of recognition that any symphony might envy."[107]

The first broadcast included music from Alban Berg's opera *Lulu* and Paul

Hindemith's Overture to the opera *News Of the Day.* Richard Rodgers and Oscar Hammerstein's *Oklahoma!* ended the first program. The broadcast brought much favorable response. Dimitri Metropolous of the New York Philharmonic, Conductor Charles Munch of the Boston Symphony, manager Arthur Judson of the New York Philharmonic, and Jascha Heifetz all sent congratulations to Conductor Alessandro and the orchestra.[108]

Programs featuring the Oklahoma City Symphony Orchestra in 26 concerts were heard over more the 700 stations. Alessandro told the Oklahomans that the Oklahoma Symphony had surprised the entire world. No one had expected anything like this to come out of Oklahoma, the home of the "Okies." Keeping in touch with the spirit of Oklahoma, which became a state in 1907, selections were to include only those composed after 1900. Radio Free Europe was also added to the broadcasts. When a contract was signed to make records with the Allegro Recording Company, Frank Buttram invited people to his home to give pledges to help finance the radio broadcast series. A total of $22,500 was raised. Stanley Draper predicted that the fund would reach $30,000 when all the money was turned in.[109]

Guest artists were sometimes included in the radio broadcast programs. Anton Karvas, a zither player, participated in one broadcast. His foot-and-a-half-long zither had many strings and was played like a guitar. A reviewer noted that Anton's ten fingers and the 34 strings of the instrument could create illusions. He cautioned Oklahomans to "Never underestimate the power of a zither . . . It can create springtime and recall romance. Its tunes are elfin little things and haunting like something almost but not quite remembered."[110]

When duo pianists Arthur Whittemore and Jack Lowe made a return appearance at a regular concert, they also took part in the radio broadcasts. A few years later, in the 1955-56 season, the two performers made a public confession to Dixie Gilliand, a reporter for *The Daily Oklahoman.* The two told Gilliand that they only "pretended" to fly into Oklahoma City when they came to work with the Oklahoma Federal Symphony Orchestra for $85 a month. Like starving musicians all over the country, they had been acutely feeling the effects of the Great Depression. Wanting to make a impressive appearance, they staged a fake arrival at Will Rogers Field where they had been told that the press planned to interview them. After a jaunty interview with Edith Gaylord, daughter of *The Daily Oklahoman* editor and publisher E. K. Gaylord, they performed with the orchestra and then "disappeared." Lowe kept out of sight at the home of an aunt in Oklahoma City. Whittemore bunked with Victor Alessandro, conductor of the WPA Orchestra.[111]

The two musicians worked diligently and prepared arrangements for the symphony. Two and a half months after their original concert, they were "brought back by popular request" to play another concert. Again they slipped out to the airport where they were interviewed by the press. They soon left Oklahoma City with their secret. They returned to the city a number of times to appear as guest artists with the symphony. Finally, after 16 years had passed, they acknowledged their secret maneuvers even to Edith Gaylord. The press and the public enjoyed their story. *The Daily Oklahoman* wrote that Whittemore and Lowe were two of the smoothest ham actors in the two-piano business. An *Oklahoma City Times* editorial observed that the duo always had something for everybody and the people of Oklahoma City always liked their presentations.

By this time, the 1950-51 radio broadcasts had been expanded to one hour for each of the 26 concerts. The last world broadcast of the season, played in Bartlesville, was a special dedicatory program to honor Canada and to show the cooperation between the two North American republics in the field of music. All of the music carried over the Mutual Broadcasting System, Canadian Network, and the Voice of America had been arranged by Canadian composers in the twentieth century.[112]

William Judd Judson of New York City made a nationwide tour that included a visit to Oklahoma City. He later sent a letter to *Oklahoma,* the official publication of the Oklahoma City Chamber of Commerce. He wrote that the music world and the public had been intrigued that such first-class programs had come over the air waves from Oklahoma. He hoped the broadcasts would continue because they provided an opportunity for the radio audience to become acquainted with Oklahoma through its symphony, "one of the state's outstanding promotional assets."[113]

Alessandro and the orchestra received favorable comments and reviews from throughout the country. Scott D. Hamilton, manager of the Greater Little Rock, Arkansas, Chamber of Commerce wrote that it was a great compliment to the Southwest to have such "a beautiful program" originate in the area. He predicted that the program would do much to overcome the outside world's misunderstanding of the region.[114]

A Chicago music critic wrote that Oklahoma City was one of the "smallest cities in the country to support a major orchestra." He also pointed out "Its membership of nearly 5,000 gives it the highest per capita group of concert goers in the country."

Maestro Guy Fraser Harrison with the Oklahoma Symphony Orchestra, ca. 1950. Courtesy Archives of Contemporary History, Oklahoma Christian University Library.

Another Chicago music critic pointed out that not only should the Chicago Symphony strive to be compared favorably with the "big three orchestras" but they should also be honest enough to recognize that there could be inspirational musical activity in Oklahoma City as well as in New York and Boston. He commended the Oklahoma Symphony Orchestra for devoting all 13 broadcast hours to music of the twentieth century. He also considered it to be "especially fitting that this summary of music of our century should emanate from Oklahoma, which became a state in 1907, and is in all ways, industrially and culturally, a product of the past fifty years."

The critic also said it took "some doing" for Alessandro to have used, with equal design, folk themes, music based on literature, drama scores from fictional and documentary films, the writings for the musical stage of Rogers and Hammerstein, as well as samplings taken from throughout Europe and the Americas. He concluded by observing that the people of Oklahoma could point to themselves as the builders, not the inheritors, of a flourishing musical environment.[115]

During the 1950-51 season, the Oklahoma City Chamber of Commerce advertised "Music of All Nations," a series that came from the geographic center and heart of America without government financing or government control. In March of the same season, Robert Rudie, concertmaster of the orchestra, conducted a forty member chorus in place of the usual Little Symphony in the Hall of Mirrors, and Spenser Asah directed a program of Indian dances and gave explanations of various Indian musical instruments.[116]

In December 1950, it cost the symphony more than $100 to keep extraneous noise out of its first recording session of the new season. Police managed to muffle motor noises, but the whistles from steam engine and diesel trains carried over through the sanctuary walls of the First Christian Church. This switching business lost the orchestra five or six minutes of time at $25 a minute. The orchestra finally prevailed and recorded three complete long-playing records that were flown to New York for processing. The compositions recorded for the first time were Claude Debussy's *Le Martyre de Saint Sebastien* with orchestra, chorus, and soloists; all 21 of the Brahms *Hungarian Dances;* and Mozart's piano concertos 17 and 19.[117]

The *Dallas Texas News* and the *Houston Chronicle* highly praised Alessandro for much subtlety and delicate balance of choirs and chorus. The reviewer considered the technical aspects to be excellent, and said that the orchestra ensemble virtually glowed. The long-playing album disc was being considered in musical circles to be a future collector's item.[118]

High School students called "Hi Notes" ushered during the 1964-65 Concert Season. Shown are Cindy Hendrick from Harding High School and Jim Henson from Classen High School. Courtesy Archives of Contemporary History, Oklahoma Christian University Library.

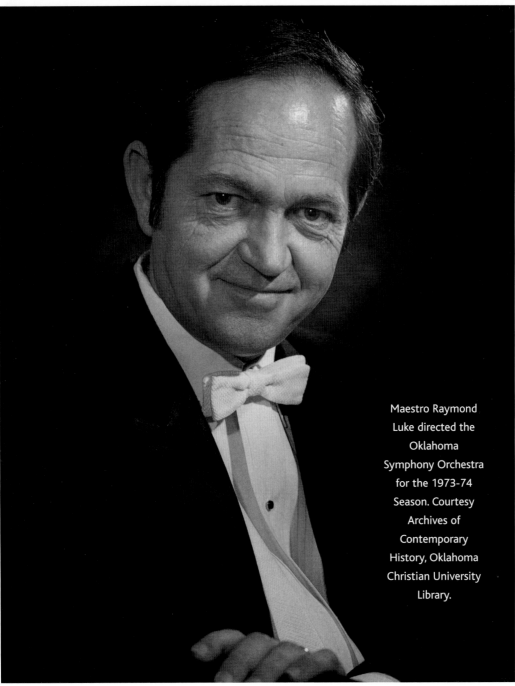

Maestro Ainslee Cox directed the Oklahoma Symphony Orchestra from 1974 to 1978. Courtesy Archives of Contemporary History, Oklahoma Christian University Library.

Maestro Raymond Luke directed the Oklahoma Symphony Orchestra for the 1973-74 Season. Courtesy Archives of Contemporary History, Oklahoma Christian University Library.

Maestro Herrera de la Fuente was known for his expressive hands. He directed the Oklahoma Symphony Orchestra (left) from 1978 to 1986. Courtesy Archives of Contemporary History, Oklahoma Christian University Library.

1979-80 Season

THE OKLAHOMA SYMPHONY ORCHESTRA

Felix Borowski of the *Chicago Sunday Times* wrote that the first complete recording of *Le Martyre de Saint Sebastien,* performed by Victor Alessandro and the Oklahoma Symphony Orchestra, was a valuable addition to recorded classical repertory. He regarded the 12-inch long-playing (LP) record to be a credit to all concerned and especially to Alessandro. He recommended it to collectors interested in the works of Debussy.[119]

The *New York Times* reported that the orchestral transcriptions of 21 *Hungarian Dances* arranged by Brahms for piano duet were on the same disc. The writer found it interesting because it demonstrated the excellence of one of the nation's younger orchestras, the Oklahoma Symphony. The critic pointed out that the orchestra entered the major class recently when its budget went over the $100,000 mark, during the 1945-46 season. He referred to the record as first-rate, with a "rich and substantial" unison tone as the orchestra played with the "flexibility and responsiveness of a well disciplined body." The critic concluded that the dances were led with "spirit, variety, and a surging songfulness by Victor Alessandro."[120]

At the end of the 1950-51 symphony season, Alessandro moved to San Antonio, Texas, to become music director of that city's symphony orchestra. Arthur Judson, Alessandro's personal manager, told the symphony board that ten years was long enough for a conductor to stay with the same orchestra. Judson believed that the Oklahoma public had been trained to listen to classical music, and the orchestra should be able to function with a new conductor. Alessandro was quoted as saying,

Hominy, Oklahoma's Mildred M. Andrews, a music teacher and concert organist, gave concerts all over the United States and conducted workshops throughout America. She was inducted into the Oklahoma Hall of Fame in 1971. Courtesy Archives, Oklahoma Heritage Association.

"There comes a time in a musical career when a change is needed . . . And this is best for the orchestra as well as the conductor."[122]

Music critic Tracy Silvester wrote a farewell letter to Alessandro. He viewed the young conductor's climb to the top of symphonic conductors to be a truly amazing feat and gave Alessandro much credit. The fact that there had been no concerns about the survival of the orchestra showed that his leadership had continued to build upon an organization that had been good when he took it over.[123]

Alessandro was remembered in musical circles for his excellence as a guest conductor, his innovative ideas, his effective programming, and his radio broadcasts that had sent messages of goodwill to the world in a way that people liked and understood. He is credited with changing the stereotype of Oklahoma as nothing but a place of wild Indians, cowboys, and outlaws. The United States Chamber of Commerce also recognized the exceptional abilities of Victor Alessandro. They nominated him as one of America's ten most outstanding young men in October 1950.[124]

Classical music kept emanating from Oklahoma City. Guy Fraser Harrison, conductor from 1951 to 1973, maintained the radio programs until funding problems prohibited further transmissions. Ray Luke (1973 to 1974), Ainslee Cox (1974 to 1978), and Maestro Luis Herrera de la Fuente (1978 to 1986), continued to provide high levels of excellence until the Oklahoma Symphony Orchestra Board closed its doors on October 31, 1988.[125]

A "Tubby the Tuba," poster rated close inspection, and then "Tubby the Tuba" music gained rapt attention at a Kinder Koncert offered by the Oklahoma Symphony Orchestra during the 1983-1984 season. Courtesy of Archives of Contemporary History, Oklahoma Christian University Library.

The symphony enjoyed increased visibility and recognition as a major cultural entity in the Southwest during the 22-year tenure of British-born Maestro Guy Fraser Harrison, in spite of recurring money problems. Harrison was a tireless speaker and lecturer. He devoted much consideration to choral music, opera, and to the popularizing of classical music. Some firsts of the musical history of Oklahoma under Harrison's direction were Kinder Koncerts for preschoolers, Brown Baggers for the downtown lunch crowd, and the Opening Doors program in public education. The orchestra was the first symphony in the nation to begin the European custom of playing in a church to highlight a coming holiday season. When show horses, including the famous Lippizaners of the Spanish Riding School of Vienna, pranced to symphonic music at the Oklahoma State Fairgrounds, another European practice had been introduced to the United States by the Oklahoma group and its versatile conductor. Harrison became involved in every aspect of his job and gave his audiences the impression that he was privileged to share a special affinity with people that had come to hear "music of all ages."[126]

After Maestro Harrison retired, Dr. Ray Luke, an instrumental music professor at Oklahoma City University, became resident conductor for the 1973-74 season. His primary interests were in teaching and composing music.[127]

Dr. Luke encouraged local talent. He brought soloists, chorus, and orchestra members to new levels of competence. Small, but appreciative, audiences enjoyed his "590 Concerts" which seated only 590 people. After Luke explained a work, virtuoso solos and dance would combine into a "potpourri" of entertainment in an intimate setting. Luke was noted for a sense of humor that drew chuckles from the audience.[128]

At the end of the season, Ainslee Cox, a protégée of Leopold Stowkowski, replaced Luke. Cox, the assistant conductor of the New York Philharmonic Orchestra, had worked with the Goldman Band in New York City and had conducted a series of concerts for young people with the American Symphony Orchestra before coming to Oklahoma City.[129]

Serious financial and union problems were a continuing concern during Cox's tenure. Various plans were considered by the Oklahoma Symphony Society to solve the issues. When Cox emphasized the need for a professional manager, the symphony board set up a search committee to find one. Cox had insisted that "many orchestras have been able to get along without a conductor, but a professional orchestra needs a manager."[130]

Cox noted that Oklahoma was famous for its vocal talent and he tried to showcase it. Although Cox was criticized locally for using too much modern music, the American Society of Composers, Authors, and Publishers (ASCAP) chose the Oklahoma Symphony Orchestra to receive a national award for "adventuresome programming" for two successive years in 1975 and 1976.[131]

Conductor Cox was followed by Mastro Luis Herrera de la Fuente, a popular guest conductor with a brilliant international reputation. He encouraged audiences to be open to their own sensitivity and reception. He conducted without a score and seemed to create a unity with the music, the orchestra, and the audience. Herrera continued to honor several previous international commitments to guest conduct in several foreign countries.[132]

During the nine years that Herrera served as musical director of the Oklahoma Symphony, the orchestra reached new musical heights. A magazine article in

Symphony concluded that the state of Oklahoma had been born with an inferiority complex and Oklahomans tended to believe that whatever they did was inferior. However, the writer declared that Oklahoma could hold its own with the best in world especially with its symphony and noted ". . .Oklahomans are brilliantly talented musicians, equal in technique and interpretive depth to their counterparts in any professional orchestra, and the element that has freed them to exhibit these qualities has been the baton of Maestro Herrera de la Fuente."[133]

The writer substantiated praise for Maestro Herrera and the Oklahoma Symphony with photos of foreign newspaper clippings. Europe's *Wein Express* called Herrera a "magnificent conductor . . . who brought out beauty and nobility of expression." The *Courier Musical* in Paris noted "a great harmony between orchestra and conductor. . . sensitive, ardent, and firm." The *Monte Carlo Journal* considered Herrera's performance "an unforgettable interpretation, a rare success, a splendid work." Other European reviews were equally full of praise for the director of the Oklahoma Symphony. In the United States, the *Rochester Democrat and Chronicle* reported that Maestro de la Fuente showed intense musical drive as he conducted from memory and left the audience applauding "convincingly." A New Orleans

Conductor Joel Levine initiated "A New Tradition of Musical Magic" when he introduced the recently organized Oklahoma City Philharmonic Orchestra to the public on October 16, 1989. Courtesy Joel Levine.

reviewer elaborated that when Maestro Herrera raised his baton, both orchestra and audience:

> . . . are made a part of the composer's emotional intent. Each musician is cued by Herrera's baton and expressive hands, the dynamic and mood of each entry is telegraphed to the musicians an instant prior to the part's entry. . .No theme or melodic line is ever lost. Each is brought forth, to speak its meaning clearly from the accompanying orchestral patterns. All combines to build together, stimulating, inspiring, satisfying, as the composer purposed, becoming whole music, for whole musicians, whether players or listeners. Oklahoma now has conducting the symphony in Oklahoma City, one of the world's superlative musicians. . .This is the verdict of critics around the world.[134]

During Herrera's tenure, the audiences had steadily increased as the orchestra continued to reach out to young people and to children. Sunday afternoon programs at the Music Hall were also popular with the older crowd, and concerts at the Oklahoma City Zoo were enjoyed by families.[135]

As the 1980s were ending, some of the dreams of the pioneer women for classical music had actually materialized in many small towns and cities all over Oklahoma. Modern transportation and technologies had made music more accessible. Local businesses and corporations became more involved in supporting symphonies, especially with corporate memberships. In the 1983-84 season, the number of Pops Concerts offered by the Oklahoma Symphony increased from eight to 16 because guest artists were usually booked for two appearances. The change increased ticket sales by 144 percent. In February, more than 2,500 children under five years of age attended the Oklahoma Symphony's Kinder Kozerts over a three-day period. Members of the Oklahoma City Symphony's Women's Committee ushered and gave the children each a "Tubby the Tuba" poster to take home. "Odyssey" and "Decorator Showhouse" projects were two particularly popular and successful fundraising efforts by the Women's Committee.[136]

Meanwhile, unrest and financial problems in symphony orchestras throughout the country, especially since the inflationary 1970s, had become persisting dilemmas. Some symphonies had been forced into bankruptcy that had led to eventual closures.[137]

The Oklahoma Symphony Orchestra was not immune from such controversies. The city and the orchestra endured prolonged efforts to settle differences between the musician's union and the symphony's board of directors. An impasse in negotiations to end the musicians' strike resulted in the disbandment of the orchestra. After a silence of two years and a determined community effort, a symphony orchestra was heard again in Oklahoma City Philharmonic Orchestra. On October 16, 1989, Conductor Joel Levine raised his baton and initiated "A New Tradition of Musical Magic."[138]

The Tulsa Philharmonic, the Tulsa Opera, the Lawton Symphony, the Enid Symphony, and the OK Mozart Festival in Bartlesville had also become well known. Several talented composers, musicians, ballet dancers, and concert singers had achieved brilliant careers. People wanted to have and to listen to classical music. They tried to provide instrumental and vocal classical music for themselves and for their families. Hundred of volunteers, especially women, had supported the efforts with

Internationally popular opera singer Barbara McAlister, mezzo-soprano, a member of the Cherokee Nation, was chosen by audition throughout the United States to attend the Wagner Seminar given by Henry Holt in 1995. She was listed in the *Gold Book of Wagner Singers* in 1997. She is also a former Muskogee, Oklahoma Rodeo Queen. Her paintings have been shown in galleries in the United States and in Europe. Much of her work is in private collections. Courtesy Five Civilized Tribes Museum.

their time and energy. Meanwhile, financial concerns, a continual pressing need, had often created crises.

A broad survey of the history of symphonic and other classical music in Oklahoma showed that the people, first of all, built on solid foundations laid out by their forefathers. History revealed that Oklahomans, in their own ways, accomplished much, and found enjoyment in their efforts to support classical music in the twentieth century.

An overview of Oklahoma's anomalous history and diverse racial traits indicated that Oklahoma's environment had produced a musical historical panorama that has contributed to the state, to the nation, and to the world. The early history of Oklahoma also revealed that the pioneers—American-Indian, African-American, European-American—who came voluntarily or were forced to come to Indian Territory or later to Oklahoma Territory, exhibited almost desperate needs for fellowship and music as they struggled to survive. The area experienced clashes between different races, tribes, and economic interests, as well as the forces of greed, politics, power, legal graft, and often loneliness. Consequently, untold stories and music about the pioneers as they rebuilt and persevered after disasters, natural or man-made, may be material for future musicals, symphonies, and operas as music continues to flow from Oklahoma.

CHAPTER 1

MUSIC IN INDIAN COUNTRY

1 Helen L. Kaufman, *The Story of One Hundred Composers* (New York: Grosset & Dunlap, 1943) xv; Arrell Morgan Gibson, *Oklahoma: A History of Five Centuries* (Norman: University of Oklahoma, 1981), 180-81.

2 *Daily Oklahoman*, 1 March 1953.

3 Robert J. Schwendinger, *The Indians Book: Authentic American Legends, Lore and Music* (New Jersey: Portland House, 1987), xi-xiii, xxiv, xxx, xxxi-xxxiii, xxxixxxiii.

4 Lillian , Woody M., and Minisa Crumbo, oral interview with author, 15 April, 1994. Woodrow "Woody" Crumbo was inducted into the Oklahoma Hall of Fame in 1978.

5 George Stevenson, Professor of Music, Oral Roberts University, "Freeing the Flute," oral presentation, Oklahoma Historical Society 1994 Annual Meeting, 16 April 1994.

6 Doris Smithee, "Nationally Honored Flutist Revives Tradition, "*The Storyteller,* The Center of the American Indian, Oklahoma City, Oklahoma.

7 William W. Savage, Jr., *Singing Cowboys and All That Jazz* (Norman: University of Oklahoma Press, 1983), 4; Alice Marriott and Carol Rachlin, *American Epic: The Story of the American Indian* (New York: G.P. Putnam's Sons, 1969), 178-181; George Catlin, "Sketching Up the Missouri River in 1835, "*American Scene: The Art and History Magazine With A Purpose* (Tulsa: Thomas Gilcrease Institute of American History and Art, 1964), 14.

8 Gibson, *A History of Five Centuries*, 27, 44, 45, 151.

9 Ibid.

10 Ibid., 47, 64, 65, 88.

11 Ibid.

12 Ibid.

13 Ibid.

14 Ibid., 84-97; Muriel H. Wright, *The Story of Oklahoma* (Oklahoma City: Webb Publishing Company, 1929-1930), 131.

15 Gibson, *A History of Five Centuries*, 95, 99.

16 Ibid., 64, 88, 89, 286.

17 Ibid., 91.

18 Ibid., 96. 95; Wright, *The Story of Oklahoma,* 120-122.

19 Gibson, *A History of Five Centuries*, 92, 93, 137.

20 Ibid., 90, 91, 96, 97.

21 Marion Thede, *The Fiddle Book* (New York: Oak Publications, 1967), 115, 141, 159.

22 Ibid.

23 Kathleen Garrett, "Music On The Indian Territory Frontier," 39 *Chronicles of Oklahoma* (Oklahoma City: Oklahoma Historical Society), 339-348.

24 Ibid., 348, 341-343.

25 Ibid.

26 Ibid. Author's Note: Some of the early music teachers at the seminary were: Miss Fannie Cummins, Miss Nell Taylor (Mrs. Clu Galager), Miss Florence Caleb, Miss Carlotta Archer, Mrs. Marlin R. Chauncey (Vera Jones), Miss Cora McNair, Miss Bluie Adair, and Miss Cherrie Adair.

27 Ibid., 345.

128 Ibid., 346.

29 Ibid., 346, 347.

30 Ibid., 347.

31 Ibid.

32 Ibid., 348.

33 Ibid., Gibson, *A History of Five Centuries*, 119, 129; "Wheelock Mission," 29 *Chronicles of Oklahoma* (Oklahoma City: Oklahoma Historical Society, 1951), 317.

34 Garrett, " Music On the Indian Territory Frontier," 348.

35 Gibson, *A History of Five Centuries,* 84, 130-135; Confederate Memorial Hall, Oklahoma Historical Society; John Thompson, *Closing the Frontier* (Norman: University of Oklahoma Press, 1986), 28, 29.

36 Ibid., 28-47; Gibson, *A History of Five Centuries,* 130-135.

37 Ibid., 139, 131.

38 Ibid., 130, 156-163.

39 Ibid.; Carlile, *Buckskin, Calico, and Lace*, 50-57; McDermott, *Oklahoma Today,* September/October, 1997, 14-19.

40 Gibson, *A History of Five Centuries,* 134-135.

41 Ethel and Chauncey Moore, *Ballads and Folk Songs of the Southwest* (Norman: University of Oklahoma Press, n.d.), viii.

42 Savage, *Singing Cowboys*, 4; Mariott and Rachlin, *American Epic*, 178-181.

43 Savage, *Singing Cowboys,* 4, 5; "Oklahoma Composers," 1-3, WPA Oklahoma Writers' Project, Library Resources Division, Oklahoma Historical Society; Alice C. Fletcher, *Omaha Indian Music* (Lincoln: University of Nebraska Press, 1994), 7, 70, 71.

44 Fletcher, *Omaha Indian Music*, 7, 8.

45 Ibid., 152.

46 Ibid.

47 Ibid., 55, 56, 71.

48 Howard L. Meredith, "Native Response: Rural Indian People in Oklahoma" 1900-1939, *Rural Oklahoma*, ed. By Donald Green, (Oklahoma City: Oklahoma Historical Society, 1977), 76-81.

49 Savage, *Singing Cowboys*, 4, 5; WPA Writers' Project, "Oklahoma Composers," 1-3.

50 Ibid.

Author's Note: During the historical time of this manuscript, any fraction of Indian heritage warranted the legal classification of Indian. Therefore, the particular tribe (family) of the Indian person will be listed if known.

51 *Johnston Country Capital-Democrat,* September 1987, Jon Denton, "Dancer Captures Indian Lore," Te Ata Family Research File, Chickasaw Council House Museum, Indian Nation, Tishomingo Oklahoma; Te Ata File, Library Resources Division, Oklahoma Historical Society.

52 Ibid.

53 Ibid.

54 Ibid.

55 Ibid.

56 Ibid.

57 Ibid.

58 *Daily Oklahoman,* 31 October 1995.

59 *Washington Post,* 1932; various typewritten unsigned articles (including a memorial write-up from Rush Hall, Idyllwild, California, March 24, 1968); undated newspaper clippings from *Washington Post, New York Sun,* a clipping written by Bee Driscoll, and miscellaneous articles, Archives of the Chickasaw Council House Museum, Indian Nation, Tishomingo, Oklahoma.

60 Ibid.

61 Ibid.

62 Ibid.

63 Ibid.

64 Ibid.

65 Ibid.

66 Ibid.

67 Ibid.

68 Ibid.

69 Ibid.

70 Ibid.

71 Ibid.

72 Ibid. Rose Henderson of the *New York Sun* tried to list the many accomplishments of Ataloa. She concluded by marveling about how she always appeared in a smart club or hotel as a sophisticated college woman wearing very chic contemporary clothes that she had made herself.

73 Emery Winn, "The World of Words," *Daily Oklahoman,* 26 April 1970; *The Encyclopedia of Opera* ed. by Leslie Orrey (New York: Charles Scribner's Sons, 1976), s.v. "Cadman, Charles Wakefield," 65; *The Metropolitan Opera Encyclopedia,* ed. by David Hamilton, (New York: Simon & Schuster, 1987). s.v.

74 Ibid.

75 Ibid.

76 Ibid.

77 Ibid.

78 Ibid.

79 Roy P. Stewart, "Pigtails to Opera, Now Hall of Fame;" *Daily Oklahoman,* 11 October 1964.

80 Ibid.; *Criterion,* 1923 Ardmore High School Yearbook, Chickasaw Library, Ardmore, Oklahoma.

81 *Criterion: 1923 Ardmore High School Yearbook,* Chickasaw Library, Ardmore, Oklahoma; Albert Kirkpatrick, "Music News and Views,"*DailyOklahoman,* 19 September, 1937; Ruth Lewis, "Ardmoreite Recognized With Honor," *The Ardmoreite,* 24 May 1964; "Mobley, Tessie," manilla folder, Library Resources Division, Oklahoma Historical Society; *Daily Oklahoman,* 27 January 1935, 18 April 1964, 8 November 1964; Marion Gridley, *Indians of Today,* 83, reprint, Library Resources Division, Oklahoma Historical Society; Sandra Walls, "Indian museum display honors Ardmoreite known internationally,"*The Ardmoreite,* d. unknown; Brunetta Griffith, " 'Lushanya,' Sweet Singing Bird," Source and d. unknown, News clippings, Archives of Chickasaw Council House Museum, Indian Nation, Tishomingo, Oklahoma; Federal Music Project Record Group 69, FMP Stock Area 11 E 4, Compartment 1, Box 74, Oklahoma, National Archives, Washington, D.C. Hereinafter cited: National Archives, FMP (OK-69).

82 Ibid.

83 Ibid.; Brunetta Griffin, "'Lushanya, 'Sweet Singing Bird, " Library Resources Division, Oklahoma Historical Society.

84 Ibid.

85 Ibid.; Ruth Lewis, "Ardmorette Recognized With Honor," *The Ardmorette,* 24 May 1964.

86 *Daily Oklahoman,* 18 November 1991.

87 Ibid.; Gibson, *Five Centuries of Progress,* 283; "Oklahoma Hall of Fame Members," Oklahoma Heritage Center; Marion E. Gridley, ed., *Indians of Today* (Oklahoma City: Oklahoma Historical Society, 1971), 4th ed., s.v.

88 Ibid.

89 Ibid.

90 Ibid.

91 Ibid.

92 Ibid.

93 Ibid.; 114.

94 Ibid.

95 Ibid.

96 "Music," Library Resources Division, Oklahoma Historical Society; *Stage Play and Song "Oklahoma!,* Library of Congress Publication, 1907-1957, 51;"Oklahoma! Is Offical Favorite," Library Resources Division. Author's Note: Lynn Riggs was inducted into the Oklahoma Hall of Fame in 1948. Movie actor Franchot Tone was discovered in "Green Grow the Lilacs."

97 Ibid.

98 Ibid.

99 Gridley, *Indians of Today,* 243, 244.

100 Ibid.

101 Ibid.

102 *Daily Oklahoman,* 12, 25 January, 6, 9, 16 February 1976.

103 Oklahoma Symphony Orchestra Program 1986-1987 (Spring); Dee E. Brown, *Bury My Heart At Wounded Knee,* (New York: Henry Holt & Co., 1970), 439-445.

104 Ibid.

Society. Other early musicians included on the list were: Clarence Burg, Lemuel J. Childers, Lucile Crist Carson, E. Edwin Crerie, Milton Dietrich, Charles F. Giard, Marie Hine, Galen Holcomb, Claude Lapman, Johnny Marvin, Gerald J. Mraz, Hugh McAmis, Edwin Vail McIntyre, Samuel McReynolds, Paul Wesley Thomas, and Joseph Wynne. Another list compiled by the WPA writers included Mayme Rabinowitz, the Reverend Father Ignatius Groll, Robert W. Wolfe, Wynn York, and Spencer Norton.

76 Ibid.

77 Ibid.

78 Ibid.

79 Ibid.

80 Ibid.

81 Ibid.

82 Ibid.

83 Ibid.

84 Ibid.

85 Ibid.

86 Ann Hogue, "Dr. Vida Chenweth," Archives of Hall of Fame, Oklahoma Heritage Center.

87 Ibid.

88 Candace Krebs, "Ressurrection and Recovery," *Oklahoma Today*, 50-59.

89 Ibid.

90 Ibid.

91 Ibid.

92 Ibid.; Interview, Music Director Douglas Newell, 24 January 2001.

93 Ibid.

94 Ibid.

95 Ibid.

96 Ibid.

97 Ibid.

98 Ibid.

99 Ibid.

100 Ibid.

101 Ibid.

CHAPTER 7

PIONEER WOMEN DARED TO DREAM

1 Tracy Silvester, *Daily Oklahoman,* 1 March 1953.

2 Carol Campbell, "Women's Idea Grew Into Musical Society," *Daily Oklahoman,* 11 October 1983; OSO Scrapbook; Original members (organizers) of the club were Mrs. Edwin L. Dunn, Mrs. C. B. Ames, Mrs. W. Frank Wilson, Mrs. Leslie Westfall, Mrs. A. C. Scott, Mrs. D. W. Hogan, Mrs. A. L. Welsh, Belzora Phillips, Amanda O'Conner, and Mrs. John A. Reck. The 25 members added later were called charter members; *Musical Courier,* 24 May 1922; OSO Scrapbook, 1922-1923.

3 Ibid.

4 Ibid.

5 *Harlow's Weekly,* 18 October 1924; OSO Scrapbook; *Daily Oklahoman,* 18 October 1924, March 1953.

6 Ibid.

7 Ibid.

8 Ibid.

9 OSO Scrapbook, 1922; *Daily Oklahoman,* 20 May 1924.

10 Ibid.

11 Ibid.

12 *Daily Oklahoman,* 14 September 1924; *Musical Courier,* 13, 14, 17, October 1924.

13 *Daily Oklahoman,* 20 May 1924.

14 *Oklahoma City Times,* , n.d.); *Daily Oklahoman,* September 1924, 18 February 1931.

15 J. Roberta Wood, *Harlow Weekly,* 18 October 1924; *Daily Oklahoman*, October 1924; *Oklahoma City Times*, 13 October 1924; Gibson, *A History of Five Centuries,* 202.

16 *Sunday Oklahoman,* 18 May 1924.

17 Edith Johnson, *Daily Oklahoman,* 3 October, 28 September 1924.

18 *Daily Oklahoman,* 28 October 1924;

Harlow's Weekly, 18 October 1924; OSO Collection; OSO Scrapbook.

19 Ibid.

20 Ibid.

21 OSO Collection; OSO Scrapbook; *Daily Oklahoman,* dates unknown.

22 Ibid.

23 Ibid.

24 *Daily Oklahoman,*16 December 1924; OSO Collection.

25 OSO Concert Program.

26 Ibid.

27 OSO Scrapbook, 1925.

28 Ibid.; *Norman Transcript,* 12 March 1926.

29 Ibid.

30 Walter M. Harrison, "Tiny Times," *Oklahoma Times,* n.d.; OSO Scrapbook.

31 *Daily Oklahoman,* 7 April 1926; OSO Scrapbook, 1926.

32 Ibid.

33 Ibid; *Harlow's Weekly,* 18 October 1924.

34 OSO Collection; OSO Scrapbook, 1926: Concert Program, 1926-1927; *Oklahoma City Times,* 18 October 1926.

35 Concert Program, 13 December 1926; OSO Scrapbook.

36 *Daily Oklahoman,* n.d.; OSO Collection; OSO Scrapbook.

37 Milton Gross and David Ewen, *Encyclopedia of Great Composers and Their Music* (Garden City: Doubleday & Co., 1962), 1, 315: OSO Scrapbook.

38 Concert Program, 1930-1931 Season: OSO Scrapbook.

39 Gibson, *A History of Five Centuries,* 220-224.

40 Ibid.; Concert Program, 1930-1931 Season; OSO Scrapbook; Letter, Dean Holmberg to Mrs. Buttram, 8 August 1932, Holmberg (Fredrik) Collection, HM-1250, F-2, Western History Collections, University of Oklahoma Library.

41 Ibid.

42 Ibid.

43 Ibid.

44 Ibid.

45 Ibid.

46 Ibid.

47 OSO Collection; Federal Music Project, Record Group 69, National Archives, Washington, D.C., (Hereinafter cited: National Archives, FP (OK-RG); Merle Montgomery, unpublished autobiography, Chapter VI, "Oklahoma WPA Music Project: Fact Sheets with Regard to the Activities of Dr. Merle Montgomery from the Desk of Mary Miley, Oklahoma Heritage Association." Note: When the WPA Projects ended, the National Office dictated that all records be destroyed. Years later, when Dr. Montgomery was sorting material she had stored in her sister's garage, she found WPA Music Project Records that had been overlooked, stored, and forgotten for years. The papers were temporarily placed in Dr. Montgomery's file. A decision was made to eventually give the materials to the Archives of the Library of Congress. Mary Miley brought a chapter about the FMP and some fact sheets about Dr. Montgomery to the Oklahoma Heritage Association.

48 Ibid.; Carol Wilmoth, "Heavenly Harmony: The WPA Orchestra 1937-1942,"*Chronicles Of Oklahoma* 64(Spring 1986), 35-51; Kenneth E. Hendrickson, Jr., "Politics of Culture: The Federal Music Project in Oklahoma," *Chronicles of Oklahoma*, 63(Winter 1985-1986), 363-369; OSO Collection.

49 Ibid.

50 Ibid.; *Daily Oklahoman*, n.d.

51 Ibid.; Concert Program.

52 Ibid.

53 Ibid.

54 Ibid.

55 Ibid.; *Oklahoma City Times*, 4 January 1938; *Daily Oklahoman*, 4 January 1938; Dean Richardson to R. F. Story, Editor of *Durant Democrat*, 5 January 1938.

56 OSO Collection; OSO Scrapbook.

57 *Oklahoma City News*, January 1938; Wilmoth "Heavenly Harmony," 41-42; OSO Scrapbook.

58 *Daily Oklahoman,* 26 January; *Oklahoma City News*, 25 January 1938; National Archives, FMP (OK-RG 69).

59 Wilmoth, "Heavenly Harmony," 42; *Oklahoma City Times*, 25 February 1938.

60 Ibid.; OSO Collection; National Archives, FMP (OK-RG69); Sandra Stanley-Bates, "Civic Center Music Hall, unpublished seminar paper, University of Central Oklahoma, 2, 18-25.

61 Ibid.

62 Ibid.

63 OSO Scrapbook; New Auditorium Advertising Brochure, 26 April 1937; National Archives, FMP (OK-69); *Daily Oklahoman*, 19 September, 7 November 1937.

64 *Oklahoma City Tribune*, 27February 1938; *Daily Oklahoman*, 17 July, 21 August 1938; OSO Scrapbook: Wilmoth, "Heavenly Harmony," 46,47. Other musicians listed were principal bassoonist Betty Sullivan Johnson, Annette Burford, Steele Hutto, Madeline Morsteller in the bass fiddler section, bass trombone player Harold Wiles, tuba player Virgil Estes, and Billy Jordan, who played the marimba.

65 *Sunday Oklahoman*, 22 January 1938. Other nations were represented by violinist Leatha Sparlin and Horace Thornburg, (Scandinavia); cellist Samuel McReynolds, (Scotland); Conductor Rose, violinist Meyer Bello, violinist Don Frankel, Walter Kessler, (Isreal); tuba and double bass player John Hugh Kaufman, cellist Eugene Roseriger, cellist Don Garlick, violinist George Unger and timpanist Robert Rigsbee, (Germany); Clarinetist Garth Cashion, trumpet player Ross Bour, Jr., (France).

66 Hendrickson, "Politics of Culture," 364-370.

67 Ibid.

68 *Daily Oklahoman*, 3 May 1938; National Archives, FMP (OK-RG69).

69 Ibid.

70 OSO Collection; National Archives, FMP (OK-RG69). The composers included Samuel McReynolds, Paul W. Thomas, Lemuel J. Childers. Robert W. Wolfe, Ingram Cleveland, Wynn Weeks, James Neilson, Theodore Dreher, Glen Holcomb, and Truman Tomlin. Symphony concerts had been given in Altus, Anadarko, Chickasha, Collinsville, Edmond, El Reno, Lawton, Muskogee, Norman, Oklahoma City, Shawnee and Tulsa.

71 OSO Scrapbook.

72 Ibid.

73 *Daily Oklahoman*, 8 September 1938.

74 National Archives, FMP (OK-RG69); Wilmoth, "Heavenly Harmony." 43-47.

75 Ibid., 47-48.

76 OSO Scrapbook; National Archives, FMP (OK-RG69).

77 Ibid.

78 OSO Scrapbook; Hendrickson, "Politics of Culture," 370.

79 Ibid.

80 Ibid.

81 Ibid.

82 Ibid.

83 OSO Collection.

84 Hendrickson, "Politics of Culture," 371.

85 Ibid.; Wilmoth, "Heavenly Harmony," 48; *Daily Oklahoman*, 29 January 1956.

86 OSO Collection; National Archives, FMP (OK-RG69); OSO Scrapbook.

87 Ibid.

88 Ibid.; Alessandro to editor of *Oklahoma Times*, 27 October 1944.

89 Hendrickson, "Politics of Culture," 373-374; National Archives, FMP (OK-RG69); OSO Scrapbook; OSO Collection.

90 Ibid.

91 Ibid.

92 Ibid.

93 Ibid.

94 Ibid., *Daily Oklahoman*, 1948.

95 Ibid.; Eunice Jenkins, Mrs. Vivian Head, Mrs. Paul Dudley, Mrs. Hugh Johnson, Mrs. Boone Jenkins and Mrs. Rose Karchner were among those present. Mrs. David Delana and her daughter-in-law of El Reno also became active in the group.

96 OSP Collection; OSO Scrapbook.

97 Ibid.

98 Ibid.; Mrs. J. M. Wilk, Mrs. Charles B. Lutz, Mrs. Carl Taggert, Mrs. Joseph Rooms, Mrs. Harvey Everest, Mrs. Winston Eason, Mrs. Oscar Monrad, Mrs. William H. Taft, Miss Edith Johnson, Mrs. Florence O. Wilson, Mrs. Richard E. Swan, Miss Bernice Lemon, Mrs. Marguerite Engle, Mrs. Mary Bordeaux, Mrs. Charles A. Vose, Mrs. Charles C. Anderson, Mrs. F. Cooper, and Mrs. Don Dow were all active members of the Women's Committee.

99 OSO Collection: *Daily Oklahoman*, 1,6, December 1948.

100 Ibid.

101 Ibid.

102 Ibid.

103 Ibid

104 *Houston Post*, 30 June 1948.

105 OSO Scrapbook; OSO Collection: *Sooner Spirit*, 13 October 1949.

106 *Houston Post*, 15 December 1949; OSO Scrapbook.

107 Ibid.; OSO Collection.

108 Ibid.; *Oklahoma City Times*, 1 January 1950; *Daily Oklahoman*, January 13, 1950; *Dallas Morning News*, 8 January 1950.

109 *Oklahoma City Times*, 1 January 1950; *Daily Oklahoman*, 13 January 1950.

110 *OSO Collection.*

111 Ibid.; *Daily Oklahoman*, 6 April 1950.

112 OSO Collection.

113 Ibid.; *Oklahoma City Times*, 28 March, 1950.; *Daily Oklahoman*, 22, 30 March 1950,

114 *Oklahoma*, 20 April 1950.

115 *Daily Oklahoman*, 3 May 1950.

116 *Chicago Tribune*, 30 April 1950; *Daily Oklahoman*, 3 May 1950.

117 OSO Scrapbook.

118 *Daily Oklahoman*, 5 December 1950.

119 *Dallas News*, 25 March 1951; *Houston Chronicle*, 3 March 1951.

120 *Chicago Times*, 27 March 1951. The soloists were Frances Yeend and Miriam Stewart, sopranos, and Anna Kaskas, contralto.

121 *New York Times*, April 1951.

122 OSO Collection.

123 Ibid.; *Daily Oklahoman,* 6 April 1950.

1224 Ibid.

125 *Oklahoma Gazette*, 2 March, 18 May, 13 July 1988; *Friday*, 4, 11 December 1987, 15 January, 12 February, 22 April, 6 May, 3, 10 June, 1, 14, 21 July 1988; Oklahoma Symphony Board of Director's Meeting, 24, 28 June 1988; OSO News Release, 28 June 1988; "City Scene," *Oklahoma City Living* May/June 1988; *Daily Oklahoman,* 7, 9 October, 5 November, 13 December 1987, 9, 13, January, 28 May, 1 16, 30 June 1988; Musicians Union hand-out. OSO Collection.

126 OSO Collection, "Members: Oklahoma Symphony Orchestra;" *Daily Oklahoma* 5, 17 November 1953, 2, 3, 7 October 1971, 12 December 1971, 15, 17 March 1972, 15, 24 April 1972, 16 July, 6 September 1972; OSO Collection.

127 OSO Scrapbook; OSO Collection; *Daily Oklahoman* 8 April 1974, 18,19, March 1974.

128 Ibid.

129 OSO Collection; *Daily Oklahoman* 29 May, 22 September 1974.

130 Ibid.; 15, 22, 26 August 1975, 1, 3 September 1975.

131 *Daily Oklahoman* 29 January 1976, 10, 29 February 1976, 2, 11 June 1976, 19 September 1976.

132 OSO Collection; *Sunday Oklahoman* 12 March 1972; *Oklahoma City Journal* 12 March 1972.

133 OSO Scrapbook, "Luis Herrera de la Fuente and the Oklahoma Symphony," Summer '79, no author nor source noted.

134 Ibid.; OSO Collection.

135 Ibid.

136 *Journal Record,* 7 November 1979; *Oklahoma City Times,* 8 October 1979; *Daily Oklahoman,* 18 December 1979; *Oklahoma City Journal,* 18 December 1979; *Oklahoma Gazette,* November 1983; OSO Collection.

137 *Oklahoma City Journal*, 7 August 1979; *Daily Oklahoman,* 9 September 1979; *Friday,* July 1980; OSO Collection.

138 Ibid.; Karen Shackenburg and Patrick Alexander, "Oklahoma: Not OK,"*Symphony*, January/February 1989, vol. 40, no.1, 28-37; *Oklahoma City Philharmonic Concert Program,* 16 October 1989; *Gazette* 27 September, 20 October 1989; *Friday* 14,21 July, 20 October 1989; *Daily Oklahoman* 27, 28 September, 1 October 1989.

Primary Sources

Archives and Manuscript Division. Oklahoma Historical Society. Collection of photographs, Pioneer, Indian, and Black Histories and WPA interviews.

Chickasaw Council House Museum, Indian Nation, Tishomingo, Oklahoma. A collection of articles, newspaper clippings, and photographs concerning Te Ata Fisher and Mary Ataloa Mclendon.

Chlouber, Carla. "Otto Gray and His Oklahoma Cowboys: The Country's First Western Bank," 1996., n.p.

Federal Writer's Project, National Archives, Washington, D. C. Record Group 69, Federal Music Project Stock Area 11 E-4, Compartment 1, Box 74, Oklahoma

Federal Writer's Project, Oklahoma Works Progress Administration (WPA). Irvin, Jesse, ed. "Music: A History of Oklahoma," "Oklahomans Write Too," "Oklahoma Composers." Library Resources Division, Oklahoma Historical Society.

Gene Autry Collection, Gene Autry Museum, Gene Autry, Oklahoma. Newspaper clippings, photographs, and memorabilia.

Gilcrease Institute of American History and Art. George Catlin, "Sketching Up the Missouri River in 1832."

Greater Southwest Historical Museum, Ardmore, Oklahoma. A Collection of photographs and quotes concerning Tessie Mobley.

Library Resources Division, Oklahoma Historical Society. Typewritten articles and letters concerning Te Ata Fisher and Hathaway Harper including Lingenfelter, N.H., "Hathaway Harper, Insurance Agent."

McAlester Building Museum Archives. Photographs and news items.

McGalliard Historical Collection, Ardmore, Oklahoma Public Library. Typewritten article about "Jubilee Singers."

Montgomery, Merle. Biography, n.p. Chapter VI, "Oklahoma WPA Music Project: Fact Sheets with Regard to the Activities of Dr Merle Montgomery From the Desk of Mary Miley, Oklahoma Heritage Association.

Okfuskee County Historical Museum. Collection of scrapbooks and memorabilia about Woodrow Wilson Guthrie.

Oklahoma Heritage Center. Oklahoma Hall of Fame Members Display.

Oklahoma Publishing Company Library. Photographs and news items.

Oklahoma Symphony Orchestra Collection, Archives of Contemporary History, Oklahoma University of Science & Arts. Oklahoma City. Scrapbooks, newspaper clippings, concert programs, news releases, symphony publications, photographs and other memorabilia.

Patterson, Zella J. Black and Lynette L. West. "Music: Langston University, A History," n.p., Langston, University.

Pittsburg County Historical Society Museum, McAlester. News items.

Santa Fe Depot Museum, Shawnee. Photographs and articles.

Washington Irving Trail Museum. Collection of photographs and memorabilia about Otto Gray and William McGinty, Stillwater, Oklahoma.

Western History Collections, University of Oklahoma. Photographs, handwritten letters, typewritten articles about Fredrik Holmberg, Joseph Benton and Western History.

Williams, Jack and Laven Sowell. *Tulsa Opera Chronicles* 1934-1992, privately printed, 1992.

Interviews

Bannister, Margaret, Okemah, Oklahoma, oral interview by author, 3 March 1997.

Chlouber, Carla, Washington Irving Trail Museum, oral interview by author, 9 November 1996.

Chlouber, Dale, Curator Washington Trail Museum, oral interview by author, 11 August 1996.

Crumbo, Lillian, Woody M., and Minisa, Oklahoma Historical Convention, oral interview by author, 15 April 1994.

Gaberino, Mary Ann Everett, McAlester Building Museum, Oral interview by author, 1 March 1999.

Hughes, Marjorie, Tulsa, Oklahoma, oral interview by author, 17 September 1996.

Kilgore, Ken, Director of Ambassador Choir, telephone interview by author, 13 September 1991.

Love, Clarence L., Tulsa, Oklahoma, oral interview, 11 October 1996.

Meredith, Jean, Okfuskee County Museum, oral interview by author, 13 June 1997.

Newell, Douglas, oral interview by author, 24 January 2001.

Sowell, Laven, Tulsa Opera, Inc., telephone interview with author, 25 June 1997.

Wessel, Kennis, Director of Poncan Theatre, oral interview by author, 3 June 1999.

Oral Presentations

Carney, George O. "Oklahoma Jazz: Deep Second to 52nd Street." 1994 Annual Meeting of Oklahoma Historical Society.

Chlouber, Carla. "Otto Gray and His Oklahoma Cowboys: The Country's First Western Band." 1994 Annual Meeting of Oklahoma Historical Society.

Crumbo, Minisa and Woody Max. "The Art of Woody Crumbo." 1994 Annual Meeting of Oklahoma Historical Society.

Ellis, Clyde. "Hearing a Different Oklahoma: Music and the Making of

Contemporary Indian Identity." 1996 Annual Meeting of Oklahoma Historical Society.

Lehman, Paul. "A New Look at the Negro Spiritual." 1994 Annual Meeting of the Oklahoma Historical Society.

Logsdon, Guy. "Woody Guthrie." Okemah's Woody Guthrie Day, 14 July 1997.

Stevenson, George. "Freeing the Flute." 1994 Annual Meeting of the Oklahoma Historical Society.

Newspapers-Articles

Atkins, Hannah D. "Jazz Men." *Oklahoma Today* 20 (Winter 1969):15-18.

Bracht, Mel. "Tulsa race riot examined in new film." *Daily Oklahoman,* 31 May 2000.

Brown, Willie L. and Janie M. McNeal-Brown. "Langston University, the Early Years." 74 *Chronicles of Oklahoma* (Spring 1996).

Campbell, Carol. "Women's Idea Grew Into Musical Society," *Daily Oklahoman,* 11 October 1983.

Carney, George O. "Oklahoma Jazz: Deep Second Street to 52nd Street." 72 *Chronicles of Oklahoma* (Spring 1994): 4-21.

Churchill, Reba and Bonnie. "Gene Autry: One of the First Singing Cowboys Is Still No. 1 In Many Ways." *Gene Autry (Oklahoma) Star Telegram,* 29 September 1996.

Denton, Jon. "Dancer Captures Indian Lore." *Johnson County Capital-Democrat,* September 1987.

Distel, Dave. "Gene Autry-From Corral to Countinghouse." *Star-Telegram,* 29 September 1996.

Driscoll, Bee. "Indian Songs, Dances, Legends." *New York Sun, n.d.*

Edwards,, John. "Escape From the South, 1861." 43 *Chronicles of Oklahoma* (1965): 58, 59.

Garrett, Kathleen. "Music On the Indian Territory Frontier." 39 *Chronicles of Oklahoma:* 339-348.

Gray, Elizabeth Gaines, *Oklahoma Indian Times '98 Tourism and Pow-Wow Guide;* 3-5.

Harrington, Gary. " Doc Tate Nevaquaya, 1932-1996." *Native Peoples* (Summer 1996): 103.

Hendrickson, Kenneth E., Jr. "Politics of Culture: The Federal Music Project in Oklahoma." 63 *Chronicles of Oklahoma* (Winter 1985-1986): 361-374.

Huffman, Emily. "Happy 50th, Tulsa Phil," *Intermission,* Tulsa Philharmonic, 10, 11.

Jenkins, William L. "Clarence Love In the Hall of Fame." *Oklahoma: Reach-Out Newspaper Publication (Tulsa),* December 1-31, 1995.

Johnson, Greg. "Words and Music." *Oklahoma Gazette,* 11 January 1996.

Kelly, Leo. "Hoxie and Acord: 'Reel' Oklahoma Cowboys." 74 *Chronicles of Oklahoma* (Spring 1996): 4-15.

Kirkpatrick, Albert. "Music: News and Views, "*Daily Oklahoman.* 19 September 1937.

Krebs, Candace. "Resurrection and Recovery," *Oklahoma Today.* 50-59.

Kudlacek, Kerry. "The Oklahoma Blues Tradition." *Juneteenth on Greenwood: A Celebration of Oklahoma's Black Traditions,* 1989, 9-11.

Lewis, Ruth. "Ardmorette Recognized With Honor." *Ardmoreite,* 24 May 1964.

McDermottt, Maura. "The Monk's Versailles." *Oklahoma Today.* September/October 1997, 14-19.

Ney, Marian Wallace. *Indian America: A Geography of North American Indians:* 3-5.

Pearson, Julie. "Doc Tate Nevaquaya," *Southwest Art,* April 1990.

Phillips, Robert W. "If Only I Still Had All of Those Gene Autry Comic Books." *Star Telegram,* 1 October 1994.

Reeves, Donald W. "Native American Cowboys: Riding For the Tribal Brand." *Persimmon Hill* Autumn 1997: 29-32.

Roth, Barbara Williams. "A Past That Would Never Live Again." *The Cowman.* February 1971.

Russell, Bill. "End of An Era Prompted Area's Last Trail Drive: Texas to Montana On Horseback." (Texas) *Prairie Dog Gazette,* Summer 1966.

Savage, William W., Jr. "Oklahoma's Jazz Heritage." *Juneteenth On Greenwood: A Celebration of Oklahoma's Black Music Traditions,* 1989, 9-11.

Schnackenberg, Karen, and Patrick Alexander. "Oklahoma: Not OK." *Symphony,* January/February, 1989, 28-37.

Shepard, Rhonda. "Frankie, Johnny Marvin Were Just Good Old Oakies." *Star Telegram,* 29 September 1996.

Smith, Barbara. "Theatrical Activities in Miami, Oklahoma: Indian Territory Days Through Early Statehood." Thesis. Kansas State College, July 1973.

Smithee, Doris. "Nationally Honored Flutist Revives Tradition." *The Storyteller.* 8 (Winter) 1991), 1, 6.

Smyth, Willie. "Oklahoma's Black Sacred Music Traditions." *Juneteenth on Greenwood: A Celebration of Oklahoma's Black Music Traditions,* 1989, 3, 4.

Spears, Jack. "Hollywood's Oklahoma." 67 *Chronicles of Oklahoma* (Winter 1989-1900): 340-380.

Stewart, Roy P. "From Pigtails to Opera. Now Hall of Fame." *Daily Oklahoma,* 11 October 1964.

Tipton, Robert. "The Story of the Jubilee Singers: You and Your Church In The World." *The Presbyterian,* 10 September 1890, repr., *Missionary Herald,* Nashville: Fisk University, November 1947.

Whalen, David Barry. "Gene Autry-No. 1 Cowboy: Exponent of Rodeo-"New Look.'" *Star Telegram,* 29 September 1996.

Wilmoth, Carol. "Heavenly Harmony: The WPA Symphony Orchestra, 1937-1942." 64 *Chronicles of Oklahoma:* (Spring 1986): 35-51.

Winn, Emery. "The World of Words." *Daily Oklahoman,* 26 April 1970.

Wooley, John. "Johnnie Lee Wills Gets His Due: Street Named For Musician." *Tulsa World,* 15 September 1996.

Wright, John. "Back In the Saddle Again." *Star Telegram,* 1 October 1994.

Wright, Muriel. Review of *Short Stories of the Bible* by Bert Hodges in *Chronicles of Oklahoma,* n.d.: 418, 419.

Wright, Muriel H. and LeRoy H. Fisher. "Civil Ware Sites in Oklahoma: 'Spencer Academy, Choctaw Nation.'" 44 *Chronicles of Oklahoma.* (1966-1967): 172.

Books

Argo, Burnis and Kent Ruth. *Oklahoma: Historical Tour Guide.* Carpentersville, Illinois: Crossroads Communications, 1992.

Autry, Gene and Michael Herskowitz. *Back In The Saddle Again.* Garden City: Doubleday & Co., 1978.

Axelrod, Alan and Dan Fox. *Songs of the Old West.* New York: Metropolitan Museum of Art, 1991.

Berendt, Joachim E. *The Jazz Book: From Ragtime to Fusion And Beyond.* Brooklyn, New York, 1992.

Berry, Lemuel, Jr. *Biographical Dictionary of Black Musicians and Music Educators.* Guthrie: Midwest Publishing Co., 1978.

Blackburn, Bob. *Images of Oklahoma: A Pictorial History.* Oklahoma City: Oklahoma Historical Society, 1984.

Brooks, Tilford. "Black Music Forms After 1900" Chap. In *America's Black Musical Heritage.* New Jersey: Prentice Hall, 1984: 120-123.

Brown, Dee E. *Bury My Heart At Wounded Knee.* New York: Henry Holt & Co., 1970.

Buchart, Bill and David Fitzgerald. *Oklahoma.* Portland Oregon: Graphic Arts Center Publishing Co., 1979.

Carlile, Glenda. *Buckskin, Calico, and Lace: Oklahoma's Territorial Women.* Oklahoma City: Southern Hills Publishing Co., 1990. *Petticoats, Politics, and Perouttes.* Oklahoma City: Southern Hills Publishing Co., 1995.

Charters, Samuel B. *The Country Blues.* New York: De Capo Press, 1975.

Collier, James Lincoln. *The Making of Jazz: A Comprehensive History.* Boston: Houghton Mifflin Company, 1978.

Cross, Milton. *The New Milton Cross's Complete Stories of Great Operas.* New York: Doubleday & Co., n.d.

Cross, Milton and David Ewen. *Encyclopedia Of the Great Composers and Their Music.* Garden City: Doubleday & Co., 1962.

Curtis, Natalie. *The Indians' Book.* New Jersey: Portland House, 1987.

Dale, Edward & Gene Aldrich. *History of Oklahoma.* Edmond: Thompson Books, 1969.

Dinsmore, Frances. *American Indian and Their Music.* New York: Women's Press, 1926.

Douglas, Clarence B. *The History of Tulsa, Oklahoma, A City With a Personality.* Chicago: S.J. Publishing Co., 1921.

Edwards, Jim and Hal Ottoway. *The Vanished Splendor: Postcard Views of Oklahoma City.* Oklahoma City: Abalache Book Shop Publishing Co., 1982.

Ellison, Ralph. *Shadow and Act.* New York: Random House, 1953, 1972.

Ewen, David. *The Complete Book of 20th Century Music.* Englewood Cliffs, N.J.: Prentice Hall, 1959.

Feather, Leonard. "Jazz Overseas" and "Sixty Years of Jazz" A Historical Survey." *Encyclopedia of Jazz.* New York: Horizon Press, 1960: 23-51, 160, 486. *The Book of Jazz: From Then Till Now.* New York: Horizon Press, 1965.

Fisher, Miles Mark. *Negro Slave Songs In the United States.* New York: Russell & Russell, 1953.

Fletcher, Alice C. *Omaha Indian Music.* Lincoln: University of Nebraska Press, 1994.

Gibson, Arrell Morgan *Oklahoma: A History of Five Centuries.* Norman: University of Oklahoma Press, 1981.

Green, Donald E., ed. *Rural Oklahoma.* Oklahoma City: Oklahoma Historical Society, 1977.

Gregory, Hugh. *Who's Who In Country Music.* London: Weidenfel and Nicolson, 1933.

Gridley, Marion E., ed. *Indians of Today.* Oklahoma City: Oklahoma Historical Society, 4th ed., 1971.

Hamilton, David E., ed. *The Metropolitan Opera Encyclopedia.* New York: Simon & Schuster, 1987.

Hare, Maud Cuney. "The Source." *The Negro Music and Art.* Lindsey Patterson, ed. New York: Publications Co., 1969:19-22.

Harrison, Daphne Duval. *Black Pearls: Blues Queens of the 1920s.* New Brunswick, London: Rutgers University Press, 1988.

Helander, Brock. *The Rock Who's Who.* New York: Shirmer Books, 1982.

Holliwell, Leslie, *Hollywood Filmgoer Companion* New York: Charles Scribner & Sons, 1988.

Johnson, Bobby H. "Pilgrims On the Prairie: Rural Life In Oklahoma." *Rural Oklahoma,* ed. Donald E. Green. Oklahoma City: Oklahoma Historical Society, 1977:6-20.

Katz, William Loren. *Black Women Of the Old West.* New York: Ethrac Publications, 1995.

Kaufmann, Helen L. *The Story of One Hundred Composers.* New York: Grosset & Dunlap, 1943.

Kohrs, Milton & Karl. Mo*re Stories of Great Operas.* New York: Doubleday & co., 1922.

Lassiter, Luke E. *The Power of Kiowa Song.* Tucson: University of Arizona Press, 1998.

Locke, Alain. "The Age of Minstrelsy." In *The Negro In Music and Art,* ed. Lindsey Patterson. New York: Publishers Company, 1969: 21-25.

Lowie, Robert H. *Indians of the Plains.* New York: McGraw-Hill Book Co., 1954.

McCloud, Barry. *Definitive Country: The Ultimate Encyclopedia of Country Music and Its Performers.* New York: Berkley Publishing Group, 1955.

Malone, Bill C. *A Fifty Year History: Country Music U.S.A.* Austin: University of Texas Press, 1968.

Marriott, Alice and Carol Rachlin. *American Epic: The Story of the American* Indian. New York: G. P. Putnam's Sons, 1969.

Meredith, Howard L. "Native Response: Rural Indian People in Oklahoma, 1900-1939." Chap. in *Rural Oklahoma,* ed., Donald Green. Oklahoma City: Oklahoma Historical Society, 1977: 14-18.

Moore, Ethel and Chauncey. *Ballard and Folks Songs of the Southwest.* Norman: University of Oklahoma Press n.d.

Orrey, Leslie, ed. *They Encyclopedia of Opera.* New York: Charles Scribner's Sons, 1976: 65.

Paige, Harry W. *Songs of the Sioux.* Los Angeles: Westernlore Press, 1970.

Richardson, Joe M. *A History of Fisk University 1865-1946.* Tuscaloosa: University of Alabama Press, n.d.

Rossi, Paul A. and David C. Hunt. "The Cowboy: Maker of the Cattle Culture." Chap. in *The Art of the Old West.* New York: Alfred A. Knopf, 1971: 266-315.

Savage, William W., Jr. *The Cowboy Hero: His Image In American History and Culture.* Norman:University of Oklahoma Press, 1979. *Singing Cowboys and All That Jazz: A Short History of Popular Music In Oklahoma.* Norman: University of Oklahoma Press, 1983."Rural Images, Rural Values and American Culture: A Comment." Chap. in *Rural Oklahoma*, ed. Donald Green, 1977: 113-127.

Schuller, Gunther. *The History of Jazz-Early Jazz-Its Roots and Musical Development.* New York: Oxford University Press, 1968. *The Swing Era, the Development of Jazz, 1930-1945.* New York: Oxford University Press, 1989.

Schwendinger, Robert J. *The Indians Book: Authentic American Legends, Lore, and Music.* New Jersey: Portland House, 1987.

Thede, Marion. *The Fiddle Book.* New York: Oak Publications, 1967.

Thompson, John. *Closing the Frontier.* Norman: University of Oklahoma Press, 1986.

Thorpe, M. Howard, *Songs of the Cowboy,* Lincoln & London: University of Nebraska Press, 1984.

Townsend, Charles. "Bob Wills and Western Swing: The Oklahoma Years. 1934-1942." Chap. in *Rural Oklahoma*, ed., Donald Green. Oklahoma City: Oklahoma Historical Society, 1977; 84-100.

Traubner, Richard. *Operetta: A Theatrical Story.* New York: Doubleday & Co., 1938.

Wallis, Michael. *Pretty Boy: The Life and Times of Charles Arthur Floyd.* NewYork: St. Martin's Press, 1992: 110-113.

White, Richard. *"It's Your Misfortune and None of My Own:" A History of the American West.* Norman: University of Oklahoma Press, 1991: 14, 37.

Wiley, Lynn M. "Dr. Brewster Higley." *The Famous and Infamous of Pottawatomie County Oklahoma.* Santa Fe Depot Museum, Shawnee, Oklahoma: 10, 11.

Wilson, James N. "Oklahoma and Midwestern Farmers In Transition, 1880-1910."*Rural Oklahoma,* ed. Donald Green. Oklahoma City: Oklahoma Historical Society, 1917: 21-36.

Work, John Wesley. *Folk Songs of the American Negro.* Nashville: Fisk University Press, n.d.

Wright, Muriel H. *The Story of Oklahoma.* Oklahoma City: Webb Publishing Co., 1920.